America's Electric Utilities: Past, Present and Future

by
Leonard S. Hyman

Third Edition

Public Utilities Reports, Inc.
Arlington, Virginia

This publication is designed to provide accurate
and authoritative information in regard to the subject matter covered. It is sold with the understanding that the publisher is not engaged in rendering
legal, accounting, or other professional service. If
legal advice or other expert assistance is required,
the services of a competent professional person
should be sought. *(From a Declaration of Principles
jointly adopted by a Committee of the American Bar
Association and a Committee of Publishers.)*

First Printing, September, 1983
Second Edition, August, 1985
Third Edition, May, 1988

ISBN 0-910325-25-1
Library of Congress Catalog Card
   No. 88-61186
Printed in the United States of America

To Judith, Andrew and Robert

TABLE OF CONTENTS

TABLES

Preface

A century ago electricity was a peculiar force that ran through telegraph lines and lit the homes of a handful of tycoons. One electric utility, built by a brash inventor, served a few customers in lower Manhattan. Today electricity illuminates and powers America, consuming one third of our fuel in the process. When the power fails, the economy stops.

Not only does electricity play a role in almost all phases of our economy, but efficiently supplying the capital to make possible the electricity is one of the critical tasks of financial markets. The electric industry has required almost $12 billion per year of new capital in 1982-1986. Investors—ranging from individuals to pension funds to insurance companies—have an enormous stake in the welfare of the industry.

Despite the fact that the lights still go on in this country, many experts argue about whether the electric utility industry is in trouble. For decades it has been buffeted by environmental opposition, turmoil in the capital markets, shifting patterns of demand for power, rising costs, insecure sources of fuel, inadequate regulatory procedures, consumerism, and technological failure. Experts differ on the industry's future. It may be a mature industry in the declining phase of its life cycle. Or, perhaps, the worst problems are over, so the electric utilities are about to enter a new phase of prosperity. The most worrisome outlook, though, is that the industry will be discouraged from meeting its responsibilities, so that America's growth will be stifled by a shortage of electric power. The future seems to offer perils as well as opportunities.

Today investors have over $300 billion in the electric utility industry. Producers of machinery and builders collect $30 billion a year from utilities. The government tries to use the utility industry to reduce America's dependence on foreign sources of energy, although this solution to a national security problem runs headlong into the environmental movement's efforts to reduce air pollution, deemphasize nuclear energy and minimize our attachment to central station power. In the meantime, consumers resist the rising cost of electricity, industrialists warily examine the question of whether electric utilities can meet the demands that will be placed on them in the future, and competitors look for ways to enter the electricity market that used to be the monopoly of the local electric utility.

The purpose of this book is to examine—in basic terms—how the electric utility industry developed, how it is regulated and financed, how it operates, and where the industry might be going.

The book is an introductory work. The required principles of accounting, engineering, finance, law and physics are explained in the text. Each section has been written to be relatively self-contained, which means that a few explanations are repeated through the book, rather than forcing the reader to double back to find the original explanation.

An *Introduction* (Part One) provides the basic concepts and terminology required to understand the industry.

The Operation of Electric Utilities (Part Two) describes how electricity is produced, why its characteristics make it different from most other products, and why shifts in patterns of demand make it so difficult to plan ahead and to assure that the supply of electricity will be adequate in the future.

Building on the knowledge of operations, *The Development and Structure of the Electric Utility Industry* (Part Three) traces the history of the industry, with emphasis on how the industry developed its present structure, and whether the cost characteristics now are such that the industry's structure is ripe for change.

Regulation (Part Four) describes the legal background of the regulatory system as well as the procedures now used in regulation.

Financing and accounting are more important to electric utilities than to most industries, due to the huge amounts of capital required in order to do business. *Financial Structure* (Part Five) explains financing and accounting procedures, how financial analysts and investors examine the utility, and what has happened to the industry, financially, in the postwar period.

Finally, we will tackle *The Future of the Electric Utility Industry,* (Part Six), a topic swirling with dogmatism and uncertainty, but of vital importance to the nation.

The Appendices include a special section on Canada, Selected Bibliography and Index.

Much of the text of the book is derived from a series of papers issued by Merrill Lynch Pierce Fenner & Smith Inc. My colleagues at Merrill Lynch aided my efforts. Rosemary Avellis developed the statistical series on regulation. Françoise Merrien collected and arranged much of the statistical material. Meava Daniels helped to put it together in an orderly fashion. Doris Kelley, Marjorie Jones, Heidimarie West and Richard Toole provided support and held the fort when necessary. Randall F. Spencer, Ms. Nina Seebeck and Wallace C. Stefany and the staff at Public Utilities Reports smoothed the way for production. Don Wallace of Public Service E&G, Michael Crew of Rutgers University, Ted Komosa of Merrill Lynch, and George Cohen of Cohen, Davis & Marks helped greatly in reading the text, providing valuable guidance and correcting many of the errors. All remaining errors are, of course, the author's.

Part One

Introduction:
Electric Utilities in One
Easy Lesson

Chapter 1

Introduction

The position that electric energy has come to occupy in our civilization is a result of its unique characteristics of ease in transportation and distribution, ease of application to the widest range of processes requiring energy, and its potential for application to almost all energy-using processes with the utmost flexibility, complete cleanliness, and safety, and with the largest and most sensitive susceptibility to control.[1]

Philip Sporn

The electric utility industry is dominated by engineers, accountants, lawyers and regulators who speak a jargon that baffles outsiders and obscures simple concepts behind a fog of specialized verbiage. Here are the basic concepts and vocabulary necessary to understand the industry, with emphasis on operations, regulation, finance, ratio analysis and capital markets.

Operations

Utilities measure the size (capacity) of a generating station in *kilowatts* (thousand of watts), abbreviated KW, or *megawatts* (millions of watts), abbreviated MW. Those measures are equivalent to saying that a factory has 10 machines, or that a hamburger stand has 10 grills. Capacity figures tell how big a plant is, but not how much it actually produces. The unit of electrical production is the *kilowatt-hour* (KWH) — the amount of electricity produced by running a generator that is one kilowatt in size for one hour. *Sales* of electricity are thus measured in kilowatt-hours. The *revenues* of an electric company are its sales in kilowatt-hours multiplied by the price per kilowatt-hour. *Voltage* is the pressure at which electricity is pushed through power lines. In general, long distance *transmission* lines carry electricity at high voltages, and local *distribution* lines carry it at low voltages. The time at which demand for electricity is highest is the *peak*. A utility must have a *reserve* — a certain amount of spare capacity available should a power station break down during the peak period. The *reserve margin* is the reserve measured as a percentage of the peak load.

Regulation

An electric utility is supposed to be a *natural monopoly:* meaning that one producer can serve customers more efficiently than can many competing producers. In addition to avoiding the obvious inconvenience of having five or six utility companies dig up the streets, the natural monopoly provides *economies of scale* — that is, one large utility can produce and sell electricity more cheaply than could a number of small producers. Because a utility has a monopoly, a *regulatory agency* in each state assures that the utilities do not take advantage of their customers. The agencies often set service standards and always set prices. The price *(rate)* is set to permit the utility to collect enough money to cover all operating expenses, including taxes, and to have enough *operating income* left to provide a *fair rate of return* on the money invested in the business. Investors' money, of course, has been used to build the plant and to buy the equipment that serves the customers (the *rate base*). The rate of return is determined from the utility's *cost of capital.* For example, suppose that a utility has invested $1,000 in facilities to serve its customers. The company borrowed $500 on which it is paying 10% interest ($50 a year). The other $500 came from holders of the utility's common stock. The regulators note that the loan costs 10%. After a lengthy hearing, the regulators decide that common stockholders are entitled to a return of 15% on their investment ($75 a year). Thus, the cost of capital, as calculated below, is 12.5%, the rate of return that the utility will be allowed to earn.

Type of Capital	*Amount of Capital*	*Cost of Capital*	*Dollar Return*		
Debt	$500 ×	10% =	$50		
Stock	500 ×	15% =	75	and	
	$1000		$125		$\dfrac{\$125}{\$1000} = 12.5\%$

Regulatory agencies usually set rates annually. Certain major expenses, however, can move up or down rapidly in the course of a year. A utility might earn too little when these expenses rise, or too much when they fall. To avoid having frequent rate hearings to adjust price for these sudden shifts in expenses, most agencies allow the use of *automatic adjustment clauses,* which provide for changes in certain expenses to be quickly passed on to customers. Fuel expenses, which eat up 30 to 40% of revenues, are volatile. Thus, the most common automatic *adjustment* is for fuel costs.

Finances

Electric utility facilities are enormously expensive to build, with some large power stations costing several billion dollars. Electric companies can rarely set aside from the year's income enough money to pay for constructing a new plant. To pay for the plants, the companies often have to borrow money and to sell new shares of stock to outsiders (*external financing*).

Thus, the profits from new business that is served by the new plant have to be shared by an increased number of holders of the company's bonds and stock. If too many new securities are sold and if business does not grow as expected, the share of profits left for the holders of old securities might actually be less than before the expansion. *Dilution* takes place when so many new shares have to be sold to pay for expansion that earnings per share of stock are less than they would have been had no expansion and financing taken place. Dilution usually occurs when the *market value* of the stock (the price at which it sells) is less than the *book value* (the amount of money per share that common stockholders have already invested in the business and any earnings that have been retained or saved by the company). As a result, investors and management carefully watch the ratio of *market* value to *book* value — the market price of the stock stated as a percentage of its book value. Other things being equal, a utility is usually better off if it can finance as much of its expansion as possible from internal sources when interest costs are high and stock prices are low.

Ratio Analysis

The financial reports of a corporation have three key parts. The *income statement* shows revenues and expenses for the year. The *balance sheet* provides a statement of assets (what is owned), money owed, and money put in by shareholders. The *statement of sources and uses of funds* tells how the company raises and disposes of cash in a particular accounting period.

The balance sheet shows the sources of all money used to build the company since it was formed (the *capital*) and the percentage of capital that was borrowed and the percentage that came from shareholders (the *capitalization ratio*). If a large percentage of funds came from borrowing, the company is said to be *leveraged*. If something goes wrong, the shareholders will not be paid dividends or get back their investments until creditors have been repaid. In general, bondholders judge the quality of their securities by whether shareholders have invested a sufficient cushion of money for bondholders to fall back on if something goes wrong and by the *pretax interest coverage ratio* ("coverage"), which measures how much income is available to pay interest charges. If $100 of income is earned and interest charges are $20, then the coverage ratio is five-to-one (5×). In addition, financial organizations rate investment quality of bonds by letter designations. Moving from highest to lowest, designations are Aaa or AAA, Aa or AA, A or A, and Baa or BBB, with a plus, minus, or number added to show gradations of quality. Many investors are not allowed to own bonds rated below Baa or BBB because they are not considered to be prudent investments.

Some companies use conservative accounting procedures that tend to overstate expenses, so their reported income is likely to be below that of a comparable company using liberal accounting procedures. Regulatory agencies establish accounting procedures for utilities, and some agencies are more cautious than others. Two key items make a big difference in determining how solid are earnings. One is the treatment of income taxes. Some companies keep income tax expenses low and show a larger profit by reporting only taxes actually paid as an expense (*flow through accounting*), a procedure becoming less prevalent. Others report not only taxes actually paid as an expense but also funds set aside for taxes that might have to be paid in the future (*normalization*). Therefore, tax expense, including taxes set aside for future payment, as a percentage of taxable income indicates how conservative are a utility's accounting procedures. The higher the percentage, the more conservative the accounting.

Financial analysts also judge utilities on the basis of another item in the income statement — the *allowance for funds used during construction* (AFUDC). Companies that are building plant must raise money to finance the plant during the construction process and must pay interest and dividends on that money. Plant that has not been completed is called *construction work in progress* (CWIP). Many regulatory agencies do not allow the utilities to recover carrying charges on the CWIP from customers during the construction process. Accountants, however, believe that a company's current earnings should not be reduced by charges for a plant that will serve customers in future years. To offset in the income statement the charges associated with money raised to finance CWIP, the utilities add AFUDC to income. For various reasons, the AFUDC added to income is often greater than interest being paid on the money for the construction project and greater than income will be from the project once it is completed. As will be explained later, the use of AFUDC is also a method of passing on to future customers the financial costs incurred during the construction period. Because AFUDC is bookkeeping income — not real dollars collected from customers — investors may be wary of companies for which AFUDC constitutes a large percentage of income. *Quality of reported earnings* is the term used to describe the overall conservatism of an income statement.

Finally, to determine how profitably stockholders' money is being used, we must find out how much income is earned on every dollar invested, or the *return on equity*. If a company earns $150 for stockholders who have invested $1,000, the return on equity is 15%.

Capital Markets

Most of the money supplied to a utility from outside sources is in the form of borrowings or of equity capital (money invested by stockholders who own the business). Borrowings usually come from banks or from investors who buy commercial paper (*short term debt*), or in the form of bonds or debentures (*long term debt*). In the case of *long term debt,* the creditor lends money for a long period (perhaps 20 years) and receives a bond that will *mature* (be paid off) on a specified date. When owners of bonds need cash before the maturity date, they sell the bonds in the marketplace. Bondholders have no assurance that the market price will equal the price paid when the bond was issued or will equal the value of the bond at maturity (*face,* or *par value*). Meanwhile, the bondholder receives a fixed interest payment (often called the *coupon*) each year. The return that the bondholder earns is called yield. The simplest yield is the *current yield,* the coupon as a return on the market price of the bond. If a bond sells for $100 and has a coupon of 12% ($12), the current yield is also 12%. If the same bond with the 12% coupon ($12 in interest) sells at $80, the current yield is 15%. When the bond is selling below par, $80 in this example, the investor will not only receive $12 a year in interest, but will also receive $20 more when the bond is finally redeemed (at $100 par) at maturity. In that case, the correct yield to use is the *yield to maturity,* a calculation of return that takes into account both the current return and the increase in price as the bond approaches the maturity date. In general, yield to maturity is lower for high rated (high quality) bonds. That is, when risk is lower, return is lower.

Preferred and *preference* stocks also pay fixed dividends. In many cases, when preferred or preference stock is not called for redemption at a given date, the investor must sell the stock in the market to raise cash. The return is measured by the *dividend yield,* which is the annual dividend divided by price.

The *common stockholders* are the owners of the business and their investment in it is called *equity.* In order of priority, interest is paid first, then preferred and preference dividends, then dividends on common stock, if anything is left. The same order applies if the company goes out of business. First all debts are paid in full. Then preferred and preference shareholders get their investments back. Finally, if any funds remain, the common stockholders take what is left. When something goes wrong, common stockholders' money is used to pay the holders of bonds and preferred stock. When business is good, the common stockholders collect the profits. If a company earns $1 million and has one million shares of common stock, it has *earnings per share* of $1. The company will keep some of the profits for the business (*retained earnings*) and pay the balance as *dividends.* The *payout ratio* is the dividend as a percentage of earnings. The price of a common stock is usually valued as a *multiple* of earnings, also called the *price-earnings* (P/E) ratio. For instance, if the stock of a company earning $1 a share sells at $7, its P/E ratio is seven-to-one, or seven times earnings (7 ×). Investors often pay a higher P/E for the stocks of companies whose earnings are expected to rise rapidly. The second common measure of value is the *dividend yield* — the dividend return on the price of the stock. The stock selling for $7 and paying a dividend of 63¢ a share annually yields 9%. Shares of companies that are expected to raise their dividends rapidly often sell at lower dividend yields. A company with a high payout ratio may not be able to raise its dividend for lack of earnings from which to pay the additional dividend. As a result, shares of that company may sell at a high dividend yield. In other words, investors will pay a higher P/E ratio and settle for a lower current dividend yield if they expect substantial improvement in the future. Investors also consider the risk level of the stock and will pay a higher P/E and accept a lower dividend yield from the investment with the lower risk.

Both bond and stock prices are affected by movements in interest rates. When investors can earn a high return on money in the bank, for instance, they will not buy a stock or bond until its price has declined to a point at which the dividend yield or the yield to maturity is high enough to compete with returns offered elsewhere. On the other hand, when interest rates decline, investors bid up the prices of stocks and bonds until returns on them drop to levels that are close to interest rates. The market is a two way street.

Notes

[1]Philip Sporn, *The Social Organization of Electric Power Supply in Modern Societies* (Cambridge, The MIT Press, 1971), p. 3.

Part Two

The Operation of Electric Utilities

Chapter 2

Watts and Volts

While the early experimenters chiefly directed their attention to the chemical effects of galvanic currents, other phenomena were not overlooked. It was soon found that, when passing through a conductor of any kind, the current evolved heat, the amount of which depended on the nature of the conductor. This thermal effect is now of great practical use in electric lighting, heating, etc.[1]

Sir William Cecil Dampier

The operating characteristics of electric utilities have changed little in this century. Power still has to be generated, transmitted, and distributed. Huge fixed assets are required and must be available at all times, although in use for only a fraction of the day, week, or year, because storage of power is expensive, and because customers expect instantaneous response to demand. Despite numerous advances in technology, most power is generated as it was at the turn of the century: by boiling water to create steam that turns a blade on a wheel that turns a magnet within coils of wire and thereby induces an electric current into the utility grid. If you understand a few simple terms and concepts, you understand the industry.

Power is "defined as the work done divided by the time during which this work is done."[2] Work, in turn, is defined as "the product of the force which acts on the body and the distance through which the body moves while the force is acting on it."[3] All that can be explained simply — i.e., if a cement block weighing 10 pounds must be pulled 10 feet, the work done is:

$$\text{Work} = \text{Force} \times \text{Distance}$$
$$= 10 \text{ lbs.} \times 10 \text{ ft.} = 100 \text{ ft. lbs.}$$

Power adds the dimension of time:

$$\text{Power} = \frac{\text{Force} \times \text{Distance}}{\text{Time}} = \frac{\text{Work}}{\text{Time}}$$

11

If the above work were done in five seconds, the power involved in the effort becomes:

$$\frac{10 \text{ lbs.} \times 10 \text{ ft.}}{5 \text{ sec.}} = \frac{20 \text{ ft. lbs.}}{\text{sec.}}$$

The *watt* (W) is the measure of power used in the electrical industry, and:

746 watts = 1 horsepower.

The watt, however, is a small quantity of power. Therefore, power is usually measured in thousands of watts, or kilowatts (KW), or even millions of watts, or megawatts (MW).

If:

$$\text{Power} = \frac{\text{Force} \times \text{Distance}}{\text{Time}}$$

and:

$$\text{Work} = \text{Force} \times \text{Distance}$$

then:

$$\text{Power} = \frac{\text{Work}}{\text{Time}}$$

and:

$$\text{Power} \times \text{Time} = \text{Work.}$$

The unit of energy or work produced by the electric utility is the watt-hour. Again, this is such a small unit of output that measurements are usually made in thousands of watt-hours or kilowatt-hours (KWH) or even millions of watt-hours, or megawatt-hours (MWH).

Confusion often exists between the output of the plant (measured in kilowatt-hours) and the *capacity* or *capability* of the generating plant, measured in kilowatts (KW) or megawatts (MW). Capacity is the ability to produce a given output of electricity at an instant in time, and output is the amount of electricity produced in a period of time. (Technically, capacity is a rating given to the generator by the manufacturers or the utility. Capability, on the other hand, refers to the load the unit can handle without exceeding limits set to prevent operating problems.)

For an example, a pipe factory has 10 machines in it, each capable of producing one pipe an hour. If each machine works, the factory has the capacity to produce 10 pipes at once, and its output is 10 pipes an hour. Similarly, an electrical generating station that has the capability of producing 1,000 kilowatts at one time will have an output of 1,000 kilowatt-hours if it runs at maximum capacity for one hour.

In a sense, the consumer of electricity makes two different calls on the electric system, one for capacity (measured in kilowatts) and one for output (measured in kilowatt-hours). If a customer owns a machine that requires 1,000 kilowatt-hours of electricity each hour to run, the utility must set aside 1,000 kilowatts of capacity to serve that machine. The customer demands 1,000 kilowatts of capacity, and that amount is fixed. The customer, however, could run the machine any amount of time up to 24 hours a day (requiring an output of 24,000 kilowatt-hours). The output taken by the customer therefore varies. That situation is one of the major problems of the electric utility industry, which must have the capacity available for the customer and must support that fixed plant, while realizing that the customer's need for power may vary greatly.

The utility industry divides its operations into three segments: *generation*, *transmission* and *distribution*. Generation is the production of the power itself, usually in a large central station. Because the power station may not be near the consumers, the power must be transmitted, sometimes over long distances. Those transmission lines often carry the electricity at high voltages. A *volt* (V) is a unit of electromotive force (pressure). It can be compared to water pressure, or to the force of water coming out of a hose. The *kilovolt* (KV), one thousand volts, is a common measure. Once the power reaches the neighborhood of the users, it is stepped down at a substation to a lower voltage, and then it is sent through the local distribution lines to the customers.

That briefly sums up the basics of electric utility operations.

Chapter 3

Generation, Demand and Storage

The building and equipment of the station and its distribution system required large outlays of capital, whereas the demand for light was confined to a relatively small portion of the running time. . . .[4]

Abbott Payson Usher

In the electric utility industry, power is produced at central generating stations and then distributed over a network to customers. The power stations are themselves interconnected by the network. Individual customers, power stations and distribution networks are not isolated from each other.

The bulk of central station power is generated in one of three ways: from the burning of fossil fuel (coal, oil, natural gas), from the burnup of nuclear fuel, or from the force of water (hydroelectricity). The principle of the production of alternating current (AC) electric power is the same for all three methods. Fuel (either fossil or nuclear) is used to heat water to steam. The pressure of the steam turns the blades on a wheel called the turbine (a super pinwheel). The shaft of the turbine is attached to electromagnets. The spinning of the turbine causes the electromagnets to turn, causing the magnetic lines of force to cut the wire, thereby inducing an alternating current of electricity into the wire coil. (As an alternative, the electric coil or loop can be turned, and the magnets remain stationary.) That coil is the beginning of the utility's grid, which carries power to the users. For hydropower, the process differs only in that the turbine is a water wheel turned by falling water rather than a pinwheel turned by steam.

For most electric utility systems, power must be produced at the generator when the customer wants it. Because in most circumstances the power cannot be produced in advance and stored for the moment it is needed, the utility must have enough production facilities available to meet the maximum demand on its system whenever that occurs. Much of that generating plant will not be in use for most of the day, but only when demand is there. Perhaps an example will demonstrate the awkwardness of such a situation.

Take the case of a toy company that makes all of its sales in December.

14

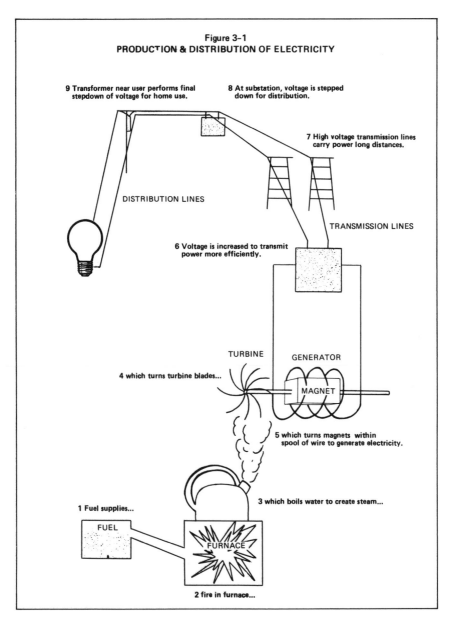

Figure 3-1
PRODUCTION & DISTRIBUTION OF ELECTRICITY

9 Transformer near user performs final stepdown of voltage for home use.

8 At substation, voltage is stepped down for distribution.

7 High voltage transmission lines carry power long distances.

DISTRIBUTION LINES

TRANSMISSION LINES

6 Voltage is increased to transmit power more efficiently.

TURBINE   GENERATOR

4 which turns turbine blades...

MAGNET

5 which turns magnets within spool of wire to generate electricity.

1 Fuel supplies...

3 which boils water to create steam...

FUEL

FURNACE

2 fire in furnace...

It will sell 12,000 toys in that month. Each toy machine makes 100 toys a month. The toy machine can be rented for $1,000 a year and only annual leases are available. The raw material costs are $1 a toy. The cost of storing toys is $100 a thousand toys a month. Should the toy company rent 120 machines so that it could produce all 12,000 toys in one month and thus save on storage costs, or should it rent 10 machines, produce 1,000 toys a month, and store the inventory until the December rush? The answer requires simple arithmetic. In the first case, machine rental would be:

$$120 \times \$1,000 = \$120,000$$

and with no storage costs likely, the production cost would be $120,000 for rental plus $12,000 for raw materials, or $132,000 in total. In the second case, machine rental would be:

$$10 \times \$1,000 = \$10,000$$

and if we assume that an average of 6,000 toys were in storage for the year, storage costs would be $7,200 and raw material costs $12,000, so total production costs would be $29,200. The answer is clearcut. There is no reason to have 120 machines on which rent is paid standing idle for 11 months of the year. It is too expensive.

The problem, however, is that the electric utility usually cannot store its production, and must have the generators ready to meet that period of maximum demand. The machines must be in place even if they are expensive to maintain and stand idle for much of the time. The utility's daily load pattern might look like that in Figure 3-2.

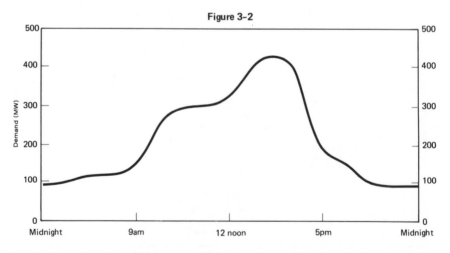

Figure 3-2

Load also varies during the year with heavy demand during the heating and air conditioning seasons, as can be seen in Figure 3-3.

The utility has to serve the entire load, but it does not need the same kind of power plant to do everything. For instance, in examining the daily and monthly charts, demand appears never to go below 100 megawatts. On the other hand, demand goes above 300 MW for only brief periods. The

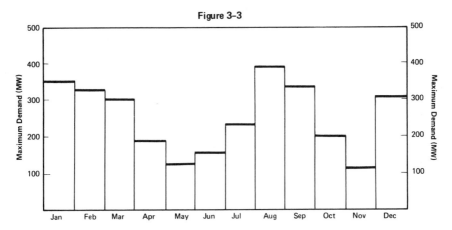

Figure 3-3

utility wishes to minimize the investment it has in plant that is likely to be idle most of the time, and wants the plant that will be in operation most of the time to be as reliable and economical as possible.

The solution is to build what are called *base load* plants to meet the minimum around-the-clock load. Because fixed costs can be spread over many hours of operation, those plants tend to be large and expensive-to-build machines that utilize low cost fuels. The base load plants are built for steady running. If demand on the system becomes unstable or unpredictable (as has been the case in recent years) and dips below the expected base load, then base load generating units have to be run below their capacity or turned on and off. That kind of use puts strains on the plants and is inefficient.

At the other extreme, the utility builds and runs *peaking units* for those brief periods of maximum (peak) demand on the system. Those units are generally inexpensive to build (because fixed costs have to be spread over a brief period of usage), but fuel costs are often high. The industry also has an intermediate category of generators that are used less than base load and more than peaking units.

In order to be able to build larger generating units, have power available at times of emergencies, plan systems without duplicating the work of neighboring companies and increase their ability to buy low cost power from others, electric utilities join in regional *power pools*. The companies in the pool work together to assure a reliable, low cost power supply for a large area.

Often power plants within the pool are owned jointly and power within the pool is dispatched from a central control point. In a sense, a number of companies run their generation and transmission operations on a joint basis.

In the production of electricity, roughly two-thirds of the caloric content of the fuel is lost up the smokestack or into waterways in the form of waste heat. In the United States, the power plants usually are situated far from potential customers for the waste heat. Perhaps if the power plant could be built where the user of heat is situated, then more of the heat that is contained in the fuel could be used. That is the principle of *cogeneration*, an old idea with a new name. A small power plant, situated at the industrial facility, produces electricity and waste heat. Some (or all) of the electricity is consumed at the industrial facility and the balance, if there is any, is sold to the electric utility. The waste heat is used in industrial processes. (Some industrial processes might produce waste heat that could be applied to help generate electricity, too, reversing the concept.) The concept behind cogeneration is to waste as little fuel as possible. Under Federal and some state laws, the price for cogeneration power to the utility is set at the utility's avoided costs (what electricity would have cost from the generating station that was displaced by the cogenerated power). Depending on the size and ownership of the cogenerator, return earned on the cogeneration investment may not be regulated.

Considering the huge sums invested in generating facilities, the utility concerns itself with the generating unit's *availability,* or the percentage of time that the unit is available for use, whether the unit is used or not. Clearly, availability is something within control of the management. How much the machine is actually used on average, however, might depend on the timing of the customers' demands for electricity. To get a good idea of usage, one calculates the *capacity factor,* or average load on the machine as a percentage of rated capacity.

For instance, if a 500 MW machine supplies 400 MW in the first hour, 300 MW in the second hour, 500 MW in the third hour, and 200 MW in the fourth hour, the average load is 1400/4, or 350 MW. The capacity factor is:

$$\frac{350}{500} = 70\%$$

Management must also consider the characteristics of demand for power in the utility's system. An effective management will want demand spread so that generators will be idle as little as possible. How the load is spread out and whether there is a great difference between the average demand on the system and the demand at peak is measured by the *load factor,* which is defined as average load in a particular period as a percentage of peak load. Consider the two electrical systems with identical generating capacity (600 MW) and peak load (500 MW) shown in Figure 3-4.

Clearly, with the same investment, Company B keeps its facilities running more and sells more electricity than Company A. A load factor, however, could get too high. When that happens, the utility is using its generators so much that it does not have the time available to take the units out of service for normal maintenance, which means that the utility might need

Figure 3-4

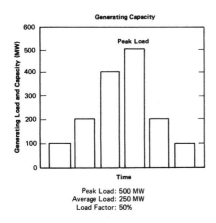

Peak Load: 500 MW
Average Load: 250 MW
Load Factor: 50%

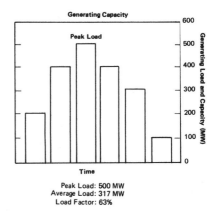

Peak Load: 500 MW
Average Load: 317 MW
Load Factor: 63%

extra generating units in reserve so that generators can be taken out of service for needed maintenance repairs.

That, in turn, leads us to the subject of the *reserve margin*. If the electric company could predict perfectly its peak demand and the times its generating units would be out of service, it could have sufficient generating capacity to meet the peak load, without wasting money on superfluous plant. Unfortunately, utility managements must be prepared for the vagaries of demand and for unexpected breakdowns of generators. They must have additional power plants that can be put into service either immediately or after a short period of preparation. The utility may not own the power plant that is held in reserve, but it might have a contract with a neighboring utility to buy extra power when needed. In its simplest form, reserve margin is the difference between peak load and capacity as a percentage of peak load. *Capacity margin* is the difference between peak load and capacity as a percentage of capacity. In the above example, capacity is 600 MW, peak load is 500 MW, reserve margin is 20% and capacity margin is 16.7%. The actual calculations account for ability to buy from or obligation to sell to other systems on a firm basis. Assuming (at time of peak load):

C	=	capacity margin (%)
R	=	reserve margin (%)
C_o	=	own system capability (MW)
C_p	=	capability under firm purchase from others (MW)
C_s	=	firm obligations to sell capability to others (MW)
P	=	own system peak load (MW)

then:

$$R = \left(\frac{C_o + C_p - C_s - P}{P}\right) \times 100 \text{ and } C = \left(\frac{C_o + C_p - C_s - P}{C_o + C_p - C_s}\right) \times 100$$

The proper generating reserve margin depends on the characteristics of the system, such as types of generators, load growth, and availability of power from neighboring companies. Theoretically, a utility with a large number of small power plants can get by with a lower margin because the odds are against having several plants out of service at the same time. A utility with a few large plants might need a high reserve margin to guard against the possibility that one plant representing a large percentage of capacity might go out of service. A utility whose plants go out of service often, would need a higher reserve margin than a utility with plants that operate well. If conditions of demand were extremely erratic (perhaps because of extremely high, low, or unpredictable temperatures), the utility might need a high reserve margin to protect it against the unexpected. Finally, some utilities make large sales to interruptible customers whose service can be turned off at will by the utility. Such a utility need not invest in a large amount of reserve capability because it has the option to cut off customers during difficult periods. The desired reserve margin is set by a loss of load probability (LOLP) analysis designed to assure that major power outages will be limited to one day in a given number of years.

Until recently, emphasis has been placed on ensuring that capacity is available to meet the peak load. That emphasis, however, has been extremely expensive because of the cost of building generation plants. Utilities have begun to experiment with the management of demand so that the peak load can be cut down to obviate the need for the generating capacity. Load can be influenced by charging more for power at certain times of the day or year, or it can be controlled directly by the electric utility (load management). In load management, the electric company connects a control device to one or more appliances on the customer's premises. During periods of high demand, the electric company turns off the appliance for a period of time, thereby making it less necessary for the utility to keep generating reserves. In a sense, the utility has created additional interruptible customers. Tests indicate that, for many systems, the cost of load management equipment per KW of demand reduction is far less than that of capacity added to meet each KW of additional demand.

So far we have discussed the electric system as if power could not be stored, and as a result generating units either had to be available to meet demand or demand had to be repressed to fit available generating capacity. Actually, power can be stored, if the utility is fortunate to have the right sort of terrain nearby. The pumped storage hydro plant is such a facility. During off peak periods, such as the middle of the night, the utility uses power from its most efficient base load generating station (probably a nuclear power plant) to pump water into a reservoir on the top of a mountain. The water is stored in the reservoir until demand rises to the level at which the utility needs additional power. At that point, the water is released, descends through pipes, and turns electrical turbines. The spinning turbine generates electricity in the same manner as in an ordinary hydroelectric facility. The pumped storage plant is like a huge rechargeable battery. Other storage research is going on based on the same principles.

In Table 3-1, we can see some of the trends of the last two decades. In the 1960s, growth in both sales and peak load was high. The industry's capacity, however, rose more slowly than peak load. That was possible because the industry started with a high reserve margin that could be allowed to fall. The load factor declined a bit. In addition, the industry was able to generate an increasing amount of electricity for each kilowatt of installed capacity. (In theory, if a generator worked perfectly all year, one kilowatt of capacity could produce 8,760 KWH of power in a normal year and 8,784 KWH in a leap year.) In the 1970s, sales and peak load growth became unstable, probably because of sharply higher prices and increased sensitivity to weather conditions (because of the popularity of air conditioning and electric heating). The industry, however, was adding capacity as if nothing had happened to demand because the plant additions had been planned years before the slowdown. Reserve margin rose, indicating that many utilities were carrying the burden of plant in excess of need. The load factor continued to drop. The worst indicator was the sharply declining amount of power generated by each kilowatt of capacity in place.

To some extent, the industry's problems became circular. It could not operate large, new base load generators as planned because demand did not materialize as projected. When the plants were operated under suboptimal conditions, they did not perform well. If plants did not perform well, higher reserve margins were required, and operating costs rose, thereby raising the price of electricity. Price was raised even more because cost of facilities had to be spread over an unexpectedly low level of KWH sales. That triggered another fall in demand and worsened the operating situation. Even today, the industry will require several more years to adjust capacity additions to the new demand situation, to put in power plants that will respond better to unstable conditions, and to control load to keep it in line with capacity. In the future, the industry will have to not only make more efficient use of its own facilities, but also do so while incorporating into the system new, non-utilities sources of electricity.

TABLE 3-1

Sales, Demand and Capacity 1960-1986
Total Electric Utility Industry

Year	% Change in KWH Sales to Ultimate Customers	% Change in Peak Load	% Change in Capacity at Peak	Reserve Margin %	Load Factor %	Ratio of KWH Generated to Average KW of Capacity (Total USA)
1960	8.9	6.1	7.0	31.5	65.5	4688
1961	5.5	6.0	8.3	31.0	64.8	4588
1962	7.7	7.3	4.8	31.0	64.9	4649
1963	7.1	6.6	6.0	30.2	65.2	4624
1964	7.2	8.5	5.5	23.7	64.2	4619
1965	7.1	6.5	5.7	22.9	65.0	4677
1966	9.0	9.2	5.2	18.4	64.7	4793
1967	6.5	5.0	7.2	20.8	65.3	4747
1968	8.6	11.5	8.1	17.2	63.5	4800
1969	8.7	8.3	7.7	16.6	64.1	4831
1970	6.4	6.6	8.9	19.0	63.9	4733
1971	5.4	6.3	8.1	20.9	63.2	4583
1972	7.6	9.3	8.1	19.6	62.5	4601
1973	8.0	7.7	8.9	20.8	62.0	4468
1974	−0.1	1.5	7.0	27.2	61.2	4122
1975	1.9	2.2	7.9	34.3	61.4	3915
1976	6.7	4.0	4.1	34.5	62.6	3943
1977	5.5	6.9	3.5	30.2	61.4	3915
1978	3.4	3.0	5.8	33.7	62.1	3879
1979	3.3	−2.4	2.3	36.7	64.4	3816
1980	2.0	7.2	2.4	30.7	61.1	3773
1981	1.2	0.5	2.4	33.3	61.6	3676
1982	−2.4	−3.2	2.5	41.0	62.1	3488
1983	2.9	7.7	1.8	33.3	59.5	3562
1984	5.6	0.8	1.3	33.9	59.7	3687
1985	1.1	2.1	2.9	35.0	62.0	3632
1986	2.1	3.4	1.9	33.0	60.7	3563
Averages:						
1960-1964	7.4	6.9	6.3	29.5	64.9	4634
1965-1969	8.0	8.1	6.8	19.2	64.5	4770
1970-1974	5.4	6.3	8.2	21.5	62.6	4501
1975-1979	4.1	3.4	4.7	33.9	62.4	3894
1980-1984	2.3	2.6	2.1	34.4	60.6	3637
1985-1986	2.6	2.8	2.4	34.0	61.4	3598

Source: Edison Electric Institute, *Statistical Year Book of the Electric Utility Industry* (Washington, D.C.: EEI, various dates), Tables 2, 7, 12, 38.

Chapter 4

Fuels

The failure to build more economical coal-fired and nuclear power plants would mean foregoing an opportunity to eliminate ... oil and gas use by utilities. The result would be higher fuel costs ... In addition, this use of oil could continue U.S. dependence on imports.[5]

Betsy O'Brien and Andrew Reynolds

The electric utility industry started by burning coal. When long distance transmission became possible, the industry exploited hydropower sites, but coal has remained the dominant fuel for the entire history of the industry.

Picking a fuel is not always a question of what burns best or what is nearby, to which recent experience attests. Many utilities in the 1960s switched from coal to oil to avoid the environmental problem involved in burning coal. In the 1980s, many of the same utilities then switched from oil to coal to cut down dependence on foreign oil. Natural gas was considered to be a clean, efficient fuel, but the short-lived natural gas shortage for a time caused the Federal Government to attempt to force electric utilities off gas to reserve that fuel for supposedly superior uses. Use of water power depends on the availability of good hydropower dam sites. Most of the major sites have been utilized or are in park areas, so few large scale hydropower projects (excluding pumped storage) have been built recently. The rising cost of fossil fuels, however, may make small hydro projects economical again. From the early 1960s, a handful of nuclear power plants produced a miniscule portion of the nation's power, but electric utilities had great hope for what appeared to be an economical and benign source of energy. Environmental opposition, changing rules for construction and safety, and skyrocketing costs have retarded the growth of nuclear power.

What else is there? Geothermal energy produces a small amount of power in California. In logging regions, burning waste wood produces some electricity. The industry is also experimenting with solar energy, windmills, agricultural wastes and just about anything else. For the near term, however, conventional power sources will dominate the mixture.

As Table 4-1 illustrates, generating mixes have changed. Some of the variation is attributable to fluctuations in water conditions, to coal strikes, and to plant shutdowns, but the trend shows a clear substitution of oil for coal between 1965 and 1973. Now there is a resurgence in the use of coal at the expense of oil. The trend for natural gas will depend on the state of legislation regulating its use and its availability. The trend seems to be down but utilities probably will push to continue to use this clean fuel. If supplies are adequate, utilities might even build new gas fired units. Nuclear power was on the upswing until plant shutdowns and operational delays associated with the Three Mile Island nuclear accident put a halt to nuclear activity for a while. Nuclear power should become increasingly important in the future, although not to the extent previously predicted by nuclear boosters. In the case of hydro, year-to-year swings are due to variation in water conditions, but hydro should account for a declining percentage of generation. If current projections are any indicator, the fuel mix in 1996 might be over 50% coal, over 20% nuclear, with the balance oil, hydro, gas and other.

Aside from experiments with sun and wind, certain developments could alter the fuel mix. Discovery of more natural gas might make a significant difference in fuel planning. Another oil emergency, of course, could speed up substitution for that fuel ("oil back out" is the term used in the trade).

Research on burning coal more cleanly might bear fruit, or environmental restrictions could be relaxed. In either case, the result would be greater emphasis on coal. More cogeneration might have a minor effect on fuel mix, too. Some cogeneration plants could conceivably burn industrial wastes. Finally, if the utilities succeed in reducing peak load (many of the peaking plants burn oil or gas), they might be able to increase the percentage of generation from base loaded coal and nuclear generating stations. On the other hand, legislation to reduce acid rain would slow the use of certain types of coal.

TABLE 4-1

Generation by Energy Source 1960-1986
Total Electric Utility Industry

(%)

Year	Coal	Oil	Gas	Nuclear	Hydro and Other
1960	53.5	6.1	21.0	0.1	19.3
1961	53.2	6.0	21.4	0.2	19.2
1962	52.9	5.5	21.7	0.2	19.7
1963	53.9	5.7	22.0	0.3	18.1
1964	53.5	5.8	22.4	0.3	18.0
1965	54.1	6.1	21.1	0.3	18.4
1966	53.6	6.9	22.0	0.5	17.0
1967	51.9	7.4	21.8	0.7	18.2
1968	51.5	7.8	22.9	1.0	16.8
1969	49.0	9.6	23.2	0.9	17.3
1970	46.1	11.9	24.4	1.4	16.2
1971	44.3	13.5	23.2	2.4	16.6
1972	44.2	15.6	21.4	3.1	15.7
1973	45.6	16.9	18.4	4.5	14.7
1974	44.4	16.0	17.1	6.1	16.3
1975	44.4	15.1	15.7	9.0	15.8
1976	46.3	15.7	14.5	9.4	14.1
1977	46.4	16.8	14.4	11.8	10.6
1978	44.2	16.5	13.9	12.5	12.9
1979	47.8	13.5	14.7	11.3	12.7
1980	50.8	10.7	15.1	11.0	12.4
1981	52.4	9.0	15.1	11.9	11.6
1982	53.2	6.6	13.6	12.6	14.0
1983	54.5	6.3	11.9	12.7	14.7
1984	55.5	5.0	12.3	13.6	13.7
1985	56.8	4.1	11.8	15.5	11.8
1986	55.7	5.5	10.0	16.6	12.2

Source: Edison Electric Institute, *Statistical Year Book of the Electric Utility Industry* (Washington, D.C.: EEI, various dates), Tables 14, 21, and 22.

Chapter 5

Environmental, National Defense, Social, and Philosophical Considerations

Thus, what confronts us is not a series of separate crises, but a single basic defect — a fault that lies deep in the design of modern society.[6]

Barry Commoner

Modern economics does not distinguish between renewable and non-renewable materials, as its very method is to equalize and quantify everything by means of a money price ... From a Buddhist point of view ... this will not do. Non-renewable goods must be used only if they are indispensable.[7]

E. F. Schumacher

For years, the electric utility industry ran its operations unchallenged. Problems had simple engineering solutions. Once the solution was found, all that had to be done was to implement it. Alas, the simple life ended in the turbulent 1960s, but that took a while to realize. The result was frustration, conflict, and financial distress.

In some ways, national policy issues are the easiest to comprehend. The nation's interest is not served by importing huge amounts of oil. The electric utility industry uses under one tenth of all oil consumed in the country, but power plants are visible and under Government control. Therefore, electric companies can be ordered to switch from oil to other fuels. When natural gas appeared to be in short supply, electric companies were ordered to cut back use of gas to make sure that gas was available for residential users. Because natural gas is itself a substitute for oil for some uses, having electric utilities change from gas frees up oil for domestic use without increasing oil imports. Thus, the operations of the electric utility industry can be affected by considerations of national interest, and any cost associated with those operating changes may be borne by the utility's customers and stockholders unless the Government provides a subsidy.

Standard objections by environmentalists to utility operations are more

26

difficult to handle, because experts cannot always decide whether the objections are valid. Furthermore, although certain operations are clearly damaging to the environment, the cost to prevent the damage may be well in excess of the cost of the damage itself.

Some objections are of a generic nature. Power plants and transmission lines are huge and often unsightly structures that obtrude into the landscape. In the early days of environmentalism, the electric utility managements saw their problems in almost cosmetic terms:

> Since utility facilities are so prevalent a part of the landscape, beautification and preservation of scenic values are elements which must be incorporated into the policies and programs of every utility.[8]

The term "beautility" came into fashion for a short while, referring to attempts to locate facilities esthetically or to place distribution lines underground.

Power stations generally require huge amounts of water. The water is discharged at a substantially higher temperature than the surrounding water. The hot water could have untoward environmental consequences for aquatic animals and plants, so electric utilities are required to build cooling ponds, canals, and enormous cooling towers to lower the temperature of the water, before discharging it.

When fossil fuels are burned, particulates and harmful gases are emitted from the smokestack. One of the earliest solutions to the problem was to build tall stacks, so that pollutants would not concentrate near the power plant, but would be spread by the wind. If enough power plants had followed that procedure, of course, the country would have turned grey. The industry installed precipitators, scrubbers and filters to prevent particles from escaping. It installed scrubbers, to remove sulfur oxides, and then had to deal with the problem of removal of the waste material produced in the scrubbers. Some companies switched from coal to low sulfur content oil to avoid the scrubber problem. Others switched to low sulfur coal. Water and air pollution control equipment adds 20% or more to the cost of a power plant and also decreases output and reliability.

High voltage transmission lines have been criticized for more than just appearance. They have been denounced for everything from bringing on headaches and nervous disorders in workers and in farmers ploughing the fields under the lines to disturbing the milking habits of local cows. Studies and counterstudies provide a confusing picture. Local opposition to routing of lines has made it extremely difficult to place transmission corridors, and transmission towers have been bombed in several places.

Finally, the creation of carbon dioxide is a problem inherent in the burning of fossil fuels. A buildup of carbon dioxide in the atmosphere might create a greenhouse effect that would warm the atmosphere sufficiently to melt some of the polar ice, thereby raising the water level of the ocean and flooding vast land areas. Research on this question is in its infancy, but the problem is made more serious by the claim that we could increase the carbon dioxide to the damaging levels before we finish the research, unless the ocean or forests could act as a sink for carbon dioxide long enough for us to come to grips with the problem.[9]

Other environmental objections are aimed at particular fuels. Even hydropower is not considered benign by some because the huge dams destroy flowing rivers, change aquatic habitats, and require long transmission lines to carry power to the load centers.

Underground coal mining may be dangerous and unhealthy. Surface (strip) mining scars the landscape if done improperly. Burning coal produces not only carbon dioxide, but also particulates, sulfur oxides, and acid rain. The waste material that comes from filtering and scrubbing at the power plant must be disposed of, too. Burning coal may be especially offensive in densely inhabited areas. Some of the difficulties, though, can be alleviated by burning coal with a low sulfur content. In addition, experimentation indicates that coal can be processed to reduce pollution.

Although many would assert that the environmental danger from coal is greater than from nuclear power, nuclear power has been a main target of environmentalists.[10] As one critic put it, in a relatively temperate statement about nuclear power:

> Again, no one knows what the chance of a major accident actually is and reassurances that cite very tiny probabilities must be taken with a grain of salt. Highly improbable events have a way of happening anyway in complicated technological systems, as the 1965 Northeast power blackout, the sinking of the "unsinkable" Titanic and the failure of other "fail-safe" and "fool-proof" systems have demonstrated.[11]

The objections to nuclear power range from solidly based to hysterical. Here are some of the main ones:

1) The estimated cost of nuclear power to society is not a true one because nuclear power has been subsidized by the Government. Thus, cost comparisons are unfairly biased toward nuclear power. This is probably true. On the other hand, public transportation and solar energy (after tax credits) — two environmental causes — are or have been subsidized.

2) The nuclear power plant can blow up like an atom bomb. Almost all experts flatly deny this as a possibility because of the dilution of the fuel within the reactor.[12]

3) The cooling system that keeps down the heat within the reactor could malfunction. This would cause the core of nuclear fuel to melt down

or to precipitate a boiler explosion, either of which could possibly penetrate the reactor's containment structure, thereby loosing radioactive materials into the environment. In America's most serious nuclear accident, Three Mile Island (1979), the containment vessel held in the radioactive material. Russia's Chernobyl plant did not have the same containment facilities. The 1986 nuclear accident there did scatter radioactive contamination.

4) Nuclear materials in transit could be hijacked or involved in accidents. This is possible, but methods of transport make it unlikely.

5) A nuclear accident near a city could harm many people. That is true to the extent that a serious accident is likely. New generating stations are placed far from population centers, although doing so does not alleviate fears about the nuclear plants already running in urban areas. Ironically, one recommendation of an environmental task force in the 1960s was "that earnest examination be conducted on the feasibility of siting nuclear plants in urban areas at the earliest possible time."[13] Doing so, it was suggested, would reduce urban air pollution and the need for long distance high voltage transmission lines.

6) Nuclear wastes produced by the power plant are poisons that will endanger the environment for thousands of years and cannot be disposed of safely. Perhaps a better argument would be that the United States Government, over four decades into the nuclear age, has not developed permanent waste storage facilities and seems years away from doing so, despite all the research on the subject. Europeans have developed disposal techniques, including encapsulation and burial, but, so far, American politicians, scientists and environmentalists have not been able to agree on satisfactory procedures for the United States.

7) The nuclear reactor, once its life has ended, will be a huge radioactive monument that will have to be taken apart, guarded, or entombed. This may be true at least until radioactivity dies down enough to allow dismemberment. It seems unlikely that the dead nuclear power plant will be the monument of our time, America's answer to the pyramid.

As for the objections to nuclear power, some seem to be based on the argument that anything can happen, so risks should not be taken. Others represent serious questions that nuclear agencies have not done enough to address. The question, though, is, what is the alternative? If the answer is coal, it may be that nuclear power is environmentally preferable. Environmentalists would counter that the real alternatives are more efficient use of energy (so that the nuclear plant is not needed at all) and so-called "soft technologies" such as solar power. Oddly enough, after trying for years to go the nuclear route, many utility executives seem to have come to the same conclusion, although their reasons are probably more economic and political than environmental.

Sociological and philosophical objections may underlie some of the fights about health and safety. Our environmental laws address matters of health, safety, and preservation. They do not consider whether centralized generation of power is socially or economically objectionable. If one believes that central generation of power is a threat to society, what better way to stop it than to raise environmental objections? A court case to preserve an obscure flower can stop a power project far better than a political campaign to replace a power station with wood stoves. If campaigning against its perceived environmental dangers is really a method to stop central station power then no amount of measures to fix the objectionable elements of the power system will succeed in mollifying the opposition. The philosophical/sociological objections to central station power fit into two categories, thermodynamic and political.

Central station power, opponents maintain, creates a mismatch between the quality of energy and the tasks for which the energy is used. For instance, boiling water to turn a turbine to send electricity to an electric motor may be the best way to turn the electric motor. It may not be the best way to heat water to lukewarm for a bath. The bath water could be heated more efficiently by applying a flame to water in the house. In other words, why heat water to several hundred degrees in the boiler of the generator to heat water several tens of degrees in the bathtub?[14] The previous question is about second law efficiency. Aside from giving us additional insight, second law efficiency may have also become fashionable because it leads to a desired answer. Low quality heat should be used to do low quality work. Solar energy is of low quality and should be used to raise temperatures to relatively low levels (i e., room, pool, and water heating needs). That analysis is correct in the sense that more energy is lost when high temperature processes are used to produce low temperatures. The problem with an analysis that only considers energy is that improvement in energy efficiency, no matter how measured, incurs costs. It may be more expensive (as measured in money) to save energy than to waste it. Perhaps that would not be the case if energy were priced properly, but there could still be instances where the cost of increasing the energy efficiency of a project exceeds the value of the energy saved.

The second argument against central station power is that it is a coercive technology that saddles us with diseconomies of scale, is unsafe militarily, puts control of our destiny in the hands of a few, and prevents the development of a benign, decentralized society based in part on soft technologies. Basically, the argument calls for the dismantling of our industrial society, which cannot last anyway because it is based on non-renewable energy resources. That attitude, unfortunately, is generally not taken seriously by utility managements, regulators and investors, which may explain, in part, why they do not fully comprehend some of their opponents. Ironically, as will be discussed later, proponents of a freer, less regulated utility environment also advocate less emphasis on central station power for economic rather than political reasons.

For the late 1980s and early 1990s, the most serious environmental and operating problems might include:

1) *Acid rain* - The term, coined in 1852 by British scientist Angus Smith, refers to the deposition of acidic emissions, some of which are dry. Acid rain has become an international issue.[15] Correction could require installation of expensive scrubbers or development of new coal cleaning technology.

2) *Location and improvement of transmission lines* -Transmission may be the bottleneck that prevents needed power transfers, economic operations of some facilities and competition.

3) *Nuclear safety* - Disputes over evacuation plans and the politics of the NIMBY (not in my backyard) syndrome could create problems for existing as well as new nuclear stations.

4) *Carbon dioxide* - With nuclear power seemingly unacceptable and with fossil fuel usage growing again, the climatic changes possibly caused by a buildup of carbon dioxide could become an issue.

No doubt a combination of more effective use of energy, more efficient production and a forward looking research effort will be needed to solve environmental problems.

Chapter 6

Operations, Demand and Planning

The market price ... is regulated by the proportion between the quantity which is actually brought to market, and the demand of those willing to pay the natural price of the commodity ... which must be paid to bring it thither. Such people may be called the effectual demanders, and their demand the effectual demand ... It is different from the absolute demand. A very poor man may be said ... to have a demand for a coach and six; he might like to have it; but his demand is not an effective demand, as the commodity can never be brought to market in order to satisfy it.[16]

Adam Smith

Electric utilities must begin to build many facilities well ahead of the time the facilities will be needed, simply because it takes so long to complete them. To further complicate matters, the new facilities will last for decades. The electric utility must have a good estimate of what the customer will buy over a long period of time or the plant that is built could prove to be either unnecessary or inadequate.

Not only must the utility estimate the amount of electricity that will be sold, but it must also project the timing of the sales. Will the customer buy the power steadily around the clock and throughout the year, or will demand for power be bunched around peak periods? If the former is the case, the utility will put in expensive to build, but inexpensive to run, base load generators. If the latter, it will install cheap to build but expensive to run peaking units. Or, as another alternative to peaking units, it may try to control demand at the peak, through special pricing or electronic devices that turn off customers for brief periods, rather than by building peaking units.

As an example, a base load generating unit costs $1,000 to build, the fixed costs and interest on borrowing the money to build it are $150 per year, and the unit burns a cheap fuel, runs efficiently, and therefore has operating costs of 5¢ per kilowatt-hour produced. A peaking unit, on the other hand, costs $300 to build, the fixed costs and interest paid for the

investment is only \$45, but the unit burns an expensive fuel, runs ineffi-
ciently and has operating costs of 20¢ per kilowatt-hour generated. Both
plants should last the same number of years. There are 8760 hours in a 365
day year. The electric utility expects to need a new generating unit 3,000
hours per year. Which one should it choose?

For the base load plant, total cost will be:

$150 for interest

plus 3,000 hours × 5¢ per hour operating costs (\$150)

or \$300 per year.

For the peaking unit, total costs will be:

$45 for interest

plus 3,000 hours × 20¢ per hour operating costs (\$600)

or \$645 per year.

Obviously, it is cheaper to build a base load plant. On the other hand, if the
utility only needed the plant for 300 hours, during the hottest hours of the
day in August, then the decision might be different.

For the base load plant, total costs are:

$150 for interest

plus 300 hours × 5¢ per hour operating costs (\$15)

or \$165 per year.

For the peaking unit, total costs are:

$45 for interest

plus 300 hours × 20¢ per hour operating costs (\$60)

or \$105 per year.

The utility must also plan ahead by choosing the right fuel for the power
station. (Stations that can burn several fuels are flexible but also more expensive to construct.) The choice of fuel depends on location, price, availability, national security and environmental considerations. Those factors can
change radically during the period of construction and the life of the plant.

In the days when demand for electricity grew at a steady pace, power plants could be completed quickly, fuel costs were stable and environmental rules almost non-existent, planning was easy. The best tool for projection was the ruler.

Between 1960 and 1973, electricity sales rose every year, never more than 9.0% nor less than 5.4% in any year. In ten of the years, the sales increase was in the 7%-9% range. Peak load grew steadily, too, going up between 5.0% and 11.5% each year. In ten years, the numbers ranged between 6% and 9%. Load factor was equally steady, staying between 62% and 66%, with nine years in the 64%-66% range. The electric company's projection might not be on target every year, but it was not likely to be far off. The companies planned and built plant with confidence. After 1973, patterns of demand became unstable, with annual changes in sales ranging from −2.4% to 6.7% and peak load growth fluctuating wildly from −3.2% to 7.7%. Load factor deteriorated, falling between 59.5% and 64.4%.

Yet, even before 1973, the Yom Kippur War and the upheaval in the oil markets, there were problems. In the early l960s, the load factor held up and reserve margin fell, indicating that the pattern of load was relatively steady and that the industry felt that it could cut down on its reserves without endangering service. In 1965, the lights went out in the Northeast. Managements had to rethink procedures and need for facilities, but power plants take a while to build, and reserve margin fell more. Then, in the 1970s, as the new capacity went into service, load patterns deteriorated and so did growth in demand, probably because economic growth slowed below expectations, service industries (which are less energy intensive than heavy industry) began to dominate the economy and because the price of electricity rose in relation to other prices. A consumer would be sensible to cut use throughout the year, but still take the usual load at peak (during periods of discomfort) if the tariff did not discourage peak use. When this explanation is coupled with increased electric heating penetration (because of the natural gas shortage) and greater air conditioning saturation, the decline in the load factor is understandable. Table 6-1 documents the trends in reserves, load factor and lessening importance of large industrial users of power. As shown in Figure 6-1, the imbalance between summer and winter reserve margins increased, despite the growth of electric heating. Clearly, making use of facilities on a year-round basis became a problem for the industry.

On a simplified basis, demand for electricity is determined by five variables:

1) Economic activity — Prosperity means more electricity used by business and more appliances bought and run by consumers.

2) The price of electricity in relation to other prices — If electricity becomes cheaper than other goods, especially competing types of energy, people will use more electricity.

TABLE 6-1

Load Factor, Reserve Margins and Energy Sales by Class of Customer
1960-1986
Total Electric Utility Industry

(%)

Year	Load Factor	Reserve Margin (Non-Coincident Winter Peak)	Reserve Margin (Non-Coincident Summer Peak)	Capacity Margin (Non-Coincident Peak for Year)	Industrial % Electric Sales (Large Light & Power)
1960	65.5	31.5	28.6	24.0	50.5
1961	64.8	34.0	31.0	23.7	48.2
1962	64.9	31.0	29.3	23.7	48.2
1963	65.2	30.2	28.8	23.2	46.8
1964	64.2	30.0	23.7	19.2	46.0
1965	65.0	30.7	22.9	18.6	45.4
1966	64.7	27.9	18.4	15.5	44.8
1967	65.3	30.1	20.8	17.3	43.9
1968	63.5	27.4	17.2	14.7	43.1
1969	64.1	31.6	16.6	14.2	42.7
1970	63.9	36.4	19.0	16.0	41.2
1971	63.2	40.1	20.9	17.3	40.4
1972	62.5	35.4	19.6	16.4	40.5
1973	62.0	46.8	20.8	17.2	40.4
1974	61.2	54.5	27.2	21.4	40.5
1975	61.4	48.7	34.3	25.6	38.2
1976	62.6	46.1	34.5	25.6	39.2
1977	61.4	49.3	30.2	23.2	38.8
1978	62.1	46.6	33.7	25.2	38.8
1979	64.4	50.3	36.9	26.8	39.2
1980	61.0	48.8	30.7	23.5	37.3
1981	61.0	47.5	33.3	25.0	38.1
1982	62.0	59.9	41.0	29.1	36.7
1983	59.5	49.1	33.3	25.0	36.3
1984	59.7	42.6	33.9	25.3	36.6
1985	62.0	50.2	35.0	25.9	35.6
1986	60.7	52.9	33.0	24.8	34.7

Source: Edison Electric Institute, *Statistical Year Book of the Electric Utility Industry* (Washington, D.C.: EEI, various dates), Tables 7, 38 and 40.

3) Weather — Air conditioning and electric heating sales are affected by weather conditions.

4) The structure of the economy — Shift of emphasis to or from energy intensive industries, or even the movement of industry to or from the country will affect the demand for power.

Figure 6-1
RESERVE MARGINS

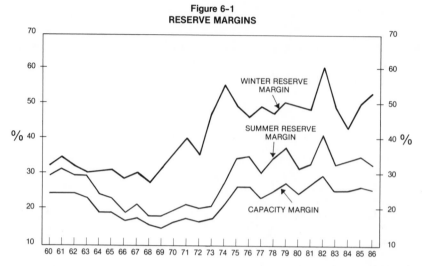

5) Technology — A stream of inventions and technological improvements will produce processes that require more electricity than old ones, or make it possible to operate with less power.

An analyst trying to determine the trend of electricity consumption in a utility's service area might also focus on demographics, the strength of the utility's conservation and insulation programs, the availability of alternative sources of energy, new businesses entering the service area and the pricing structure of the utility's electricity.

In the 1950s and 1960s, sales of electricity steadily increased. Planning ahead seemed an easy job. Sales would continue to grow the way they had grown. Power plants could be added to the system with the assurance that they would be needed. You did not need a complicated model to predict demand for electricity. Even if sales and peak load growth could not be forecast exactly, capacity often lagged requirements, so the worst that could happen was that a few utilities on occasion had slightly more plant than they needed for a year or two.

By the 1970s, demand for electricity reacted to destabilizing influences, such as the unavailability of other fuels, environmental rules that encouraged users to take electricity instead of burning their own fuels, and sharply higher prices for electricity that discouraged consumption. How can you build for the future when you do not know what the future will bring? Two basic methods are now used for projections: they could be characterized as the "bottom up" and "top down" methods.

The bottom up method is conceptually simple, but complicated in practice. The analysis examines all major uses of electricity and then predicts how these uses will grow over time, taking into account technological change, structural modifications of the economy, demographic trends, availability of fuels, price of electricity and alternatives, environmental restrictions, consumer preferences, new industrial processes, conservation, economic conditions and other factors. All the uses of electricity are then added up to derive total consumption of electrical energy. Hence the bottom up name. The approach has the advantage of focusing attention on the individual uses of electricity, but the disadvantage of forcing the analyst to predict structural and technological changes. The bottom up analyses — if not carefully prepared — may contain engineering or ideological biases in that they assume that users will take certain steps to increase or decrease demand, when in reality it may not be economical to do so. (Two examples come to mind. A metals manufacturer might be shown to increase demand because a new, efficient process uses more electricity. In reality, though, the manufacturer might choose to move manufacturing to a less developed country where energy costs are lower rather than improve processes in the United States. A residential consumer, according to the analysis, will reduce consumption of electricity by putting in a more efficient heating system. Unfortunately, in the real world, the price of electricity may be set below its real value, so perhaps the residential customer will not put in the initially more expensive heating unit, because the long term savings are not evident to him. In either case, the analysis could go wrong.)

The bottom up method usually begins with extremely detailed breakdowns of current usage for each sector of the economy. Unfortunately, the estimates of end use are often based on surveys whose results vary from one another, so the bases for the projections are rough. Let us begin with the household sector, whose usage (based on studies by Oak Ridge National Laboratories and other sources) we will approximate as:

Space heating	15%
Air conditioning	15
Water heating	15
Refrigerators	20
Freezers	10
Cooking	5
Lighting	5
Other	15
	100%

The analysts will estimate growth in number of households, the saturation level of each appliance (how many households have the appliance), whether new appliances will be larger or smaller or more energy efficient, the availability and price of competing fuels, the number of residents in each household, changes in the living space per household and insulation techniques. They will also attempt to gauge the impact of new uses for electricity and for substitutes for electricity (such as solar heating) and even the impact of shifting patterns of consumption (such as from watching television to playing computer games).

For the commercial sector the analysis will focus on the growth of floor space, new building, heating, cooling and insulation techniques, trends in usage per square foot or per employee, and the overall direction of the economy.

Analysis of the industrial sector will be more complex. Some industries use a great deal of electricity and are likely to react to a change in its price or availability by redesigning manufacturing processes or even moving the facility elsewhere. Certain industries, such as aluminum, iron and steel and industrial chemicals not only are among the biggest consumers of electricity but electricity also accounts for a significant percentage of their expenses. Analysts will look into that part of the manufacturing process that uses the most electricity and determine how new techniques will affect consumption of electricity. They will examine the price and availability of electricity relative to other fuels. They will also look into whether foreign countries can offer better conditions for these industries. Then these engineering and industrial analyses will be joined to an examination of how the industry will fare given certain rates of growth for the economy as a whole.

Several years ago, the Department of Energy produced an energy model that took into account assumptions about (among other things):

Oil, gas, tar sands and shale oil production
Imports of natural gas
Coal production and exports
Railroad traffic
Completion of power plants
Conservation programs
New technologies
Prices of fuels
Elasticities of demand

The assumptions were detailed enough to include a discussion of oil tanker rates from Alaska to the Gulf of Mexico. The final results for the three major electricity sectors came out as follows (in quadrillion BTUs per year):[17]

	Historic		*Projected*	
	1972	*1977*	*1985*	*1990*
Residential	1.74	2.23	2.83	3.34
Commercial	1.44	1.83	2.61	3.09
Industrial	2.18	2.58	3.96	5.02
Total	5.36	6.64	9.40	11.45

Reaching the 1985 projection would have required growth in sales of electricity to average close to 5% per year between 1977 and 1985. In 1978-1985, sales increases only once exceeded 4% in any year. The compound rate of growth for the period was 2.4% per year, and the industrial sector had the lowest (not the predicted highest) increase in demand. This is not to denigrate the detailed effort, but rather to point out the uncertainties involved in such an effort. Wrong assumptions could doom the effort to error even if the model itself is a good one.

In order to avoid the complications of the bottom up approach, one can, instead, start with a measure of economic activity, such as the gross national product, and observe the past relationship between energy consumption, GNP, and the price of electricity and its substitutes. Then, one can determine demand for electricity in the future based on projections of growth in GNP and change in prices of electricity and its substitutes. In other words, start with the biggest variable and then work downwards to the amount of electricity that will be demanded as a result of a given level of economic activity. That is the top down approach. It, too, has hazards. Can we be certain that past relationships between economic activity and electricity usage will hold in the future? Can we make good projections for GNP and energy prices? Unfortunately, the record of our econometric seers is not perfect.

Perhaps one should use both methods and understand the uncertainties involved. Coming to grips with the uncertainties, though, may mean that what was a rational capital investment policy when demand seemed more certain is no longer as rational today. Perhaps utilities will no longer seek the supposed economies of scale derived from the operation of large power stations because they will be uncertain whether demand for power will require the large station, or whether the large station could be completed for when it will be required. They might, instead, build smaller generating units that could be built more quickly if needed, and if not needed, less money will be at risk and less plant will stand idle.

Econometric analyses can provide us with guidance, although the results from study to study are not that consistent, which should not be surprising because the studies rarely deal with the exact same questions or

TABLE 6-2

Range of Values for Elasticity of Demand of Electricity to Price and Income (or Economic) Variables[a]

| | Price | | | | | | Income or Economic Activity | | | | | |
| | Short Run | | | Long Run | | | Short Run | | | Long Run | | |
	High	Low	Mean	High	Low	Mean	High	Low	Mean	High	Low	Mean
Residential	-0.80	-0.54	-0.23	-4.54[b]	-0.46	-1.17[b]	2.00	0.10	0.44	1.08	0.22	0.61
Commercial	-0.66	-0.25	-0.40	-1.54	-0.56	-1.08	—	—	—	1.38	1.15	1.27
Industrial	-0.20	-0.10	-0.15	-1.24	-0.74	-0.94	0.87	0.07	0.47	0.70	0.68	0.69

Notes

[a] 25 studies published after 1975.

[b] Excluding -4.54 outlier, high is -2.1, mean is -0.98.

Source: Resources for the Future, *Price Elasticities of Demand for Energy — Evaluating the Estimates* (Palo Alto: Electric Power Research Institute, September 1982), pp. 3-68 to 3-72, 3-88, 3-99.

time periods. Table 6-2 shows the results for 25 studies of the reaction of electricity users to changes in price of electricity (price elasticity of demand) and reaction to changes in economic conditions (income elasticity). Because there is often a delay between the time the price of electricity changes (or economic conditions improve or decline) and the time that the consumer reacts to the change, we must consider the immediate reaction of the consumer of electricity (short run) and the delayed reaction (long run). As an example, if the price of electricity goes up sharply, consumers will immediately turn off lights or reduce the thermostat (short run) but will not replace lighting fixtures or put in a more efficient furnace (long run) until the fixtures or furnace wear out.

Weighing the values in Table 6-2 by electric sales, and assuming that commercial customers are sensitive to economic activity (in the short run) in a manner similar to residential customers, the elasticities for electricity demand as a whole would be about:

- 0.2 for short run price elasticity
- 1.1 for long run price elasticity
  0.5 for short run economic or income elasticity
  0.8 for long run economic or income elasticity

A negative number indicates (as would be expected) that energy sales move in the opposite direction of price. That is, a 10% increase in the price of electricity would produce a 2% (0.2 times 10%) decline in demand for power. Over the long term, though, a 10% increase in price could lead to an 11% (1.1 times 10%) drop in electricity sales. If economic activity (or income) rises 10%, though, this has a positive effect on demand for electricity, pushing up sales by 5% (0.5 times 10%). In the long run, perhaps after new equipment and appliances are purchased, that 10% rise in income will help push up sales of electricity by 8% (0.8 times 10%).

In reality, just as with the engineering-oriented bottom up analysis, the top down econometric studies are complex, and the investigator must often settled for out-of-date or inadequate data.

Having introduced all the caveats, it is worth examining trends over time, in order to see some of the factors that influence the demand for electricity. The examples that follow are designed to give the reader an idea of some of the analyses and problems involved in studying the variables. They are not a substitute for a thorough and rigorous statistical analysis.

We begin with the most difficult question: how to predict peak load. Utilities must have enough capacity to meet demand at the peak period, or customers will have to be cut off. Looking only at the summer peak, we surmise that demand varies with economic activity, weather conditions, and the price of electricity. Different companies, though, do not reach peaks in demand simultaneously because heat waves do not hit the entire country at once, and because economic activity is not equally strong everywhere at the same time. The nationwide peak demand shown for the summer is actually based on the non-coincident peak loads of all the reporting companies. So, the peak load figure for the U.S.A. is an approximation of reality, possibly a fiction, and we are not sure when it takes place. For this analysis, we will assume that the peak takes place during July when kilowatt-hour sales tend to be high. Obviously, the individual utility can do a more precise analysis for its own peak period.

Our measure of economic activity will be the GNP in the quarter of peak summer sales, almost invariably in the third quarter of the year.

Weather affects demand for electricity, but what measure represents weather conditions at the peak when peak load throughout the country is non-coincident? The proxy for weather selected was cooling degree days in the month of the peak. (A cooling degree day is the number of degrees by which the average temperature on the day exceeds 65 degrees Fahrenheit.) This is an imperfect measure for many reasons, but especially because peak demand is affected by number of days of heat buildup, whether the hottest days come on the weekend or during the work week, or when factories are on vacation, not to mention such factors as humidity, time of day, wind, rain, etc.

Price of electricity affects demand, but its price in isolation is not helpful. After all, if the price of electricity goes up 5% when all other prices rise 10%, the real price of electricity in relation to other goods would fall. An analysis can tackle the question by comparing the price of electricity to alternatives such as oil or gas, on the assumption that customers switch fuels depending on price. Or, we can assume that electricity is just one more commodity competing for the consumer's dollar and look at its price action relative to that of all prices. For the sake of simplicity we will take the latter course, showing the change in price of electricity relative to the change in price of all goods and services as measured by the GNP deflator. (I.e., if electricity prices rises 5% when all other prices rise 3%, then the real price of electricity moves up 2%.)

Reaction to today's price change might also be delayed until an appliance wears out and can be replaced by a more efficient one. That is, the relationship between price and usage might be a lagged one. Table 6-3 includes the change in price from last year's peak quarter to this year's, and the compound annual change in price during the four years preceding the immediate past year. (That is, for 1970, we show the percentage change in price that took place in 1970, and then another price change that has the effect of averaging the price change that took place in 1966, 1967, 1968, and 1969.)

The raw data tell us little. There are too many variables influencing demand for electricity at the peak period. Various statistical techniques can help us sort out which variables seem to be associated more with the moves

TABLE 6-3

Peak Load, Price, Economic Activity and Weather, 1962-1986

(% Changes)

Year	Summer Peak From Previous Year	Real GNP 3rd Quarter To 3rd Quarter	Cooling Degree Days In July	Real Price of Electricity 3rd Quarter to 3rd Quarter of Previous Year	Compound Annual Rate of Change In Price 3rd Quarter to 3rd Quarter of Four Preceding Years
	(1)	(2)	(3)	(4)	(5)
1962	5.7	6.0	− 10.0	− 1.3	− 0.2
1963	7.0	4.3	12.2	− 1.9	− 1.0
1964	9.7	5.0	6.6	− 2.6	− 1.1
1965	6.5	5.9	− 14.8	− 2.6	− 1.6
1966	9.2	5.7	− 27.5	− 3.4	− 2.0
1967	5.0	2.9	− 23.0	− 2.2	− 2.6
1968	11.5	4.8	11.8	− 1.9	− 3.0
1969	8.3	2.0	7.6	− 3.7	− 2.9
1970	6.6	− 0.1	− 2.5	− 1.3	− 3.1
1971	6.3	2.7	− 11.0	3.5	− 2.6
1972	9.3	6.0	3.9	0.3	− 11.3
1973	7.7	4.9	7.1	1.0	− 0.9
1974	1.5	− 1.6	− 0.3	14.6	0.4
1975	2.1	0.3	− 5.1	3.9	4.1
1976	4.0	5.2	− 7.4	2.3	4.3
1977	6.9	6.0	24.7	3.8	4.8
1978	3.0	3.9	− 12.6	− 0.9	6.0
1979	− 2.4	1.8	− 4.9	0.7	2.2
1980	7.2	2.2	28.4	8.2	1.4
1981	0.5	4.2	6.5	4.9	2.8
1982	− 3.2	− 3.0	− 23.8	2.3	3.2
1983	7.7	4.9	12.0	− 0.7	4.0
1984	0.8	6.5	− 19.0	4.4	3.6
1985	2.1	2.9	8.4	− 1.4	3.0
1986	3.4	2.6	10.0	− 2.6	1.1

Notes

Column 1:   % change non-coincident summer peak from previous year.

Column 2:   % change in real GNP, third quarter to third quarter.

Column 3:   % change in cooling degree days to July in current year from July in previous year.

Column 4:   % change in real price of electricity third quarter to third quarter. Price changes determined for industrial users from Producers Price Index and for all non-industrial users from Consumers Price Index. Quarter price is unweighted mean for three months. All price changes

TABLE 6-3 Continued

deflated by GNP deflator for quarter. Price change for peak determined by weighting industrial and non-industrial price changes by percentage of total sales accounted for by each group in year.

Column 5:   Above procedure repeated for four years preceding immediate past year. Compound annual rate of growth for four year period.

Sources:

Column 1:   Edison Electric Institute. *Statistical Year Book* (various issues).

Column 2:   Merrill Lynch Economics, U.S. Department of Commerce.

Column 3:   U.S. Department of Commerce. National Oceanic and Atmospheric Administration. *State, Regional, and National Monthly and Seasonal Cooling Degree Days. Weighted by Population (1980 Census).* (Asheville, N.C.: U.S. Dept. of Commerce, Sept. 1981, May 1985 and June 1987). Energy Information Administration.

Column 4:   Bureau of Labor Statistics. *Monthly Labor Review* (various issues).

Column 5:   Bureau of Labor Statistics. *Monthly Labor Review* (various issues).

---

of peak load. One such technique is known as multiple regression, which attempts to derive a formula that accounts for the movement of one series of numbers (the dependent variable) by the influences of various factors (the independent variables) on the dependent variable. As an example, we would use this technique to determine whether the sale of peanut butter (dependent variable) is influenced by television commercials, the price of peanut butter, and the number of five year olds in the population (independent variables). In reality, this analysis does not tell us for sure that one variable causes movement in another. It just shows that there could be an influence and how much confidence we can place in this influence.

The variables used in the first analysis are:

PK = % change in peak load (dependent variable)
GNP3 = % change in GNP, third quarter to third quarter
CDD = % change in cooling degree days in July.
Ppl = % change in relative price of electricity from third quarter last year to third quarter this year.
Pp4 = % compound rate of change in relative price in third quarter in four years preceding the immediate past year. (Period begins five years before current year.)

The analysis produces a formula (or regression equation) with the results in percent. The coefficients (the numbers by which each variable is multiplied in the equation) are like the elasticities given in Table 6-2.

$$Pk = 3.50 + 0.58(GNP3) + 0.10(CDD) - 0.06(Pp1) - 0.69(Pp4)$$

The regression explains only 74% of the movement of peak ($r^2 = 0.74$). Pp1 makes the least statistically significant contributions to the equation. (The coefficient of determination is often used as a quick test of the value of the equation. The higher the r^2, the better the regression, up to a perfect 1.00. Other tests, though, should be used before accepting the analysis.) As for price changes in the current year, it may be that customers replace air conditioning equipment only after it has worn out, or modify their habits of use only after several years of high bills.

An analysis excluding Pp1 produces:

$$Pk = 3.32 + 0.62(GNP3) + 0.10(CDD) - 0.72(Pp4).$$

The $r^2 = 0.74$ again, and statistical analysis indicates that weather may be the least important variable, which seems improbable. No doubt a similar analysis, using local weather data and the load of a single utility would produce better results. There are two conclusions to be drawn from this unsuccessful analysis. The first is that the analysis must be approached critically, with common sense prevailing. The second is that the utility must design a system that can deal with highly variable peaks caused by an unpredictable factor, the weather. It may be cheaper to attempt to control the peak demand through load management than to always have the generating capacity available to meet uncontrolled peak demand.

Looking at trends in KWH sales is a more satisfactory process. Again, we assume that consumption of electricity is affected by economic conditions, weather, price increases in the current year, and price increases during the preceding four years. We also add to the analysis the price action of natural gas, a competitor for electricity's market. All data appear on Table 6-4.

The weather proxy consists of the total cooling degree days plus the total heating degree days in the year. (A heating degree day is the deviation of the mean temperature of the day below 65 degrees Fahrenheit). This should capture both air conditioning and heating sales. Economic activity is represented by change in real GNP. The change in the real price of electricity and for natural gas is shown for the current year, and on a compound basis for the four preceding years.

Where:

KWH = % change in KWH sales

C&HDD = % change in sum of cooling and heating degree days in year
GNP = % change in real GNP
P1 = % change in average real price of electricity in year
P4 = % annual change in real price of electricity in four preceding years
G1 = % change in average real price of natural gas in year
G4 = % annual change in real price of natural gas in four preceding years.

The equation is:

$$KWH = 1.95 + 0.05(C\&HDD) + 0.77(GNP) - 0.30(P1) - 0.60(P4) + 0.17(G1) + 0.04(G4)$$

The regression explains 92% of variation of KWH from its mean value, but not all variables are statistically significant at a high level of confidence. Using the equation, anyway, as an example, assume that degree days rise 5%, GNP decreases 10%, electricity price rises 10%, the four year increase is 5%, and gas prices rise 5% this year and 10% over four preceding years. Then the equation produces the following gain in KWH sales:

$$KWH = 1.95 + 0.05(5) + 0.77(10) - 0.30(10) - 0.60(5) + 0.17(5) + 0.04(10) = 5.15\%$$

This sort of statistical analysis must be carried much further, though, before its results can be accepted. It may be that some of the variables interrelate with each other, to some extent, so that they are not all working independently. It may also be that while the equation gives the general picture, it does not work well in all years studied. As an example, it may explain well the early years of the period studied but not the later years, so it might not prove to be a reliable guide to making predictions. At least, though, the coefficients are not far from those indicated in Table 6-2, so we may be moving in the right direction. But we still do not know whether past

TABLE 6-4
Sales of Electricity, Economic Activity, Weather and Price, 1962-1986
(% Change)

Year	KWH Sales	Real GNP	Cooling and Heating Degree Days	Real Price - Current Year		Compound Annual Rate Change for Real Price For Preceding Year	
				Electricity	Gas	Electricity	Gas
	(1)	(2)	(3)	(4)	(5)	(6)	(7)
1962	7.7	5.8	2.8	− 1.7	0.5	− 1.5	2.0
1963	7.0	4.0	1.1	− 2.7	− 2.7	− 1.6	1.3
1964	7.2	5.3	− 4.3	− 3.3	− 1.5	− 1.7	0.6
1965	7.1	5.9	0.3	− 4.5	− 2.6	− 2.2	− 0.4
1966	9.0	6.0	2.7	− 5.3	− 5.2	− 3.0	− 1.5
1967	6.5	2.7	− 2.9	− 2.5	− 2.5	− 3.7	− 3.0
1968	8.6	4.6	2.7	− 5.4	− 4.8	− 3.8	− 3.0
1969	8.7	2.8	1.9	− 5.6	− 3.6	− 4.5	− 3.6
1970	6.4	− 0.3	− 0.3	− 2.2	− 1.8	− 4.8	− 4.0
1971	5.4	2.8	− 2.8	0.6	1.1	− 3.9	− 3.2
1972	7.6	5.0	2.1	0.0	3.2	− 3.3	− 1.0
1973	8.0	5.2	− 5.4	− 1.3	2.3	− 1.8	− 0.3
1974	− 0.1	− 0.5	− 0.4	13.4	11.7	− 0.8	1.2
1975	1.9	− 1.3	2.1	6.9	21.8	3.0	4.5
1976	6.7	4.9	2.5	0.6	16.1	4.6	9.5
1977	5.5	4.7	2.0	4.1	13.5	4.8	12.8
1978	3.4	5.3	5.1	0.5	3.6	6.2	15.7
1979	3.3	2.5	− 4.7	1.4	8.5	3.0	13.6
1980	2.0	− 0.2	2.3	7.8	14.1	1.6	10.3
1981	1.2	1.9	− 4.6	4.7	9.9	3.4	9.9
1982	− 2.4	− 2.5	− 5.5	5.5	15.7	3.6	9.0
1983	2.9	3.6	9.1	− 0.3	7.4	4.8	12.0
1984	5.6	6.4	− 2.6	0.7	− 3.1	4.4	11.7
1985	1.1	2.7	1.0	− 0.1	− 5.8	2.6	7.2
1986	2.1	3.7	− 4.6	− 2.2	− 15.1	1.4	3.2

Notes:

Column 1:   % change in total KWH sales to ultimate customers.

Column 2:   % change in real GNP.

Column 3:   % change in sum of heating and cooling degree days in year.

Columns
4 and 5:   % change in real price of electricity (natural gas), deflated by GNP deflator. Price of electricity (gas) is average price in year for ultimate customers.

TABLE 6-4 Continued

Columns
6 and 7:   Above procedure repeated for four years preceding current one.
             Compound annual rate for four year period.

Sources:
Column 1:   Edison Electric Institute. *Statistical Year Book* (various issues).

Column 2:   Merrill Lynch Economics. U.S. Department of Commerce.

Column 3:   U.S. Department of Commerce. National Oceanic and Atmospheric
              Administration. *State, Regional, and National Monthly and Seasonal
              Cooling Degree Days. (Heating Degree Days). Weighted by Population
              (1980 Census).* (Asheville, N.C.: U.S. Dept. of Commerce, Sept. 1981,
              May 1985, Nov. 1985 and June 1987).

Columns
4 to 7:   Edison Electric Institute, American Gas Association.

---

relationships, as shown in the equations, will hold in the future. Further study might show that the relationships are changing, in which case sophisticated techniques might be used to forecast these structural shifts.

As crude as this analysis is, it shows that sale of electricity is sensitive to weather, economic conditions, and price. The analysis also shows that a rising price for a competitive fuel (natural gas) aids the sale of electricity. Even the price analysis leaves much to be desired, because we are not examining price at the margin, i.e., what the last KWH taken costs the customer. Furthermore, if the impact of price is lagged, then today's price hike may dampen sales for years to come. This is an uncomfortable conclusion for utilities that will have to hike prices sharply to pay for large, new power stations. The vague notions that consumption of electricity fell off due to "conservation" must be replaced by a hardheaded analysis of the factors that affect demand if utilities and regulators are to engage in realistic planning. Electricity sales seem unlikely to take off until prices can be brought under control and economic growth resumes. That conclusion might lead to another: that electricity sales might be controlled by price even if economic activity does take off. Both regulators and utility managements have been reluctant to use price to clear the market, but doing so could be an alternative to meeting unfettered demand by building huge power stations.

What is the moral of the story? Forecasting is an imperfect process, but good statistical techniques, combined with reasonable assumptions and common sense should provide guidance to managements and help to prevent multi-million dollar mistakes. Furthermore, simply going through the pro-

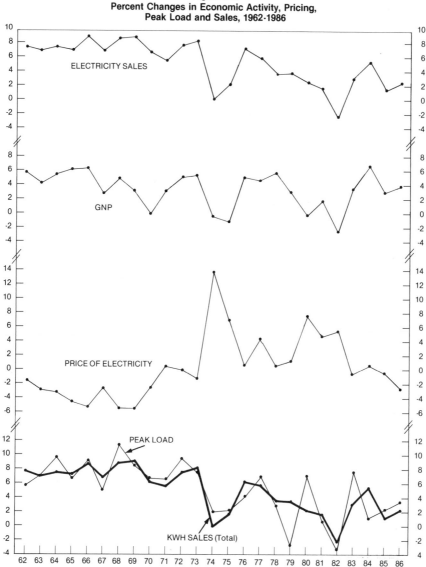

Figure 6-2
Percent Changes in Economic Activity, Pricing,
Peak Load and Sales, 1962-1986

ELECTRICITY SALES

GNP

PRICE OF ELECTRICITY

PEAK LOAD

KWH SALES (Total)

cess of deciding on the assumptions to be used, and then the statistical analysis, helps to clarify the range of uncertainty in the forecast, which, in itself, may be valuable. Some of the industry's problems in the past came about because of bad forecasts. The answer, though, is to improve the forecasts and understand the forecasting process better, not to eschew the technique altogether.

Chapter 7

Summary

Electricity seems destined to play an important part in the arts and industries. The question of its economical application to some purposes is still unsettled, but experiment has already proved that it will propel a street car better than a gas jet and give more light than a horse.[18]

Ambrose Bierce

Electric utilities had one rule for decades: bigger meant more efficient. By the 1970s, the rule seemed less and less true. For years, costs declined, prices could be reduced, and demand was strong and growing steadily. In the 1970s, growth of demand flattened as the price of power shot up. The industry used to enjoy an environment in which its activities were praised. In the late 1960s, environmentalists attacked the "living better electrically" concept, sales promotion, smokestacks, and a supposed nuclear peril. Industry leaders were now on the defensive. The world had truly been turned upside down for utility employees and security holders. Change had to take place.

If predicting the path of operations were simply a matter of forecasting technological change or fuel availability, the job would be hard enough. But that is only a small part of the job. Utilities will choose technologies because of economic and financial limitations. The Federal Government will force changes for reasons of national security. Some choices will be made because they represent the path of least resistance to environmental, regulatory or economic pressures. The only certainty is that the electric utility industry will continue to be buffeted by what the Edison Electric Institute referred to euphemistically as the "transitional storm."[19] The transition, to the EEI, is the period between the fossil age of yore and the era of inexhaustible fuels in the future.

From the standpoint of generation, most of the generating capacity for the coming decade has either been built or is under construction. The prescription calls for slightly more coal and far more nuclear energy. (The nuclear energy comes from facilities under construction. Few, if any, new orders can be expected for years to come.) Small scale sources, such as geothermal, low-head hydro, cogeneration, the fuel cell, solar and wind should play an increasingly important role, especially if they are constructed for deregulated (hence more profitable) operations, as seems to be the thrust of present policy. Whether the flowering of small scale, decentralized generation leads to the demise of central station power is another question. One could argue that a breakthrough in photovoltaic energy could reduce or eliminate the need for central station power, and that possibility alone ought to encourage electric utilities to reduce their exposure to such risk by cutting down commitment to expensive central generating facilities. At the same time, when comparing the cost of a new technology (such as solar photovoltaics) to that of the existing central station power (which is not fully utilizing its capacity), the comparison should be between the fully allocated costs of the new technology and the incremental costs of central station power. If that is understood, it will be a while before a new technology takes hold. (The implication for the profitability of the utility would not be healthy, but letting the market go to competitors might be even more unhealthy.)

Two types of nuclear power could extend the nuclear age. Building breeder reactors would vastly increase the fuel available, but the breeder program is controversial and has been stalled in this country. Fusion power would make it possible to use seawater as a fuel, but commercial fusion reactors seem decades away.

The utility industry seems to have backed off from its love affair with mammoth size. A large power plant that works poorly can put a strain on an electrical system. Putting huge sums into one machine increases the risk of doing business. Putting in a massive plant could leave the utility with a large amount of unused capacity until demand grows into the capacity, which could take years. Perhaps, when money costs were low, the carrying costs on the temporarily excess capacity were more than offset by the economies of scale inherent in larger units. Whether that is the case now is another question. Large plants have still another problem: they are built for the base load, not for on-and-off use. Unfortunately, load has been more unstable than expected in some systems, so the large unit has to be operated under less than optimal conditions. Finally, the biggest question of all is whether size has reached a point at which economies of scale are no longer meaningful.

Many utilities could reduce the increasing risk of their present mode of operations by putting more emphasis on small power units, cogeneration, conservation measures, and load management techniques. Admittedly, managements will have ambivalent feelings about such courses. On one hand, they will want to use conventional facilities already in place or under construction. On the other hand, they may not want to launch major construction projects beyond what is already under way. Non-standard measures, however, may not work everywhere. Much will depend on the characteristics of the service area. Diversity of energy source will be an important consideration if reliability is to be maintained.

The electric utility industry has not been known for its quick response or imaginative actions (in part because of the nature of the construction and regulatory processes). Under pressure now from regulators and investors and facing high capital costs and greater risks, though, the industry may be responding faster than many realize, although the results of the new policies may not be seen for several more years.

Notes

[1] Sir William Cecil Dampier, *A History of Science and Its Relations with Philosophy and Religion* (Cambridge: University Press, 1948), p. 217.

[2] Henry Semat, *The Fundamentals of Physics* (New York: Rinehart, 1957), p. 110.

[3] Semat, *op. cit.*, p. 104.

[4] Abbott Payson Usher, *A History of Mechanical Invention* (Boston: Beacon Press, 1959), p. 403.

[5] Betsy O'Brien and Andrew Reynolds, U.S. Department of Energy, Energy Information Administration, Office of Coal, Nuclear, Electric and Alternate Fuels, *Impacts of Financial Constraints on the Electric Utility Industry* (Washington, D.C.: U.S. Government Printing Office, 1982), p. xvii.

[6] Barry Commoner, *The Poverty of Power: Energy and the Economic Crisis* (New York: Alfred A. Knopf, 1976), p. 3.

[7] E. F. Schumacher, *Small Is Beautiful: Economics As If People Mattered* (New York: Harper & Row Perennial Library, 1975), p. 60.

[8] Electric Utility Task Force on the Environment, *The Electric Utility Industry and the Environment, Report to the Citizens Advisory Committee on Recreation and Natural Beauty by the Electric Utility Industry Task Force on the Environment* (no place or date of publication. Library of Congress Card No. 68-57661), p. 11.

[9] For discussion see: W. B. Broecker, T. Takahashi, H. J. Simpson, T. H. Peng. "Fate of Fossil Fuel Carbon Dioxide and the Global Carbon Budget," *Science*, Vol. 206, 26 October 1979, p. 409; Ronald A. Madden and V. Ramanathan, "Detecting Climate Change Due to Increasing Carbon Dioxide," *Science*, Vol. 209, 15 August 1980, p. 763.

[10] For a discussion of studies of relative risk, see John H. Herbert, Christina Swanson, and Patrick Reddy, "A Risky Business," *Environment*, July/August 1979, p. 28.

[11] John Holdren and Philip Herrera, *Energy: A Crisis in Power* (San Francisco: Sierra Club, 2nd printing, 1973), p. 77.

[12] Holdren and Herrera, *op. cit.*, p. 75.

[13] Electric Utility Task Force, *op. cit.*, p. 13.

[14] This argument about efficiency depends on the laws of thermodynamics. The first law (conservation of energy) states that work done by a machine equals the value of the heat applied to the system less the heat given up. In an engine it is not possible to transform into work all the heat applied, so efficiency is measured as the work done by the machine as a percentage of heat applied. This is first law efficiency, and it is generally 30%-to-40% for a power station. The second law of thermodynamics (entropy) states that energy becomes less and less available. Thus, although energy is never lost (first law), it becomes less available to do work. Measurement of second

law efficiency focuses on the end use of the work. Going back to the original example, if two-thirds of the energy content of the fuel is lost in the generation process, and then the electric coils in the water heater at home push up the temperature of the water to a level that is so hot that the hot water must be diluted with cold, a lot of energy has been wasted to produce lukewarm water. Perhaps a more efficient method would be to heat some cold water with a flame in the house. Second law efficiency often is as low as one-tenth of first law efficiency. The argument basically concludes that since the universe will eventually run out of energy that can be converted to work, we should stop wasting energy now.

[15]D. W. Schindler, "Effects of Acid Rain on Freshwater Ecosystems," *Science*, 8 January 1988, Vol. 239, p. 149.

[16]Adam Smith, *An Inquiry into the Nature and Causes of the Wealth of Nations* (New York: The Modern Library, 1937), p. 56.

[17]Office of Integrative Analysis, Midterm Analysis Division, U.S. Department of Energy, Energy Information Administration, *Analysis Report, Energy Supply and Demand in the Midterm: 1985, 1990, and 1995* (Washington, D.C.: U.S. Government Printing Office, April 1979), p. 52.

[18]Ambrose Bierce. *The Devil's Dictionary* (New York: Dover Publications, 1958) p. 35.

[19]Edison Electric Institute, *31 Answers to 32 Questions About the Electric Utility Industry* (New York: Edison Electric Institute, 1976), unnumbered.

Part Three

The Development and Structure of the Electric Utility Industry

Chapter 8

Introduction

. . . the dynamo became a symbol of infinity . . . he began to feel the forty-foot dynamo as a moral force, much as the early Christians felt the Cross . . . Before the end, one began to pray to it; inherited instinct taught the natural expression of man before silent and infinite force . . . Between the dynamo . . . and the engine house . . . the break of continuity amounted to abysmal fracture . . . No more relation could he discover between the steam and the electric current than between the Cross and the cathedral.[1]

Henry Adams

The Victorian naturalists believed that *"natura non facit saltum,"* nature does not leap. By that they meant that evolution or progress was a gradual affair. Unfortunately, the fossil record did not show such a gradual sequence, but seemed to be discontinuous, indicating sudden change or cataclysmic events rather than gradualism. The Victorians, however, persisted in their theory, asserting that the apparent discontinuity resulted from the connecting fossil links not yet having been discovered. Who can beat that argument? Fossil hunters still have not found some of those links, and some modern scientists theorize that perhaps nature does make leaps.

The development of electric power was one of those enormous events that changed our history, affected our engines, transportation, home life-styles, communications, science, distribution of population and industry, and tied us to a central source of energy. Although many of the components existed before Edison, it was he who discovered how to put together and make workable the components to create the electric power industry.

The following chapters trace the development of the industry and argue that the present structure is the result of historical, political, accidental as well as economic causes, rather than the inevitable result of natural peculiarities of the industry. The concept of the regulated natural monopoly, if not already obsolete, may soon be. The dinosaur, a highly successful beast for a long time, disappeared relatively quickly, some say, apparently unable to cope with changes in the environment. Some think that the electric utility, in its present form, may not have adjusted to the sudden changes in environment during the last two decades and that without such adjustment it could, like the dinosaur, become extinct. Fortunately, changes seem to be occurring and, as a result, survival may be a lot likelier than would have seemed possible a few years ago.

Chapter 9

Edison

I saw for the first time everything in practical operation. I saw that what had been done had never been made practically useful.[2]

Thomas A. Edison

Electric utilization technology is important since it is sometimes overlooked that electric energy cannot be produced and stored; electric energy can only be developed and used if the utilization equipment and technology for its use have first come into being.[3]

Philip Sporn

Neither electricity nor electric lighting began with Edison. The English led the way in the early years of the nineteenth century. In 1808, Sir Humphrey Davy sent a battery powered electric current through the space between two carbon rods and produced a blue-white arc of light. In 1831, Michael Faraday invented the dynamo, which, when turned by a steam engine, supplied a cheap electric current by means of electromagnetic induction.

America spawned a host of electricians, inventors, and tinkers. The telegraph, invented in 1844, depended on batteries and the wits of an army of itinerant, hard living telegraphers who learned about electricity first hand, improved the product, and took their knowledge elsewhere. Thomas Edison started as a telegrapher, improved the instrument, worked on the phonograph, and made viable that instrument of doubtful paternity, the telephone, before he went on to create the incandescent light and the electric utility industry.[4]

Davy's arc light caught on, despite drawbacks: the carbon burned up, the fumes were disagreeable and dangerous, the battery power was expensive, the light glared, and the lamps were wired in series. The arc lamp was used in a production of the Paris Opera in 1844, in English lighthouses in the 1860s, was exhibited in the Philadelphia Exposition of 1876, and lit the streets of Paris in 1877. The arc lamp, however, clearly was unsatisfactory for ordinary illumination. The gas light industry's monopoly seemed safe.

Beginning in 1820, a string of Frenchmen, Russians, British, and Americans tried to build an incandescent lamp. The electricity would light up a filament enclosed in a glass bulb that contained a vacuum or an inert gas. Because of a combination of imperfect vacuums and poorly chosen filaments, the experimenters could not create durable, workable lights. Perhaps the development of the high vacuum Crookes tube served to respark the interest that produced incandescent lamps from Joseph Swan in England and from Edison in the United States.

In 1878, Edison was looking for a new project for his Menlo Park laboratory, but decided against the intense arc light. With a characteristic insight that distinguished him from his competitors, Edison worked not only on the light but on the entire system of delivery. He described to reporters a system of central station power, with small household lights attached to meters. He decided that a slum district should be the first served because of the potential electric motor load. Edison said, "The same wire that brings the light will also bring power and heat — with the power you can run an elevator, a sewing machine, or any mechanical contrivance, and by means of the heat you may cook your food."[5] Scientists and rival inventors predicted failure, but Edison had a long string of successes behind him. Gas light stocks fell.

Grosvenor Lowrey, Western Union's lawyer, put together Edison's financial backing, a Morgan-Vanderbilt syndicate, after telling them that "Edison has discovered the means of giving us an electric light suitable for every day use, at vastly reduced cost as compared with gas."[6] The claims were grossly exaggerated. Nevertheless, on October 15, 1878, preliminary papers were drawn for the Edison Electric Light Co. Edison assigned to it all the electric light devices that he would invent in the next five years. The articles signed on November 15, 1878 said the company's "objects . . . are to own, manufacture, operate and license the use of various apparatus used in producing light, heat and power from electricity."[7]

In the year that followed, Edison worked on the vacuum, the filament, and a dynamo that maintained a constant pressure. By October 1879, Edison had a working incandescent lamp. Months later, he patented an electric distribution system. In 1880, Edison continued to improve his product and spent a great deal of time on the entire electric system while competitors stole his lighting ideas. He also made his first big sale, to Henry Villard of the Northern Pacific. Villard became an investor in the electric utilities and a founder of one of the great holding companies. Villard bought for the ship S.S. *Columbia* the first isolated lighting system sold.

Edison soon discovered that his backers wanted to collect patent royalties, not to invest new money in manufacturing facilities. (His backers also discovered that Edison was difficult to deal with, prone to making promises, did not keep to a schedule, and made no attempt to control expenditures.)

Consequently, Edison had to set up on his own the Edison Lamp Co. to manufacture lamps, and the Edison Machine Works to manufacture dynamos. Both companies paid royalties to the Light Co.

The next question was: who would buy the lights and equipment? Edison conceived of the large central power station that would distribute through lines to the customers. That meant large capital expenditures, negotiations with city councils to get use of the streets, bribes, and delays in sales until the system was completed. Edison's backers instead favored sale of isolated power stations (for factories, hotels, yachts, and the residences of the rich). The Light Company organized the Edison Co. for Isolated Lighting and the Edison Electric Illuminating Co., the latter being its first electric utility. In the beginning, the electric utility industry had plenty of competition, despite the uniqueness of the product. Edison's lamp had to compete with gas light in the cities and with other forms of illumination elsewhere. And his utility had to compete with his isolated power plants.

Edison carefully planned the New York utility system. He picked an area in downtown New York because it had 1,500 gaslight customers and the potential for 750 electric motors, so power could be sold both day and night. He wanted to serve the financial district for the prestige involved in doing so.

In characteristic Edisonian fashion, the great man's plans were over ambitious, schedules fell by the wayside, the project came in at a cost several times over the estimate, and meters were not ready, all of which resulted in no bills for months. Investors were discouraged. September 4, 1882, however, the day on which the Pearl Street Station went into business to serve 85 customers with 400 lamps, marked the beginning of the electric utility industry.

By the end of 1883, only two cities had central station power. The banks would not lend money to finance the projects. Electricity was too expensive for the average customer, and remained so into the early 1900s. The isolated power plant (especially in small towns that did not have gas light) was the big seller (334 by the spring of 1883). Because some of the purchasers of equipment did not have enough cash to pay for all equipment or royalties, the Light Co. or its affiliates had to take for payment the securities of many local lighting companies. To develop the electric utility industry would require a great deal of cash, and Edison's financiers were not eager to put up cash. Edison described the Light Co. as "the leaden collar."[8] He took control of the company in 1884.

While Edison was seizing control of the Light Co., he was losing control of the technology of the industry. Thompson-Houston, a company that infringed on his patents, overtook Edison in building central stations. More important, in a technological sense, Westinghouse Electric embraced the idea of Nikola Tesla (who had worked for and been fired by Edison) and developed the alternating current (AC) motor. Westinghouse's system produced AC power at 1000 volts for transmission and had a transformer to step down the power to 100 or 50 volts for domestic use. The Edison direct current (DC) system could only transmit power two miles. Westinghouse saw the potential for locating a central station at the source of water power or coal, shipping the power for great distances at high voltages, and then stepping down the power for distribution. Edison, with his investment in DC, opposed the new system, saying it was dangerous, which he decided to prove. Edison always had a good public relations sense. In 1888, he opened up his laboratory to Harold P. Brown, who developed the AC electric chair, as proof that AC was dangerous. Names were suggested for the process: electromort, dynamort, electrocide and Westinghoused (this last from Edison himself). But in 1893, the backers of a revolutionary plan to move electric power from Niagara Falls to Buffalo chose AC power. George Forbes, a British engineer involved in the project, commented: "The greatest step ... in the distribution of electricity since ... 1878 was the use of alternating currents ... which was simply achieved ... against the opinions of everybody who seemed to be capable of giving an opinion."[9] In the early age of the electric utility, another form of competition developed: AC vs. DC. In some cities, as will be noted later, there were utilities that supplied AC power and others that supplied DC. Edison backed the wrong horse and stubbornly clung to his notions, possibly because he could not accept the ideas of others.

Edison also developed the first electric railroad, but he never pursued the concept because he was too busy setting up the Pearl Street Station. Draper, Van De Poele, and Sprague took up the idea and in 1886 the first electric street railway went into service. By 1889, there were 154 street railways in the United States. The street railway load soon exceeded that of electric lighting. Edison had always understood the importance of a power load to the success of his central station system. Ironically, that load came from a product whose development he dropped. Some of those railways produced their own power. The street railway company had the potential to serve other electric customers. The utility, on the other hand, could get the street railway's business if its price was sufficiently low. One could argue that the electric utility had to compete against the street railway's ability to produce power.

In a little more than a decade, Edison put more than a half century of research into practical application, conceived and invented an entire industry and then became a reactionary who hampered the industry's progress and threatened to fossilize it at a primitive stage of development. Edison's role in the industry ended bitterly. Henry Villard returned from Europe with the backing of powerful German firms and, in 1889, combined all the Edison ventures into the Edison General Electric Co. Villard wanted to create an international electric trust. The new holding company was to manufacture and sell central stations and to form new central station companies in which it owned 80% of the stock. The problems compounded themselves.

The new central stations would not show returns for several years. Edison did not develop new electrical products and fought AC systems. Thompson-Houston and Westinghouse grabbed away business until Edison General Electric only had about 40% of the industry's volume. The company needed cash and it needed an AC system. Villard discussed merger terms with Westinghouse, then with Thompson-Houston. At that point, in 1892, J.P. Morgan stepped back into the picture. He not only forced a merger with Thompson-Houston, but he put Thompson-Houston's management in charge. Villard was out. He devoted his time thereafter to running what became one of the huge utility holding companies, The North American Co. Another dispossessed Edison associate, Samuel Insull, took over the presidency of a small Chicago utility. Edison General Electric became General Electric. The age of Edison had ended.

Chapter 10

The Industry Organizes

We will make electric light so cheap that only the rich will be able to burn candles.[10]

Thomas A. Edison

The early years were confused ones. Franchises in a city often were non-exclusive and sometimes competitive. Each manufacturer would give a particular franchisee the exclusive right to use that manufacturer's equipment in a given territory. Some companies operating in the same city provided AC, while others provided DC. Areas served varied from a city block "each way"[11] to the entire city. Companies had different purposes: arc lighting for streets, lighting for houses, power for industrial uses. In the same city, voltage and frequencies differed. In Chicago between 1882 and 1905, 29 franchises had been granted, three of which were citywide.

In Chicago, the city council was notoriously corrupt and the franchise negotiation centered around payoffs. At one point, a citywide franchise was granted to a group for no other purpose than to have the franchise bought out by a competitor. Such confusion and fragmentation made it difficult to develop standardized products, limited the mobility of large users of power, and — it later became evident — prevented the electric utility from achieving the benefits of load diversity and economies of scale. In a perverse way, however, the confusion and fragmentation created a healthy competition that prevented the technology of the electric industry from ossifying in its first decade and that caused the entrepreneurs who ran the utilities to experiment in the way they did business.

By 1892, Samuel Insull and other leaders of the Association of Edison Illuminating Companies had formulated an understanding of the economics of the electric utility business that has remained basic to the industry to this day. Those leaders realized that the industry had high fixed costs because of the investment needed to meet peak load and to distribute power. At the same time, the cost of operating the plants was fairly low. The question became how to translate that into profits, especially in an industry in which managements had already concluded that they were selling a luxury item. (The Welsbach mantle had been introduced for gas lighting and gas was substantially less expensive than electricity.)

Insull of Chicago Edison was a leader. He began a sales campaign, cut prices below published schedules when necessary to get customers, and wrote long term contracts for large customers. Yet, did he know his costs? On a trip to England, Insull discovered the answer in Brighton, where Arthur Wright of the municipal power company had invented a demand meter. He set the price of electricity to cover two costs: fixed and operating. The price of the initial block of electricity would cover the fixed costs involved in meeting the maximum demand. The charge thereafter would largely cover operating costs. That meant that the price for the first block of usage would be high but that it would decline thereafter as quantity sold increased.

As Insull continued the analysis, he concluded that profit was determined not by load but by the percentage of time that the power plant was in use. The idea was to keep that plant running as much as possible and to find electric customers who would need power when other customers did not. As an example, the buildup in the traction load occurred during the rush hours, and the lighting load occurred at night after the traction load had fallen off.

The load for engines, motors, elevators, and other modes of business demand was sandwiched between the twin peaks of the traction load. The same power plant could serve all three loads because they did not occur simultaneously. The traction company, however, had its own power plant, the industrial user could have had its own isolated power plant, and the lighting customer depended on the utility. Three power plants could be replaced by one, thereby producing substantial savings in overhead costs. Diversity of load created savings.

An additional saving could result from the use of large power plants, which seemed to be more economical than smaller ones. The utility could not only gain the savings from diversity of load, but it could also produce the power more cheaply (with its large generating unit built to serve many customers) than could the isolated customer with its small generating unit. The utility could benefit from diversity of load and from economies of scale.

How did the utility encourage customers to connect to it? One way was to reduce the charge for utility service. Of course, some of the utilities were small and some of the other producers of electricity could have offered competitive prices in an attempt to muscle into the utility's business.

Why did the industry evolve as it did in the image of the gas industry? Edison controlled only one central station company, which was not a financial success for years, so one cannot attribute the industry's structure to him, although he did conceive the setup. Could the traction company have expanded its generation to non-rush hours and sold the load over the electric utility's lines? Could the isolated industrial plant have done the same? Was there an inherent advantage to one company having a monopoly over all aspects of electric power production, transmission, and distribution? Several possible answers exist:

1) An inherent advantage existed in load diversity, economies of scale in generation, and economies of scale in serving many customers (such as in billing and maintenance).
2) The technology of the time did not allow for a system with power derived from various sources.
3) Potential competitors had so many problems with their principal businesses that they could not worry about ancillary activities.
4) The electric utility business was insufficiently profitable to warrant the attention of potential competitors.
5) The electric utility pursued a low price policy—either because it did not know its true costs or because it was sufficiently farsighted to give up current profits for future gains—that forced out the competition.

Despite its acceptance in industry folklore, the first and easiest explanation is not completely convincing as the sole explanation. Competition between generators of energy (in sales through a common distribution grid) might have been a problem, given the many kinds of equipment in existence in the early days. The traction companies were shaky financially, heavily in debt on a short-term basis, and the panic of 1896 sent a number of them into bankruptcy. The traction magnates may have had their hands full with their own ventures. Electric utilities were not extraordinarily profitable, borrowed heavily to produce a decent return on equity, and did not have what would now be considered to be sound accounting practices. In addition, some of the electric utility managements were determined as well as farsighted, and pushed their service at every opportunity. Finally, that was the age of the trust. The Sherman Act, passed in 1890, was rendered toothless by unenthusiastic enforcement and later by a Supreme Court ruling that reasonable trusts were legal. For a businessman to attempt to drive out or to buy out his competitors was not unusual. Those who did so did not need to develop a natural monopoly rationale. Traction and lighting companies often fell under common ownership, and that either destroyed the possibility of competition or helped those companies to realize the benefits of natural monopoly, depending on one's outlook. Clearly, the industry's structure developed for a variety of reasons.

Table 10-1 demonstrates the importance of the non-utility producer of electricity. Because the category of power produced by industrial plants omits small isolated power units in hotels and other commercial and institutional organizations (because information was unavailable), the table understates the percentage of power produced outside the utility industry.

So far as profitability is concerned, the utility industry's record is not

Table 10–1

Capacity and Generation by Ownership

1902–1932

	1902	1907	1912	1917	1922	1927	1932
Generating Capacity							
(KW millions)							
Utility	1.2	2.7	5.2	9.0	14.2	25.1	34.4
Industrial	1.8	4.1	5.8	6.5	6.3	9.5	8.5
Total	3.0	6.8	11.0	15.5	20.5	34.6	42.9
Utility % of Total	40%	40%	47%	58%	69%	73%	80%
Generation							
(KWH billions)							
Utility	2.5	5.9	11.6	25.4	43.6	75.4	79.4
Industrial	3.5	8.2	13.2	18.0	17.6	26.0	20.0
Total	6.0	14.1	24.8	43.4	61.2	101.4	99.4
Utility % of Total	42%	42%	47%	59%	71%	74%	80%

Source: *EEI Pocketbook of Electric Utility Industry Statistics* (Washington, D.C.: Edison Electric Institute, 1979), pp. 5-6.

Table 10–2

Rates of Return and Dividend Payout 1912–1932

	1912	1917	1922	1927	1932
Return on average capitalization	5.24%	5.66%	7.45%	7.35%	6.26%
Return on average common equity	5.68*	6.64*	10.25	11.18	7.91
Dividend payout ratio	53.7*	62.7*	60.4	88.9	95.0

*Merrill Lynch estimate
Source: *EEI Pocketbook,* pp. 10-11.

impressive, despite inadequate depreciation expenses which caused profits to look higher than they really were. (See Table 10-2).

Perhaps the triumph of the electric utility over the isolated supplier occurred because the utility was willing to settle for (or consistently ended up with) a lower return than the isolated supplier. Under those circumstances, there would be little point in competing with the utility.

Financing patterns for the industry evolved during that period. Originally, the industry sold 20 year sinking fund mortgage bonds, with the mortgage on a particular property. That was not ideal for an industry constantly in need of cash. Insull innovated by developing an open-ended mortgage not linked to a particular property, with no limit on amount outstanding, without sinking fund, and with a 45 year maturity. The debt outstanding could reach 75% of the completed plant. Insull also had peculiar notions of depreciation: "The Insull theory was that there was no such thing as depreciation until definite action was taken to retire facilities as obsolete or inadequate. Then the retirement was spread out over future years."[12]

To pull off that kind of financing, one had to be able to convince the investor that the utility would be around for a long time. Unfortunately, the franchise handed out by the city council was often for a shorter period than the life of the utility plant. The city councils of that day were notoriously corrupt. Franchises were granted on receipt of payoffs and franchises were not renewed when the franchisee fell out of political favor. Perhaps if the granting of the franchise and the regulation (what little there was) of the utility were in the hands of a non-partisan state agency instead of a partisan city council, financing would have been easier and cheaper.

That raised the question: would it be easier to sell all those securities, which depended on the unchanging character of the industry and the permanence of the utility, if the utility had no competition? With no sinking funds, no depreciation to speak of, and no funds set aside to pay debt, the industry could only pay off debt by selling new debt. The investor had to have confidence in the long term future of the utility to make such an investment.

In 1897, Charles Tyson Yerkes, the streetcar magnate of Chicago, got fed up with paying off the city council. He had introduced in the state legislature a reform bill to extend the streetcar franchise for 50 years and to put streetcar companies under the jurisdiction of a non-partisan state agency. Unfortunately, a reporter got wind of a fund Yerkes had set up to buy votes, and the legislation was killed. That may have been the first serious attempt to bring about state regulation.

In 1898, in his presidential address before the National Electric Light Association (NELA), Insull proposed that electric utilities be regulated by state agencies that would fix rates and set service standards. If a community did not like the service it was getting, it could buy the utility at the depreciated value of the plant. The idea did not go over well, and NELA set up a committee to discuss the matter.

The idea became increasingly appealing as a movement grew to make the electric utility business municipally owned. Between 1896 and 1906, the number of municipal systems more than tripled. If the public favored the municipally owned system as opposed to the unregulated investor owned utility, perhaps the public would drop opposition to the investor owned utility if the latter were regulated so that it could not take advantage of consumers. In 1907, both NELA and the National Civic Federation came out in favor of state regulation of electric companies. In that year also, three states established regulatory agencies. By 1916, 33 states had such agencies.

The electric industry was regulated, partly because of economies of scale and partly because of political needs. In fact, Anderson, in a study of the origins of regulation, concluded that:

> the concept of state regulation was both compatible with the ideas and political needs of progressives and expedient for safeguarding the material interests of the utilities. From 1907 to 1913, philosophical compatibility and commercial expediency combined to produce a political necessity.[13]

Was the electric utility industry regulated because it was a monopoly, or did it become a monopoly because it was regulated? The standard texts always assume the former and never ask the question. Perhaps the answer is not as self-evident if the question is asked.

Competition in the electric utility industry had all the hazards expected in an industry with high fixed and low variable costs. The competitors could cut prices until only variable costs were covered. "Cutthroat competition" it was called. If a utility had overexpanded, it would have every reason to cut prices to induce as much demand as possible to cover at least part of its fixed costs, possibly thereby ruining a competitor. (That analysis could have applicability to today's overexpanded utility system.) As Clemens put it:

> Before the passage of the public utility laws competition was looked upon with favor and the resulting rate wars were seen as the only means of escaping from outrageous monopoly prices. Any advantages were purely of short duration. . . .[14]

Why? Because the price war ended with the destruction of one competitor, or with a merger of the competitors. The war ended and the winner jacked up prices to recoup losses.

At another point, Clemens notes:

> Some industries may seek regulation and public utility status to escape the rigors of a competitive life. Other industries may prefer the profits of the open market and may be more or less forcibly placed in the public utility category. . . .[15]

The business cycle must also have had some effect on the utility executives. Perhaps prices could be adjusted upward by regulation during the slack periods to protect profitability. That would only work, however, if the regulators prevented would-be competitors from undercutting the utility's higher price. That is, a monopoly would help to preserve profitability. As J.M. Clark wrote:

> It soon became evident that railroads were not the only industry using

large fixed capital and subject to the "peculiarities" of constant and variable costs. It became evident that economic law did not insure prices that would yield "normal" returns on invested capital, because the capital could not get out if it wanted to, and so had to take whatever it could get.[16]

In other words, the utility management may have sought regulation to maintain profitability. The origin of regulation, thus, may not simply be the inevitable result of a natural monopoly situation.

Chapter 11

Expansion and Holding Companies

Corporations have always been susceptible to control by concentration of voting power . . . But it is elemental . . . that, the larger the number of shareholders, the more easily may a small concentrated block of minority shares exercise sway over the all the rest . . . But the more important point to note is that, the wider the diffusion of ownership, the more readily does effective control run to the intermediaries. Financially, the matter is dangerous, for it tends to transform a contingent outstanding charge upon earnings into virtually fixed charges thereon. The cessation of dividends, either to employee holders or to consumers, is bound to be so productive of discontent and unrest that every nerve will be strained to the utmost, even overlong, to prevent their cessation.[17]

William Z. Ripley

The industry expanded in every way. Managements pushed for increasingly large and efficient equipment. New transmission lines made it possible to move service out of the central cities and into rural areas. Sales promotion efforts pushed the use of electricity for more than lighting. Rationalization of franchises, diversity of load, the economies of scale that occurred with larger units, improved transmission facilities, and attempts by utility managements to forestall potential competition by buying up competitors all reduced the number of electric power systems. The price for electricity fell, both absolutely and relatively. Manufacturers developed new uses for electricity. Demand skyrocketed.(See Table 11-1.)

Originally, the electric utility industry was urban-oriented. DC power could not be distributed far from the central station. Isolated generating stations served the small towns even after the systems within a city had been tied together. Yet there were clear advantages to tying together the urban and rural loads, as Samuel Insull discovered. He noted that Chicago had a winter peak and the farm towns a summer peak. Although transmission costs were high between towns, large scale central station generation was cheaper than having numerous isolated power plants.

Therefore, taking control of a number of smaller systems and putting them together would be profitable and would help to consolidate the overly fragmented industry. Furthermore, raising money and engineering the best

Table 11–1

Electric Output and Pricing
1902=100

Year	Electric Power Output	Total Energy Consumption	Price of Elec. (Resid.)	Price of Coal (Bitum.)	Price of Oil (Crude)	All Prices (GNP)	All Prices (Wholesale)	Consumer Price Index
1902	100	100	100	100	100	100	100	100
1907	237	159	65	101	90	101	111	113
1912	415	180	56	103	93	103	117	120
1917	728	225	46	202	195	202	200	160
1920	948	227	46	335	384	336	262	250
1925	1,418	240	45	182	210	183	176	219
1930	1,921	255	37	89	149	152	147	208

Sources:
Sam H. Schurr and Bruce C. Netschert, *Energy in the American Economy, 1850–1975* (Baltimore: Johns Hopkins Press, 1960), pp. 182, 533, 545–46.
Francis X. Welch, *Cases and Text on Public Utility Regulation* (Washington, D.C.: Public Utility Reports, 1968), pp. 239-40.

systems could be facilitated by means of centralized ownership. The electric utility holding company, which could be traced to Edison's original plans and similar efforts of United Gas Improvement, blossomed.

The original electric utility holding companies were established as a result of diverse reasons. The North American Company was the creation of Henry Villard, who enthusiastically invested in utility operating companies and who attempted to turn Edison General Electric into a worldwide trust. The North American Co., established in 1890, was reorganized from Villard's old Oregon and Transcontinental Co. (its steamship *Columbia* had the first isolated power plant in 1880). Villard wanted to take over all the electric utilities in a thickly populated area and to gain profits from the economies associated with unitary control. He started with Milwaukee, bought traction lines in St. Louis, and purchased a minority interest in Detroit Edison. In the same year, Thompson-Houston set up United Electric Securities to own the holdings of companies that had paid for equipment with securities.

American Light and Traction was founded in 1900 to buy local utilities. From that point, the holding company was on its way. Electric Bond & Share, which held securities paid to General Electric for equipment was established in 1905.

The original reasons to set up a holding company were as different as the companies themselves:

1) Engineering firms received stock in utilities for services rendered.

(If the utility failed, the engineers might end up with the whole utility.)

2) Investment banking firms might be forced to take over companies that they promoted and that performed poorly.

3) Equipment manufacturers took securities instead of cash.

4) Operating gains could be derived from consolidation or common ownership.

The profits to the holding company also were derived in diverse ways:

1) The obvious way: efficient operation increased the value of the securities owned.

2) The holding company provided engineering services to subsidiaries at an inflated cost.

3) The holding company collected big fees for arranging financing for the subsidiaries.

The operating subsidiaries that sold electricity were regulated by the states and their expenses were passed on to customers. The holding companies were unregulated. Nobody could stop them from overcharging the subsidiaries. There was a definite advantage to controlling large congeries of subsidiaries because the bigger and more numerous the subsidiaries, the more money that could be milked from them for the benefit of the parent holding company. Naturally it was good business to control the greatest possible assets with as little capital as possible. The best way to do so was to engage in pyramiding and to see to it that outside shareholders had as few rights as possible. Some holding companies were solid operations run for no other purpose than to coordinate and make efficient the operations of the subsidiary companies. But the holding company movement became a craze because of the promotional profits to be made. The holding companies were condemned and fell because of the excesses committed. The present structure of the electric utility industry is the direct result of legislation designed to destroy the holding company that did not have an operating rationale for its existence.

As promoters saw the huge profits to be gained from the holding company business, they began to bid against each other to buy operating properties to put into the holding companies. Sometimes the promoters had to resort to odd measures to make things look good. One could, for instance, combine electric and ice properties, hiding the fact that most of the earnings were coming from the competitive, unsafe, and dwindling ice business. A good promoter could put together a combination of companies, sell preferred stock and bonds to the public to pay for the properties, take 10% or more as a commission, and keep the bulk (or all) of the voting common stock of the holding company, thereby remaining in control without having paid a cent into the business.

The mania for acquisition finally led, in 1928, to the beginning of an investigation by the Federal Trade Commission. In 1932, the eight largest holding companies controlled 73% of the investor owned electric business.

The structure of Insull's empire gives an idea of how things worked. The Insull interests controlled 69% of the stock of Corporation Securities and 64% of the stock of Insull Utility Investments. Those two companies together owned 28% of the voting stock of Middle West Utilities. Middle West Utilities owned eight holding companies, five investment companies, two service companies, two securities companies, and 14 operating companies. It also owned 99% of the voting stock of National Electric Power. National, in turn owned one holding company, one service company, one paper mill, and two operating companies. It also owned 93% of the voting stock of National Public Service. National Public Service owned three building companies, three miscellaneous firms, and four operating utilities. It also owned 100% of the voting stock of Seaboard Public Service. Seaboard Public Service owned the voting stock of five utility operating companies and one ice company. The utilities, in turn, owned eighteen subsidiaries.

The Insull empire operated in 32 states, and owned electric companies, textile mills, ice houses, a paper mill, and a hotel. With a capital investment of about $27 million, Insull controlled at least half a billion dollars of assets in 1930. What made that job so easy was that voting stock constituted a small portion of the capitalization of the constituent corporations within the empire. One could argue, in fact, that Insull controlled the lowest level operating companies by means of an investment equivalent to less than 0.01% of the securities issued by those subsidiaries.

The following figure shows the structure of the empire. (See Figure 11-1.)

That structure also served to magnify the fluctuations in income shown at the subsidiary level. Even worse, however, was that investors might forget their standing in the structure. The common stockholders of a subsidiary operating company might be safer than the debt holder of the top tier holding company. We can illustrate that with a simple example. (See Figure 11-2.)

All the voting stock of the top holding company, Universal Electric Holding Co., is owned by the promoters who set up the deal. With a $50 investment, they control, through the Eastern States Securities subholding company, two electric operating companies and one ice company (Down East Electric, White Mountain Power, and Hudson River Ice) with $12,000 of assets. Those companies have to sell (altogether) $400 a year of securities, which is arranged (for a fee) by the holding company and sold through the promoter (for a commission). The fee and commission amount to $40 a year. The two operating companies also pay an inflated service charge to Universal for engineering advice and services. Furthermore, Universal's promoters have just bought another electric company for $3,000 and they intend to sell it to Eastern States Securities for $4,000 (the extra $1,000 being a finder's fee). On top of all those benefits, there were opportunities

Figure 11-1
The Insull Organization

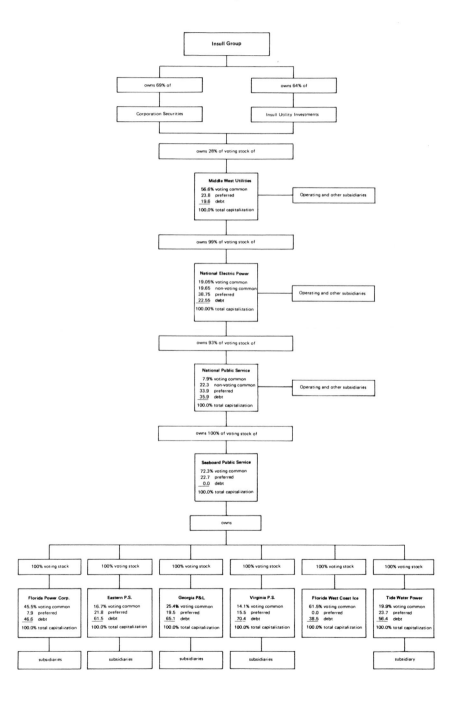

Figure 11-2
A Typical Holding Company

```
                    ┌─────────────────────────────────────────────┐
                    │         Universal Electric Holding Co.       │
                    │                Capitalization                │
                    │                                              │
                    │   $  50 voting common                        │
                    │       50 non-voting common (6% dividend      │
                    │          preference)                         │
                    │      100 preferred (6% dividend)             │
                    │      200 debt (6% interest rate)             │
                    │   ────                                        │
                    │   $400                                       │
                    └─────────────────────────────────────────────┘

                         ┌─────────────────────────────────┐
                         │ owns 100% of voting common of   │
                         └─────────────────────────────────┘

                    ┌─────────────────────────────────────────────┐
                    │         Eastern States Securities            │
                    │                Capitalization                │
                    │                                              │
                    │   $   400 voting common                      │
                    │         400 non-voting common (6% dividend   │
                    │             preference)                      │
                    │       1,200 debt (6% interest rate)          │
                    │       ─────                                  │
                    │   $2,000                                     │
                    └─────────────────────────────────────────────┘

                         ┌─────────────────────────────────┐
                         │ owns 100% of voting common of   │
                         └─────────────────────────────────┘
```

Down East Electric Capitalization	Hudson River Ice Capitalization	White Mountain Power Capitalization
$ 950 voting common 1,050 preferred (6% dividend) 2,000 debt (6% interest rate) $4,000	$ 100 voting common 900 preferred (6% dividend) 3,000 debt (8% interest rate) $4,000	$ 950 voting common 1,050 preferred (6% dividend) 2,000 debt (6% interest rate) $4,000

to misrepresent the financial picture of the system by creating fictitious profits from the sale (at inflated prices) of one company to another within the system.

If we exclude all the extras and look at the leverage inherent in the business, the cardinal principles of holding company finance would be as follows:

(a) The senior securities of the top holding company are junior to the junior securities of the operating company.

(b) Everything that happens at the operating company level is magnified by the time it reaches the holding company level.

We can trace the flow of income from the three operating companies to the parent holding company, starting with a good year. (See Figure 11-3.)

Figure 11-3
The Flow of Income in Good Times

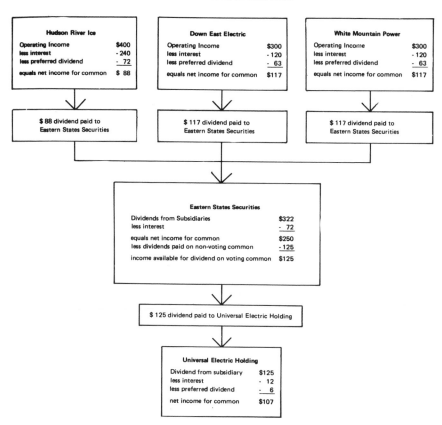

Then earnings decline because the economy slows down and the ice business suffers from a cool summer and from the inroads of the electric refrigerator. The consequences are catastrophic. In tracing the flow of income, keep in mind that the non-voting common stock has a preference for dividends over the voting common, so that it might be paid a cash dividend while the voting common gets nothing. (See Figure 11-4.)

Thus, a 25% decrease in operating income at the operating subsidiary level wipes out the ability of the top holding company, Universal, to pay its preferred and common dividends as well as its interest obligations. Note that owners of preferred stock and non-voting common of Eastern States were paid but not the preferred stockholders or debt holders of Universal. Junior security holders of subsidiaries are ahead of senior security holders of the parent.

Figure 11–4
The Flow of Income in Bad Times

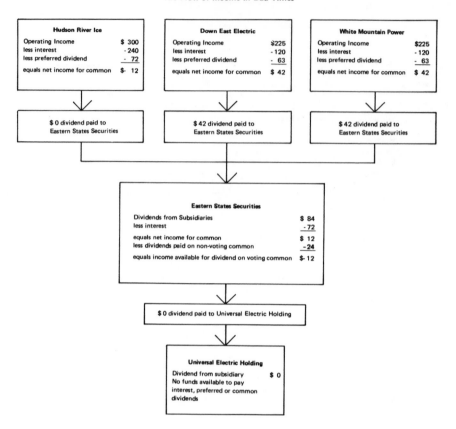

Promotion of securities from within the holding company group became big business. Not only did the investment bankers sell securities to the general public, but the companies also sold securities to employees, and the meter readers peddled securities to unsuspecting customers of the utility. Many of the purchasers did not understand what they were buying, thereby increasing their bitterness when the securities proved to be poor investments.

Why did the holding companies fail?

1) Financial leverage like that explained above magnified the effect of the economic downturn on the successive layers within the holding company system.

2) Continued expansion of facilities into the Depression created liabili-

ties that became a strain to the system when new demand for service did not materialize to produce a return on the new facilities.

3) Overpayment for operating properties created obligations that could not be met when the income from the properties did not rise at the expected rate.

4) Banks called loans that already had been invested in fixed assets, so no cash was available to pay off the loans.

5) Excursions into non-electric businesses were often unsuccessful and proved disastrous when the Depression came.

6) Some money was raised by the holding company, which used securities of the subsidiaries as collateral. When the market declined in 1929, the value of the collateral fell below the level required by the collateral agreement, thereby triggering demand for payment. The holding companies lacked ready cash, so they defaulted on the loans.

7) The questionable transactions of some managements reduced investor confidence and encouraged punitive action from the Government.

Many of the holding companies might have survived the Depression and continued in business to this day if left alone. The mood of the times was against them, however, and legislation shattered those giant combines into hundreds of component parts.

Chapter 12

The Breakup of the Holding Companies and the Rise of Public Power

A Holding Company is a thing where you hand an accomplice the goods while the policeman searches you.[18]

Will Rogers

The idea of Government ownership of utilities did not spring forth Athena-like and fully developed from the collective heads of Franklin D. Roosevelt's Brain Trust. At the turn of the century, there were numerous municipally owned electric utility systems. In fact, in terms of numbers, municipally owned systems outnumbered privately owned ones through the mid-1920s.

Until 1905, Congress let utilities build and operate dams "for ever and for nothing," to quote Gifford Pinchot, Theodore Roosevelt's Chief Forester.[19] Under Roosevelt, the Federal Government began to charge fees for the erection of dams on navigable rivers and it limited the period of use through licenses. In 1920, the Federal Power Commission was set up to regulate the rates, financing, and services of its hydropower licensees.

The Federal Government took a small role in the generation of electric power, even under Herbert Hoover, who sponsored the Boulder Dam, but who argued that the Government generated power should be sold to investor owned utilities. The Federal Government also owned a dam at Muscle Shoals in Alabama, a dam built to supply power to a World War I nitrate works. Republicans hoped to sell the dam to private interests, but Senator Norris of Nebraska led the opposition that kept Muscle Shoals in Federal hands.

George Norris typified the opposition to private power. He fought for public ownership of power facilities in Nebraska, and he saw "the dawn of the electric age," but he did not want to see it develop by means of private ownership. "The power trust is the greatest monopolistic corporation that has been organized for private greed," he declared, and then went on to accuse it of buying legislatures, clergymen and even the Boy Scouts.[20] Al

Smith wanted New York State to own and operate hydropower facilities. Franklin Roosevelt, the next Governor of New York, planned to have the state build a hydro plant on the St. Lawrence River. John Dewey and Felix Frankfurter saw electric power in terms of a great social issue.

To what did those leaders object? From an objective standpoint, the electric utility industry—despite a jerry-built financial structure and the exploitation of subsidiaries—had a good record of lowering prices and extending service, although only about two-thirds of the population and 10% of farms had electricity. Perhaps the feeling was that electric power was an extraordinary force the development of which had to be pushed beyond the limits set by the need to make a profit. Perhaps the anti-utility sentiment was opposition to the excesses of the holding company craze. Perhaps it was nothing more than a continuation of populism. Whatever the reason, private power was a political issue, as was Government exploitation of hydroelectric sites. (It may be a simplification, but some might have argued that the rivers belonged to the people and so should the power.)

On September 21, 1932, in Portland, Oregon, Democratic candidate Franklin D. Roosevelt delivered a speech in which he presented his power policies. Roosevelt denounced the "Insull monstrosity" and implied that other public utilities operated at the same level. He then proposed that the Federal Government establish four hydropower projects: the St. Lawrence, Muscle Shoals, Boulder Dam, and the Columbia. "Each of these in each of the four quarters of the United States will be forever a national yardstick to prevent extortion against the public and to encourage the wider use of that servant of the people—electric power."[21]

Within a year, the Roosevelt Administration began to implement the promises. The huge projects, which furnished work to the unemployed, combined power generation, flood control, navigation, and area development. Boulder Dam, begun in 1928, was finished in 1936. The Tennessee Valley Authority and Bonneville Power Administration built dams on the Tennessee and Columbia River systems. Ironically, Roosevelt could do little in his home state because the Senate would not confirm a treaty with Canada to develop the St. Lawrence.

The Federal agencies sold their power first to publicly owned distribution systems. The lure of cheap Federal power convinced many municipalities to take over the local power distributor. In addition, the Rural Electrification Administration poured money into farmer owned cooperatives formed to bring electricity to the hinterlands. For years thereafter, investor owned utilities lived in fear that they would lose customers to Federally supplied distribution systems.

Was Roosevelt's yardstick a fair one by which to judge the performance of investor owned utilities? Not really, because the Government agencies could be financed entirely by low cost Government debt and because the apportionment of costs among navigation, flood control, and power production could be adjusted to change the bookkeeping cost of power. Whatever the validity of Roosevelt's rationale, his push for public power created jobs, remade the physical, social, and economic faces of two river valleys, and set investor owned utilities on notice that they no longer had the markets to themselves and could lose business if they could not put up a good show against what was probably unfair competition.

Public power was the first part of the New Deal's campaign against the investor owned utilities. The second part was The Public Utility Holding Company Act of 1935. For years, regulators, scholars, and financiers noted that the operating electric companies were supervised by local regulatory agencies, but that nobody supervised the holding companies that controlled (and often exploited) the operating companies. The collapse of several holding company systems added to the worry about those far-flung creations.

In 1928, the Federal Trade Commission (FTC) began a long investigation of the holding companies that led to the Act of 1935. The FTC criticized all the abuses: control of an entire system by means of a small investment at the top of a pyramid of companies, sale of services to subsidiaries at excessive prices, buying and selling properties within the system at unreasonable prices, intra-system loans at unfair terms, and the wild bidding war to buy operating companies. Those abuses tended to raise the cost of electricity to the consumers. When the operating company was overcharged for services, it attempted to pass on the overcharge in the form of higher rates. When the holding company (or its subsidiaries) paid an inflated price for a property, that property had to earn a higher income than otherwise would have been the case in order for the purchaser to meet the interest and dividend charges associated with the overpriced purchase. (Although the holding company organization should have been a means to reduce costs, introduce efficiencies, and add to the investment the safety derived from diversity, it often added to both costs and risk.)

The FTC noted that within 18 holding company systems, there were 42 subholding companies and 91 utility operating companies. Of the $8.6 billion of assets held by that sample, $1.5 billion represented purchase prices above the original cost of the assets. If we assume that the cost of capital on the excess purchase price was the same as on previously existing assets, we could argue that the total utility system's return had to be 22% higher than would have been the case for the component parts.

The Holding Company Act accomplished the following:

(1) Interstate holding companies had to register with the Securities and Exchange Commission (SEC). By definition, a company that owned 10% or more of the voting securities of a gas or electric utility was a holding company. The holding company fell under the jurisdiction of the SEC and had to conform to certain rules.
(2) The "death sentence" clause of the Act broke up holding company systems that were not contiguous and eliminated the intermediate holding companies from the financial structure.

Some holding company systems had broken up anyway, but others were dismembered by the SEC. Between 1935 and 1950, 759 companies were separated from the holding company systems. Between 1938 and 1958, the number of registered holding companies declined from 216 to 18. Since the passage of the Act, only one holding company has been formed.

With the passage of the Public Utility Holding Company Act of 1935, the electric utility industry's emphasis shifted from razzle-dazzle finance and enrichment by questionable means to providing service to the customer at a reasonable profit.

Chapter 13

The Good Old Days: 1945 - 1965

Public utility ... stocks are susceptible ... of valuation ... within precise limits. ... This results from the high degree of stability of utility earnings, the reasonable predictability of growth trends, and the general improbability of any sudden or unexpected developments ... continued and substantial long-term growth can be looked forward to with a high degree of confidence.[22]

Graham, Dodd and Cottle, with Tatham

The breakup of the holding companies began in the Depression and ended in the postwar period. In those years, the industry began to assume its present structure. Despite rapid growth in demand during the inflationary period between World War II and the Korean War, the electric utility industry managed to lower prices. The key savings seem to have been derived from power generation. The industry increased the size of power plants, and those new plants utilized fuel more efficiently. (The heat rate measures the energy, in British Thermal Units, required to produce one kilowatt-hour of electricity. The heat rate fell steadily from 1945 to 1965.) That increased efficiency offset the rising cost of coal. The cost per kilowatt of capacity rose moderately between 1948 and 1956, and then declined. In the production part of the business, the industry seemed to be on a declining cost curve. (See Table 13-1.)

The cost of transmission picture is not as clear. Construction costs increased on a cost per mile basis, but because the industry raised the voltage of the lines, it did get more capacity per mile. Nevertheless, in the early years after the war, the cost of transmission, either on a per mile or per volt-mile basis, seemed to rise, at least until late in the 1950s. Transmission expense per kilowatt-hour sold rose through the Korean War and then declined. A certain percentage of electric production is not recorded as sold because it is lost over transmission lines, stolen, or just unaccounted for. If we assume that the bulk of the loss was in transmission, then transmission became increasingly efficient—after a brief postwar move in the wrong direction—as losses declined. (See Table 13-2.)

84

Table 13-1

Investor Owned Electric Utilities

Generation 1945-1965

Year	Av. Size of Generating Plants (1000KW)	Heat Rate (Millions BTUs/KWH)	Cost of Fuel per Ton of Coal Equivalent	Fuel Cost per KWH	Av. Cost of Generating Plant ($/KW)	Cost of Incremental Gen. Plant ($/KW)	Consumer Price Index	Handy & Whitman Electric Constr. Index (North Atlantic)
	(1)	(2)	(3)	(4)	(5)	(6)	(7)	(8)
1945	19.6	15,800	$ 4.45	0.29 ¢	—	—	62.7	65
1946	19.6	15,700	4.89	0.32	—	—	68.0	76
1947	20.3	15,600	5.60	0.37	—	—	77.8	88
1948	21.2	15,738	6.49	0.42	116	151	83.8	94
1949	23.6	15,033	6.21	0.38	120	173	83.0	100
1950	25.9	14,030	5.95	0.35	124	163	83.8	104
1951	28.8	13,641	6.05	0.34	128	170	90.5	116
1952	31.6	13,361	6.21	0.34	130	161	92.5	119
1953	35.0	12,889	6.32	0.33	133	153	93.2	125
1954	39.6	12,180	6.26	0.31	135	165	93.6	128
1955	44.3	11,699	6.27	0.30	138	181	93.3	132
1956	47.0	11,456	6.51	0.31	140	130	94.7	143
1957	50.5	11,365	6.94	0.32	139	109	98.0	152
1958	59.0	11,090	6.76	0.31	135	152	100.7	156
1959	65.1	10,879	6.58	0.29	137	139	101.5	159
1960	70.6	10,701	6.62	0.29	137	126	103.1	158
1961	76.5	10,552	6.45	0.28	138	115	104.2	155
1962	83.1	10,493	6.58	0.28	137	103	105.4	157
1963	88.2	10,438	6.41	0.27	136	101	106.7	157
1964	95.4	10,407	6.30	0.27	134		108.1	162
1965	102.9	10,384	6.23	0.27	132		109.9	167
% Change 1945-1965	+425	−37	+40	−7	+14[a]	−37[b]	+75	+157

a 1948-1965
b 1949-1965

Sources:

For columns 1, 4, 5, 6: Federal Power Commission, *Statistics of Privately Owned Electric Utilities in the United States* (Washington, D.C.: U.S. Government Printing Office, various years).

For columns 2, 3, 7, 8: Edison Electric Institute, *Statistical Year Book of the Electric Utility Industry* (Washington, D.C.: EEI, various years).

Table 13–2

**Investor Owned Electric Utilities
Transmission 1945–1965** [a]

Year	Transmission Plant/Circuit Mile of Transmission	Incremental Transmission Plant/Incremental Mile	Transmission Expense per KWH Sold (mills)	KWH Losses as % of Generation, Purchase and Interchange
	(1)	(2)	(3)	(4)
1945	—	—	0.24	9.6%
1946	—	—	0.27	10.4
1947	—	—	0.26	10.3
1948	$11,109	—	0.26	10.2
1949	11,902	$32,228	0.28	10.1
1950	12,526	25,198	0.26	10.0
1951	13,226	28,712	0.26	9.7
1952	14,284	42,101	0.28	9.8
1953	15,456	45,958	0.28	9.4
1954	16,986	65,701	0.28	9.3
1955	17,949	47,692	0.26	8.7
1956	18,816	57,916	0.24	8.9
1957	20,072	68,412	0.25	8.7
1958	21,685	72,192	0.26	8.8
1959	22,880	69,384	0.26	8.6
1960	23,906	61,831	0.25	8.4
1961	24,584	46,851	0.24	8.2
1962	25,822	73,334	0.24	8.0
1963	27,020	76,083	0.22	8.0
1964	28,007	78,422	0.22	7.8
1965	29,513	111,833	0.21	7.7
% Change 1945-65	+166% [d]	+247% [e]	−12%	−20%

Year	Average Trans. Plant per Circuit Volt Mile [b]	Period	Incremental Trans. Plant per Incr. Circuit Volt Mile [b]	Year	Percent of Transmission Circuit Miles By Voltage [b] 22-50KV	51-131KV	132-800KV
1948	$0.1603	—	—	1948	45.0	42.1	12.9
1950	0.1763	1948–1950	$0.3123	1950	42.9	42.5	14.6
1955	0.2301	1951–1955	0.4003	1955	38.0	43.0	19.0
1960	0.2878	1956–1960	0.5571	1960	34.8	43.4	21.8
1965	0.3273	1961–1965	0.5034	1965	31.8	42.6	25.6

[a] 22KV and over.
[b] Circuit volt-miles defined as miles of transmission x voltage of transmission line. Assumes same mix of voltage for investor owned industry as for total industry.
[c] Total industry.
[d] 1948–1965
[e] 1949–1965

Sources: Federal Power Commission *Statistics* (columns 1,2,3,4), Edison Electric Institute *Year Book* (columns 1,2).

Capital expenditures associated with the distribution of power showed a rising trend, on a per customer basis, but remained fairly unchanged on a per kilowatt of capacity basis. Distribution expense per customer increased, but at a minimal rate after the Korean War. (See Table 13-3.)

Electric utility sales, measured in kilowatt-hours, grew rapidly each year through 1965, with the exception of 1945-46. Although sales were influenced by economic fluctuations, they showed strength even in recession years, as did growth in demand for electricity at peak periods. The industry could take advantage of all the economies offered to it by the declining costs associated with new equipment and with increasing economies of scale. It could build new plants confident that the customer would use the new facilities. Furthermore, with the exception of a few tight years in the 1940s, the industry had sufficient reserve capacity to encourage new demand without fear of being unable to meet the needs of the customer. From the end of the Korean War to 1960, the industry increased its reserve margin, which then was allowed to decline to a low point in 1969. Also during that period, the industry was taking a larger share of the electric market, as evidenced by the decline in percentage of generation from non-utility sources. (See Table 13-4.)

From an operational standpoint, everything was going well. The electric industry was providing increasingly cheap power. The industry's costs were under control and actually declined in some instances, although prices within the economy were rising. Price for power fell despite a moderate amount of rate relief through 1961 that averaged less than 1% a year. From 1962 on, rate reductions exceeded rate increases. (See Table 13-5.)

A good operating record, however, could conceal serious financial problems, especially if actions were forced on the industry by regulatory agencies that put short term customer benefit over long term corporate solvency. Some good indicators of financial well-being tell the story.

In 1945-65, dollar investment in utility plant rose at a good rate, but not one out of line with the gains in sales. Capital spending rose rapidly after World War II but reserve margins did not rise to satisfactory levels until after the Korean War. Late in the 1950s and early in the 1960s, spending tapered off as a result of the large amount of plant that had been put into service, apparently in anticipation of future demand. Academic economists of the time asserted that utility managements had an incentive to raise the rate base to increase the earnings potential of the company. That is the Averch-Johnson effect, first discussed in a 1962 paper.[23]

For a period of time, raising capital to pay for the expansion must have been the full-time occupation of financial executives within the industry, because a large part of the capital expenditures had to be paid for with new offerings of securities. As spending tapered off and returns on investment rose, however, the need for outside financing declined. (See Table 13-6.)

Return on the book equity of common stockholders rose moderately, in line with the returns offered by investment in new utility bonds. The utility's return on equity was well below that earned in industrial investments at the time, but the stock market performance of utility stocks was not out of line with that of industrial shares. As a result, investors probably were satisfied

Table 13–3

Distribution 1945–1965
Investor Owned Electric Utilities

Year	Average Cost of Distribution Plant/Customer	Cost of Incremental Distribution/ Incr. Customer	Distribution Expense per Customer [a]
	(1)	(2)	(3)
1945	—	—	$8.33
1946	—	—	9.37
1947	—	—	10.47
1948	$187	—	11.30
1949	199	$444	11.60
1950	208	425	12.04
1951	217	444	12.46
1952	228	552	13.05
1953	241	616	13.66
1954	255	761	14.23
1955	272	797	14.18
1956	288	799	14.64
1957	306	890	14.97
1958	322	1,051	15.27
1959	336	876	15.65
1960	355	1,204	16.19
1961	370	1,294	15.62
1962	386	1,252	16.00
1963	403	1,362	16.36
1964	420	1,645	17.18
1965	437	1,303	17.48
% Change 1945–1965	+134% [b]	+193% [c]	+110%

Year	Average Distribution Plant per KW of Capacity	Period	Incremental Distribution Plant per Incremental KWH of Capacity
1948	$134		—
1950	133	1948–1950	$130
1955	129	1951–1955	123
1960	125	1956–1960	117
1965	126	1961–1965	130

[a] $ per year.
[b] 1948–1965
[c] 1949–1965

Sources: Federal Power Commission *Statistics*.

Table 13–4

Electricity and the Economy 1945–1965

Year	% Change KWH Sales	% Change Peak Load	% Change Real GNP	Electricity Made Available in the U.S.A. (%)		
				% Total US Elec. Gen. by non-Utility Sources	Supplied by All Utilities	Supplied by Investor-owned Utilities
	(1)	(2)	(3)	(4)	(5)	(6)
1945	−2.3	−2.7	−2.8	18.0	81.3	66.1
1946	−2.4	13.6	−12.4	17.2	82.1	66.6
1947	14.0	10.2	−0.2	16.8	82.7	67.2
1948	10.7	8.5	3.9	16.1	83.6	67.5
1949	3.2	5.0	0.1	15.6	84.0	67.2
1950	12.9	13.8	8.5	15.3	84.3	68.3
1951	13.4	10.6	8.1	14.5	85.1	69.3
1952	7.7	7.0	3.7	13.8	85.8	69.2
1953	12.2	9.0	4.6	13.9	85.8	68.6
1954	6.9	14.4	−2.0	13.4	86.2	67.8
1955	17.1	4.5	8.0	13.0	86.4	66.5
1956	10.3	9.5	2.1	12.3	87.1	66.6
1957	5.3	6.2	1.8	11.8	87.8	66.8
1958	1.9	7.3	−0.2	11.0	88.6	67.3
1959	10.1	6.0	6.0	10.7	88.9	68.1
1960	9.0	6.1	2.3	10.5	89.0	68.4
1961	5.5	6.0	2.5	9.9	89.9	68.7
1962	7.8	7.3	5.8	9.7	90.3	69.0
1963	7.1	6.6	3.9	9.4	90.6	69.3
1964	7.4	8.5	5.3	9.2	90.6	69.6
1965	7.0	6.5	5.9	8.8	91.2	69.9

Sources: U.S.Dept. of Commerce (column 3). Edison Electric Institute *Year Book* (columns 1,2,4,5,6).

with the utility returns, given the presumed risk differential between utility and industrial investments.

The bondholder did not fare as well, in the sense that income available to meet long term debt interest expense declined moderately as a multiple of that expense. Because a large proportion of the industry had high bond ratings by 1965, investors apparently were willing to accept slightly lower quantitative protection because of the high quality they saw in the industry. (Table 13-7.)

Finally, the industry's method of accounting for some of the costs of financing construction can disguise the real pattern of operations. The prac-

Table 13-5

Price and Usage 1945-1965
Total Electric Utility Industry

Year	Price of Residential Electricity (¢/KWH)	Price of All Electricity (¢/KWH)	Consumer Price Index	GNP Deflator	Net Rate Increases (Decreases) as % of Electric Revenue[a]	Electric Usage per Residential Customer (KWH)	Electric Usage per Customer (KWH)
	(1)	(2)	(3)	(4)	(5)	(6)	(7)
1945	3.41 ¢	1.73 ¢	62.7	59.1	NA	1,229	5,762
1946	3.22	1.81	68.0	66.6	NA	1,329	5,422
1947	3.09	1.77	77.8	74.2	NA	1,438	5,828
1948	3.01	1.79	83.8	79.1	1.0	1,563	6,073
1949	2.95	1.86	83.0	78.6	0.8	1,684	5,937
1950	2.88	1.81	83.8	79.9	0.3	1,830	6,377
1951	2.81	1.78	90.5	85.4	0.6	2,004	6,922
1952	2.77	1.79	92.5	86.9	1.4	2,169	7,183
1953	2.74	1.77	93.2	87.5	0.3	2,346	7,815
1954	2.69	1.77	93.6	88.7	0.8	2,549	8,127
1955	2.64	1.67	93.3	90.0	0.4	2,751	9,265
1956	2.60	1.64	94.7	92.9	0.1	2,969	9,944
1957	2.56	1.67	98.0	96.4	0.7	3,174	10,214
1958	2.53	1.71	100.7	98.4	0.9	3,389	10,227
1959	2.50	1.69	101.5	100.0	0.6	3,618	11,020
1960	2.47	1.69	103.1	101.8	0.4	3,854	11,704
1961	2.45	1.69	104.2	102.6	0.1	4,019	12,099
1962	2.41	1.68	105.4	104.5	-0.1	4,259	12,763
1963	2.37	1.65	106.7	106.1	-0.3	4,442	13,366
1964	2.31	1.62	108.1	107.7	-0.8	4,703	14,015
1965	2.25	1.59	109.9	112.3	-0.9	4,933	14,694
% Change 1945-1965	-34	-9	+75	+90	—	+301	+155

[a]Investor owned electric utilities. Annual aggregate amounts granted as % of year's electric revenue. Sources: Edison Electric Institute *Year Book* (all columns). *Electrical World* (all columns).

Table 13–6

Capital Spending and Reserve Margins
Investor Owned Electric Utilities 1945–1965

Year	% Increase in Gross Electric Utility Plant (1)	Capital Spending ($ Millions) (2)	New Permanent Capital Raised as % of Capital Spending [a] (3)	Reserve Margin % [b] (4)
1945	−1.8	350	15	26.5
1946	3.2	650	29	11.4
1947	7.0	1,235	49	6.1
1948	10.8	1,830	73	6.6
1949	10.1	2,190	64	14.2
1950	9.3	2,050	61	10.3
1951	9.3	2,134	70	11.8
1952	10.1	2,599	67	11.9
1953	11.3	2,876	82	17.8
1954	9.1	2,835	60	20.4
1955	7.8	2,719	50	18.6
1956	8.1	2,910	50	19.7
1957	9.7	3,679	67	22.2
1958	8.8	3,764	60	27.1
1959	7.7	3,383	57	30.2
1960	7.4	3,331	54	31.5
1961	5.8	3,000	52	31.0[c]
1962	5.5	3,037	48	31.0
1963	5.6	3,240	35	30.2
1964	5.4	3,558	43	23.7[c]
1965	6.1	4,055	36	22.9[c]

[a]Investor owned public utility long term financing as percentage of reported capital expenditure series. May understate percentage of capital raised externally to the extent that non-electric utility expenditures are excluded from column 2 or to the extent that short term debt becomes an increasing percentage of external financing.
[b]Total industry.
[c]Summer non-coincident peak reserve margin. All others winter.

Sources: Federal Power commission *Statistics* (column 1). Edison Electric Institute *Year Book* (columns 2,3,4).

tice capitalizes the financing charges associated with construction of new facilities by creating a credit in the income statement called interest during construction (IDC) for the period being discussed. The accounting concept makes sense. When the credit is large in relation to reported earnings, though, the investor or regulator may be misled into believing that things are better than they appear to be because IDC brings no cash from sale of power, but rather is an expectation of future earnings. Investors who prefer

Table 13-7

Financial Ratios Investor Owned Electric Utilities 1945-1965

Year	Return on Aver. Common Equity (%)	Interest Cost Newly Issued Bonds (%)	Interest Coverage Ratio (Long Term Debt) (×)	IDC % Net Income[a]	Average Stock Price[b]	Average Book Value[b]	Market/Book Ratio[b]
	(1)	(2)	(3)	(4)	(5)	(6)	(7)
1945	8.2	2.87	4.2	0.6 %	26.29	26.65	99
1946	10.5	2.74	4.6	0.9	34.05	27.16	125
1947	10.3	2.79	4.6	2.4	29.53	27.68	107
1948	9.9	3.07	4.2	4.3	27.34	28.08	97
1949	10.6	3.06	4.2	5.0	28.37	28.38	100
1950	10.6	2.86	4.0	4.6	31.23	29.09	107
1951	9.5	3.25	4.0	4.4	32.55	30.27	108
1952	10.2	3.36	4.1	5.2	35.48	31.00	114
1953	10.2	3.75	3.8	7.0	37.80	31.33	121
1954	10.5	3.11	3.8	6.2	44.30	31.85	139
1955	11.0	3.30	3.9	4.4	49.24	32.71	151
1956	11.1	3.86	3.9	3.6	49.62	33.90	146
1957	11.0	4.80	3.7	5.9	49.42	35.43	139
1958	11.0	4.18	3.4	8.0	57.96	36.77	158
1959	11.2	4.92	3.4	6.2	66.35	38.00	175
1960	11.3	4.72	3.4	5.5	69.82	39.52	177
1961	11.2	4.72	3.4	4.5	90.55	41.22	220
1962	11.7	4.40	3.5	4.3	91.50	43.29	211
1963	11.8	4.40	3.6	3.6	102.79	45.36	227
1964	12.3	4.55	3.6	3.6	108.76	47.67	228
1965	12.6	4.61	3.7	3.6	117.08	49.85	235
% Change 1945-1965	+54	+61	-12	+500	+345	+87	+137

aInterest during construction credit, later allowance for funds used during construction.

bMoody's Electric Utility Average.

Sources: Federal Power Commission *Statistics* (columns 1,3,4). Edison Electric Institute *Year Book* (columns 2,5,6,7). Moody's (columns 2,5,6,7).

cash to bookkeeping credits would discount the earnings of utilities that have a high percentage of income derived from IDC. Because in the 1945-65 period, IDC accounted for a minimal proportion of earnings, the quality of reported earnings held up during the period, another indicator that the overall situation was solid.

For electric utilities, the postwar period was one of reorganization out of the holding companies, mergers for some smaller utilities, minimal need for rate relief, declining costs and prices, motivation to add to the rate base, satisfied investors, and acceptable (although unspectacular) returns for owners. Although the development of the Averch-Johnson analysis questioned whether the situation was ideal, one could still argue that results were good. That environment of few operating problems and little need to question prevailing regulatory methods, left few people prepared to react quickly to or understand well the problems that followed.

14

The Decline of the Industry: After 1965

He has walled up my way, so that I cannot pass,
and he has set darkness upon my paths.
He has stripped from me my glory,
and taken the crown from my head.
He breaks me down on every side, and I am gone,
and my hope he has pulled up like a tree.[24]

The Book of Job, XIX, 8-10

Surely, as the period after 1965 unfolded, electric utility investors and managers must have felt like the puzzled Job. After so much success, what did they do to deserve such a series of misfortunes?

Before examining the problems of the industry, consider the industry in relation to the economy. In 1945-1965, America's energy consumption moved in line with its economic activity, and demand for electricity grew at roughly twice the rate of the economy. Some might attribute that fast pace to the development of electrical appliances, to the discovery of the convenience and cleanliness of electricity, and to smart marketing by electric utilities. The above elements helped to create demand, which in turn allowed utilities to reach for greater economies of scale and operation, which in turn sufficiently lowered the price of power to encourage the development and marketing of new electrical devices. Whether the development of new markets occurred because of the drop in the price for electricity or vice versa is a chicken or egg debate. The reality is that the price for electricity declined not only on an absolute basis but also in relation to prices as a whole and to the price for competing fuels. And electricity usage grew far faster than energy usage as a whole.

In 1965-1970, the trend toward increased use of electricity continued. The price for electricity remained flat despite a sharp upturn both in the overall cost of living and in the price for coal (the most important fuel for generating electricity). Other energy sources showed greater increases in price. In part, the continuing push toward electricity occurred because electricity prices declined in relation to other prices. In part, it occurred because of fears that the supply of natural gas was inadequate, and because increasing environmental awareness caused some users of energy to push their environmental problems onto the electric utility by switching to central station power.

In a way, the inability (or unwillingness) of the electric utility industry to raise prices when costs of operation and capital began to rise (possibly because neither managements nor regulators realized that a fundamental change in costs was taking place) triggered the deterioration in the industry. Moreover, the process of deterioration was accelerated because the uneconomically low price for power induced increased demand, which became increasingly difficult to meet profitably at then current rates. To make matters worse, electricity was priced on a declining block basis. Each additional increment of demand was sold at a lower price than the previous increment. The declining block tariff had been designed to take advantage of economies of scale and to encourage consumption. As a result, the industry faced a new situation. Cost of production had started to rise, but electricity was priced as if costs were still declining. Sale of that incremental kilowatt-hour was becoming increasingly less profitable.

Table 14-1

Electricity and Other Energy 1945-1986

Year	Energy Consumption in USA	Real GNP	Generation of Electricity	Price of Electricity	Price of Natural Gas	Price of No. 2 Fuel Oil	Price of Bituminous Coal	Cost of Living (CPI)
1945	100	100	100	100	100	100	100	100
1950	108	99	143	105	105	146	155	134
1955	133	122	232	97	118	174	153	149
1960	142	137	311	98	136	180	178	164
1965	171	173	427	92	141	192	174	175
1970	215	200	605	92	145	223	278	215
1975	228	222	738	156	293	470	715	299
1980	245	269	880	252	709	1206	866	457
1985	239	303	947	357	1150	1299	1013	597
1986	239	314	957	357	1001	857	997	608

Relative Rates of Growth

Period	Electricity to All Energy	Electricity to Real GNP
1945-50	132	144
1950-55	134	134
1955-60	125	120
1960-65	114	109
1965-70	114	122
1970-75	116	110
1975-80	111	98
1980-85	110	96
1980-86	111	93

Source: American Gas Association, Edison Electric Institute, Dept. of Energy, Merrill Lynch estimates.
Notes: Price of Electric — total usage. Price of Natural Gas — all usage. Price of No. 2 Fuel Oil — residential. Price of Bituminous Coal — to producers.

From 1970 on, the industry began to raise prices. Although the price for electricity did not rise as much as that for competing fuels, it increased more than prices as a whole throughout the economy. In that period, energy consumption grew at a slower rate than GNP as a whole, while use of electricity continued to grow faster than GNP, although the relative rate of growth between electricity and GNP was less than in any other postwar period. (See Table 14-1.)

As can be seen in Table 14-1, the utility industry after 1965 supplied an increasing percentage of the electricity generated in the United States. Why did industrial generators produce a decreasing percentage of the total, despite the rising cost of central station power? Two possible reasons were that utility power did not reflect the true cost of production and therefore was a bargain, and that industrial producers were not interested in becoming regulated utilities or dealing with the environmental roadblocks to the production of electricity. In addition, the investor owned utilities continued to gain market share. (See Table 14-2.)

Table 14-2

Electricity and the Economy 1965-1986

					Electricity Made Available in the U.S.A. Generated by Domestic Electric Utilities	
Year	% Change KWH Sales	% Change Peak load	% Change Real GNP	% Total US Elec. Gen. by non-Utility Sources	Supplied by All Utilities	Supplied by Investor-Owned Utilities
	(1)	(2)	(3)	(4)	(5)	(6)
1965	7.0	5.4	5.9	8.8	91.2	69.9
1966	8.9	7.4	6.0	8.4	91.5	70.4
1967	6.6	5.0	2.7	7.8	92.2	71.0
1968	8.6	11.5	4.4	7.5	92.6	71.0
1969	8.7	8.3	2.6	7.1	92.8	70.9
1970	6.4	6.6	−0.3	6.6	93.3	72.0
1971	5.3	6.4	3.0	6.0	93.8	73.2
1972	7.5	9.2	5.7	5.6	94.0	73.0
1973	7.9	7.7	5.5	5.2	94.1	73.4
1974	−0.1	1.6	−1.4	5.2	94.2	72.8
1975	1.9	2.2	−1.3	4.3	95.5	74.0
1976	6.6	4.0	5.9	4.1	95.5	74.2
1977	5.5	6.9	5.3	4.0	95.3	75.5
1978	3.4	3.0	4.4	3.5	95.7	74.7
1979	3.3	0.9	3.2	3.1	95.7	74.8
1980	2.0	6.5	−0.4	2.9	96.0	75.1
1981	1.2	0.3	2.5	2.7	96.3	74.6
1982	−2.4	−3.1	−2.1	2.7	96.1	73.4
1983	2.9	7.7	3.6	2.4	96.1	73.4
1984	5.6	0.8	6.4	2.9	95.6	73.1
1985	1.1	2.1	2.7	3.7	94.8	73.6
1986	2.1	3.4	3.7	4.6Est.	94.1Est.	72.9Est.

Source: U.S. Dept. of Commerce (Column 3). Edison Electric Institute *Year Book* (Columns 1, 2, 4, 5, 6).

Nineteen sixty-five was a watershed year for the electric utility industry. In that year, electric utility stock prices peaked, rate reductions were at their greatest levels, interest coverage ratios reached a height not seen since, the Vietnam War began in earnest, and the Northeast Blackout showed that all was not well in the electric utility industry. In the period that followed, conditions turned against the industry, which made mistakes that compounded the difficulties.

Capital spending soon became a problem. In November 1965, an equipment failure at Ontario Hydro caused the collapse of the interconnected power pools throughout the Northeast, plunging that region into darkness. The Northeast Blackout forced soul-searching within the industry. Perhaps the individual electric companies had insufficient generating capacity in reserve to meet emergencies. Reserve margins had been falling for several years. Perhaps the system of high voltage interconnections between utilities or regions was inadequate to meet emergencies. Although money had to be spent to improve reliability of service, doing so would mean investment that would not necessarily lower costs nor be automatically associated with increased revenues — as would be the case if the money were being spent to meet new demand for service.

Capital expenditures rose for other reasons as well. As the environmental movement gained popularity, utilities beautified plants, converted generating units to less polluting fuels, and put on line equipment that brought them into compliance with new environmental regulations. None of those moves, however, made plants more efficient or helped the utilities to meet the needs of new customers. Furthermore, environmental opposition to utility activities caused delays and revisions in construction programs, thereby adding to costs. Those who ran the companies probably found it difficult to understand and to adjust to the new constraints, with the result that conflicts were frequent. Many in the industry saw the situation in superficial terms. They thought that meeting environmental demands meant beautifying substations, putting power lines underground, and designing esthetic, sky blue towers to carry the transmission lines.[25]

Furthermore, not only did the cost of electric plants rise because of inflation, but also because the industry was building a more expensive (more capital intensive, that is) kind of power plant. The difficulty in securing gas supplies discouraged utilities from building low cost gas burning plants. Instead, they turned to fuels that required more elaborate generating units. Environmental protection devices added to the cost of equipment. Construction delays and labor productivity problems surfaced during the overheated Vietnam War economy. In addition, the industry had plunged into the nuclear age, and nuclear generating plants cost more to build per kilowatt of capacity, although the higher capital costs were supposed to be offset by lower fuel costs. The industry, however, was dealing with an unfamiliar technology, and one that was feared and opposed by a vocal segment of the population. As a result of technological and political roadblocks, nuclear generating units took longer to build and were more costly than expected, and in many instances proved to be disappointing performers. (See Table 14-3.)

Table 14-3

Capital Spending and Reserve Margins
Investor Owned Electric Utilities 1965-1986

Year	% Increase in Gross Electric Utility Plant	Capital Spending ($ Millions)	New Permanent Capital Raised as % of Capital Spending	Reserve Margin %[b][c]
	(1)	(2)	(3)	(4)
1965	6.1	$ 4,055	36	22.9
1966	7.4	4,941	55	18.4
1967	8.6	6,204	53	20.8
1968	9.2	7,118	53	17.2
1969	10.1	8,357	58	16.6
1970	11.5	10,264	77	19.0
1971	11.8	12,218	73	20.9
1972	13.7[a]	13,728	63	19.6
1973	8.7[a]	15,291	59	20.8
1974	13.3	17,192	67	27.2
1975	10.1	16,191	74	34.3
1976	10.5	18,158	64	34.5
1977	10.8	21,297	61	30.2
1978	10.8	24,030	49	33.7
1979	11.2	26,819	48	36.9
1980	10.2	28,335	49	30.8
1981	9.7	30,690	45	33.6
1982	10.0	35,350	44	41.3
1983	8.3	35,565	33	33.3
1984	8.4	35,285	31	33.9
1985	9.1	33,294	34	35.0
1986	5.5Est.	31,023	38	33.0

[a]Revised.
[b]Total Industry.
[c]Summer.

Sources: Federal Power Commission Statistics; Energy Information Administration, *Statistics of Privately Owned Electric Utilities in the United States* (Washington, D.C.: U.S. Gov't Printing Office, various years) (column 1). Edison Electric Institute *Year Book* (columns 2,3,4). Merrill Lynch estimates. May differ slightly from Table 13-16 due to revisions in series.

Consequently, capital spending accelerated, the rate base (using utility plant as a proxy) rose considerably faster than sales (and the income derived from sales), and a large percentage of the needed funds had to be raised by selling new capital. Unfortunately, the sale of securities occurred as interest rates were rising. Paying out increasingly high interest rates on an increasing amount of debt when income was not rising proportionately caused the decline of the pretax interest coverage ratio. That meant that the industry's debt was declining in quality, and that, in turn, necessitated payment of even higher interest rates. In short, not only were interest rates as a whole on a secular uptrend, but interest costs of utilities rose even more because utility bonds were becoming increasingly risky. (See Table 14-4.)

The way to stop the squeeze on margins was to raise the price for electricity or to reduce costs. The industry's costs previously had fallen sufficiently fast to maintain profitability levels even after reducing (or only minimally raising) the price for power. Productivity was on a downtrend, however, and could not be relied on as in the past.

> Improvements in labor productivity have been . . . dramatic . . . In the subperiod for 1947-53, the average growth rate was 7.2 percent; it slipped to 7.0 percent for 1953-66 and then declined to only 4.8 percent . . . for 1966-72. . . .

> Since there has been a shift in the direction of capital-intensive nuclear power and a rapid increase in the expenditure for cooling towers and air pollution control equipment, it seems likely that capital productivity in the electric power industry has been negative in recent years. These trends combined with a phasing out or rapid conversion of gas- and oil-fired generating plants to coal burning plants will probably insure that aggregate capital productivity will continue to be negative in the years ahead. . . . The peak in the efficiency of new fossil-fired electric generating units was apparently reached around 1967. . . .[26]

Neither regulators nor management seem to have caught the trend, and critics of the industry showed as little prescience. Metcalf and Reinemer italicized their view of the world:

> *With few exceptions . . . the price of electricity should be decreasing steadily. Electric power is a classic example of an industry in which mass production and distribution are decreasing the cost per unit.*[27]

Positive rate relief did not materialize for several years. In the interim, both the pretax interest coverage for debt and the return on stockholder investment dropped. Subsequent rate relief was insufficient to raise the ratios to previous levels. Because bond ratings also fell, the utilities had to pay higher interest charges than they would have otherwise, and during crisis periods in the bond markets, some of the poorly rated utilities had difficulty raising money at all.[28]

The common stockholder, the owner of the business, also fared poorly. Return on equity investment tapered off. In reality, however, the drop in return was greater than the numbers indicated because an increasing proportion of that declining return was derived from a non-cash credit in the

Table 14-4

Price and Usage Total Electric Utility Industry 1965-1986

Year	Price of Residential Electricity (¢/KWH)	Price of All Electricity (¢/KWH)	Consumer Price Index	GNP Deflator	Net Rate Increases (Decreases) as % of Electric Revenue[a]	Electric Usage per Residential Customer (KWH)	Electric Usage per Customer (KWH)
1965	2.25¢	1.59¢	94.5	81.3	-0.9	4,933	14,694
1966	2.20	1.56	97.2	84.0	-0.2	5,265	15,678
1967	2.17	1.56	100.0	86.5	-0.2	5,577	16,384
1968	2.12	1.55	104.2	90.4	0.0	6,057	17,445
1969	2.09	1.54	109.8	94.9	0.8	6,571	18,563
1970	2.10	1.59	116.3	100.0	2.2	7,066	19,380
1971	2.19	1.69	121.3	105.1	3.6	7,380	19,956
1972	2.29	1.77	125.3	109.5	3.3	7,691	20,964
1973	2.38	1.86	133.1	115.8	4.0	8,079	21,955
1974	2.83	2.30	147.7	127.4	6.3	7,907	21,488
1975	3.21	2.70	161.2	139.3	8.6	8,176	21,417
1976	3.45	2.89	170.5	146.4	5.5	8,360	22,361
1977	3.78	3.21	181.5	155.0	4.8	8,693	23,052
1978	4.03	3.46	195.3	165.3	3.9	8,849	23,315
1979	4.43	3.82	217.4	179.4	4.2	8,843	23,481
1980	5.12	4.49	246.8	196.1	7.4	9,025	23,167
1981	5.80	5.14	272.4	214.5	8.7	8,825	23,026
1982	6.44	5.79	289.1	227.4	7.4	8,743	22,197
1983	6.83	6.00	298.4	236.3	4.9	8,814	22,479
1984	7.17	6.27	311.4	245.3	6.6	8,978	23,152
1985	7.39	6.47	322.2	253.4	3.6	8,906	22,903
1986	7.44	6.49	328.4	260.0	1.8	9,038	22,925
% Change 1965-1986	+231	+308	+248	+220	—	+83	+56

[a]Investor-owned electric utilities.

Sources: Edison Electric Institute (all columns). *Electrical World* (all columns).

income statement—the allowance for funds used during construction (AFUDC), also known as interest during construction (IDC). To make matters worse, numerous companies adopted increasingly liberal accounting procedures in other respects to maintain a pattern of gains in reported earnings. One could argue, therefore, that the overall quality of reported earnings also had fallen and that the decline in return on stockholders' equity was much greater than was apparent from the bare numbers.

Common stockholders faced two problems, sensitivity of the stock price to the movement of interest rates, and the inability of the companies to raise return earned while the return on competitive investments rose. Prices for utility stocks tend to move with changes in interest rates. A stockholder usually buys a utility stock because it furnishes a combination of a reasonable current dividend and moderate but steady growth in dividends and earnings. The total return on the investment (current dividends plus increase in the price for the stock) should be higher than the interest received on a bond, because the common stockholder assumes a greater risk than the bondholder. Investors, however, also consider utility stocks to be safe investments and substitutes for the purchase of bonds so long as the stock provides something extra to compensate for risk. Therefore, when the expected total return from the stocks becomes too low in relation to the return available from bonds, the investors sell the stocks (thereby depressing stock prices and raising the return on the stock investment) and buy bonds. The process is reversed when the bond yield is too low in relation to the return on the stocks. If we consider the market situation after 1965, the return on bonds continued to rise, but the return earned on the stockholders' investment in the electric utility continued to fall. Investors sold the stocks, thereby causing prices to decline until the return on the stocks was commensurate with returns offered elsewhere.

To use representative numbers, in 1965, the stockholders' investment in Average Electric Company was $49.85, on which the company earned 12.6% or $6.28. If we assume that the investor considered these earnings as his total return, and the investor paid $117.08 in the marketplace for that stock, then the investor was willing to settle for a 5.4% total return at a time when he could have gotten 4.6% by buying bonds. (These numbers are not correct conceptually but will be used to illustrate the dilemma faced by utility investors.) In 1970, the Average Electric Company earned 11.8% on $62.32 of stockholders' investment, or $7.35. Bonds returned 8.8%. The buyers of utility shares demanded a return higher than that available on bonds, so they would only pay $79.06 for the share. At $79.06, the shares offered a return of 9.3% ($7.35/$79.06), which was more than the bond return. In both instances, the stockholders took a return less than 1% greater than the bond yield. By the early 1970s, investors began to worry that utility stocks might be a lot riskier in relation to bonds than previously thought. Therefore, the stocks had to offer a higher return differential than before.

In 1975, Average Electric Company earned 11.2% on stockholders' investment of $74.52, or $8.35, while bonds paid 9.97%. Purchasers paid only $51.25 for the stock, for a return of 16.3% ($8.35/$51.25). In 1980, the company earned 11.5% on its investment per share of $82.72, or $9.51, while bonds yielded 13.46%, The stock sold at $54.80, for an earnings yield of 17.4%. By 1985, the industry had recovered enough for its stocks to reach book value, and in 1986, the stock sold at $111.11 to produce an earnings yield of 10.5% as opposed to 9.61% available from bonds. (It took a continued recovery of earnings, sharply lower interest rates and a higher stock market to bring utility stocks back well above book value.)

The result of that combination of lower return on stockholders' equity and higher interest rates was to cause stock prices to drop until they were well below book values. Utility Companies had to raise money by selling common stock below book value (true of almost all electric companies by the mid 1970s), thereby diluting the interests of their shareholders, and those companies probably invested the funds for a return unfairly low according to regulatory theory. Bonbright, for instance, held that the "current cost of common-stock capital", which is the rate of return that should be allowed by the regulators, should permit the utility "to issue more . . . stock . . . at prices . . . not less than the per-share book value of the old stock. In this way it can . . . [issue] new common stock at prices high enough to avoid 'impairing the integrity' of the investment of the old stockholders."[29]

Returns being earned were insufficient to meet Bonbright's standard of profitability. Investors were discouraged by the level of profitability in the industry. Electric utility shares declined on an absolute basis (halving between 1965 and 1975), did worse than the average industrial share, and fell to prices at which new financing was dilutionary and probably damaging to existing shareowners. (See Table 14-5.)

The industry ran into problems on all fronts when, after 1965, it continued to do what had served so well before: it added increasingly large generating plants. Heat rate did not improve, however, and the cost of incremental generating capacity rose far faster than either the cost of living or the utility construction index. New plant was more expensive but not more efficient than old plant. The variability in cost of new facilities after 1978 is due to scheduling problems and wide diversity of costs of nuclear plants after the Three Mile Island accident. Power plants scheduled through the late 1980s will have costs per kilowatt well over that shown in 1982 and 1983. Fuel prices rose sharply, especially after the 1973-1974 oil embargo. The inability to utilize fuel efficiently, or to offset the effect of the dwindling importance of hydropower with the addition of nuclear power, also led to a sharp rise in the cost of fuel per kilowatt-hour, but the energy glut of the mid 1980s finally brought down fuel costs. (See Table 14-6.)

The distribution sector offered little solace. The cost of incremental distribution plant per customer rose more than the cost of living, while

Table 14-5

Financial Ratios Investor Owned Electric Utilities 1965-1986

Year	Return on Common Equity (%)	Interest Cost Newly Issued Bonds (Moody's) (%)	Interest Coverage Ratio (Long Term Debt) (FERC) (×)	AFUDC % Net Income[a]	Average Stock Price (Moody's)[b] ($)	Average Book Value (Moody's)	Market/ Book Ratio (Moody's) (%)
	(1)	(2)	(3)	(4)	(5)	(6)	(7)
1965	12.6	4.61	3.7	3.6	117.08	49.85	235
1966	12.8	5.53	3.6	4.6	102.90	51.47	200
1967	12.8	6.07	3.4	6.4	101.87	53.55	190
1968	12.3	6.80	3.1	9.2	98.37	56.41	174
1969	12.2	7.98	3.0	12.6	94.55	59.24	160
1970	11.8	8.79	2.7	17.3	79.06	62.32	127
1971	11.7	7.72	2.6	21.1	84.16	65.23	129
1972	11.8	7.50	2.6	24.2	80.20	68.39	117
1973	11.5	7.91	2.6	24.8	71.21	71.04	100
1974	10.7	9.59	2.4	28.9	48.26	72.45	67
1975	11.2	9.97	2.4	26.5	51.25	74.52	69
1976	11.5	8.92	2.4	25.8	60.10	76.37	79
1977	11.3	8.43	2.4	28.2	67.55	77.88	87
1978	11.3	9.30	2.4	31.5	63.54	79.47	80
1979	11.2	10.85	2.4	38.0	60.28	80.87	75
1980	11.5	13.46	2.3	41.2	54.80	82.72	66
1981	12.5	16.31	2.3	41.3	55.41	82.87	67
1982	13.6	14.93	2.4	43.3	63.56	82.34	77
1983	14.2	12.70	2.5	43.4	74.04	82.84	89
1984	14.5	14.25	2.5	39.9	71.16	83.99	85
1985	12.5	11.83	2.3	42.4	87.08	86.42	101
1986	13.1E	9.61	2.4E	32.0E	111.11	89.06	125
% Change 1965-1986	+4	+108	-35	+788	-5	+79	-47

[a]Allowance for funds used during construction (FPC, FERC).

[b]Moody's Electric Utility Average.

Sources: FPC, EIA *Statistics* (columns 1,3,4). Edison Electric Institute *Year Book* (columns 2,5,6,7). Moody's *Public Utilities Manual,* 1987 (columns 2,5,6,7). Merrill Lynch estimates.

Table 14-6

Power Generation 1965-1986 Investor Owned Electric Utilities[a]

Year	Av. Size of Generating Plants (1000KW)	Heat Rate (Millions BTUs/KWH)	Cost of Fuel per Ton of Coal Equivalent[b]	Fuel Cost per KWH	Av. Cost of Generation Plant ($/KW)	Cost of Incremental Generation ($/KW)	Consumer Price Index	Handy & Whitman Electric Constr. Index (July, North Atlantic)
	(1)	(2)	(3)	(4)	(5)	(6)	(7)	(8)
1965	102.9	10,384	$ 6.23	0.27¢	$ 132	$ 101	94.5	167
1966	108.0	10,399	6.22	0.27	130	94	97.2	172
1967	113.6	10,396	6.29	0.27	128	103	100.0	179
1968	121.1	10,371	6.40	0.28	125	94	104.2	184
1969	127.4	10,457	6.58	0.29	126	132	109.8	195
1970	135.0	10,508	7.38	0.34	127	147	116.3	212
1971	147.9	10,536	8.64	0.40	125	107	121.3	229
1972	157.3	10,479	9.31	0.42	130	192	125.3	245
1973	169.0	10,429	10.65	0.49	134	166	133.1	262
1974	184.9	10,481	18.49	0.87	142	247	147.7	313
1975	199.6	10,383	21.60	1.03	152	332	161.2	362
1976	202.9	10,369	22.58	1.07	159	309	170.5	379
1977	210.6	10,449	25.50	1.24	172	425	181.5	403
1978	224.6	10,495	27.34	1.35	187	678	195.3	421
1979	231.0	10,470	31.85	1.56	196	647	217.4	466
1980	241.3	10,489	37.60	1.85	211	553	246.8	505
1981	247.1	10,506	43.64	2.16	221[a]	611[a]	272.4	547
1982	251.1	10,517	45.44	2.25	235[a]	1064[a]	289.1	581
1983	254.7	10,547	43.83	2.16	248[a]	1521[a]	298.4	605
1984	266.0	10,385	43.46	2.14	269[a]	1406[a]	311.1	639
1985	271.0	10,429	40.37	1.98	294[a]	1141[a]	322.2	652
1986	278.0	10,423	34.30	1.68	346[a]	2325[a]	328.4	665
% Change 1965-1986	+170	+4	+451	+522	+162	+2202	+248	+298

Sources: FPC, EIA Statistics (columns 1,5,6). Edison Electric Institute Year Book (columns 2,3,4,7,8). Electrical World. Merrill Lynch estimates.

[a]EIA capacity data to 1980, EEI capacity data thereafter.

[b]Excludes hydro.

distribution expense per customer and incremental distribution plant per KW of capacity moved with inflation. (See Table 14-7.)

Despite all the attention paid to transmission, results were a mixed bag in that area as well. Power losses declined, which was good news. Transmission expenses per kilowatt-hour rose about as much as the cost of living. Investment in plant per unit of transmission capacity moved at the same pace. (See Table 14-8.)

The overall trends indicated a rising cost of capital, inadequate rate relief, inability to raise productivity, a declining financial situation, and a general inability on the part of regulators and managements to cope with the economic and societal problems at hand, until the early 1980s.

The utilities faced even more than constant erosion as six major events shook the foundations of the industry.

1) *The Northeast Blackout of 1965*—On November 2, 1965, a broken backup relay on the Ontario Hydro system set loose a series of power disconnections and surges:

It took twelve minutes from the time the operational interruption knocked out the relay in a little box at the Sir Adam Beck facility to produce the worst power failure in the age of electricity, engulfing 30 million people over an area of 80,000 square miles in one form or another of dark reality.[30]

After that event, the Federal Power Commission launched an investigation and instituted new reporting procedures to keep track of power outages. In its report, the FPC commented that "the initial reaction of the Northeast failure was one of general disbelief that such an incident could happen."[31] Further investigation showed that minor outages had not been uncommon in the past, and that in the years that followed the blackout, there were several noteworthy power failures. Obviously, all was not well. New power pooling procedures, an increased number of transmission lines, and more generation equipment all were needed to bring service up to standards. Moreover the Northeast blackout shook managements and regulators out of their complacency, an attitude caused by years of fairly smooth operations and good press. The money required to improve operations was the beginning of an expenditure program that had to be independent of the direction of demand, for what utility people like to call "non-revenue producing" plant. (That term also is often used in reference to pollution control equipment. Of course, all plant is revenue producing in the sense that it goes into the rate base.)

2) *The Arab Oil Embargo of 1973-1974*—In the wake of the Yom Kippur War, Middle Eastern oil producers cut off shipments to the United States and the OPEC nations multiplied the price for oil several-fold. In response to that action, Americans reduced their consumption of electricity. As the

Table 14-7

Distribution 1965-1986
Investor Owned Electric Utilities

Year	Average Cost of Distribution Plant/Customer	Cost of Incremental Distribution/ Incr. Customer	Distribution Expense per Customer[a]
1965	$ 437	$1,303	$17.48
1966	454	1,226	17.84
1967	477	1,799	18.67
1968	501	1,672	19.31
1969	526	1,913	20.56
1970	554	1,828	22.14
1971	582	1,910	22.82
1972	645[b]	2,296[b]	24.13
1973	610[b]	−600[b]	25.51
1974	670	3,228	26.46
1975	702	2,683	27.63
1976	730	2,381	29.51
1977	760	2,198	31.76
1978	794	2,504	34.81
1979	825	1,921	37.68
1980	861	2,516	41.90
1981	903	3,211	45.19
1982	950	4,726	50.62
1983	993	4,030	54.10
1984	1,050	5,123	57.71
1985	1,102	5,552	60.53
1986	1,161E	6,202	61.49E
% Change 1965-1986	+ 166	+ 376	+ 252

Year	Average Distribution Plant per KW of Capacity	Period	Incremental Distribution Plant per Incremental KW of Capacity
1965	$126	1961-1965	$130
1970	121	1965-1970	109
1975	113	1971-1975	98
1980	128	1976-1980	200
1985	157	1981-1985[c]	425
1986	165	1981-1986	430

[a]$ per year.
[b]Revised Series.
[c]EIA data for capacity to 1980. EEI data 1981-1986.
Sources: FPC, EIA *Statistics.* Merrill Lynch estimates.

Table 14-8

Transmission 1965-1986
Investor Owned Electric Utilities[a]

Year	Transmission Plant/Circuit Mile of Transmission	Incremental Transmission Plant/Incremental Miles	Transmission Expense per KWH Sold (mills)	KWH Losses as % of Generation Purchase and Interchange (%)
1965	$29,513	$111,833	0.21	7.7
1966	31,151	86,795	0.21	7.6
1967	33,611	99,343	0.21	7.5
1968	35,985	125,137	0.21	7.4
1969	38,753	146,504	0.22	7.1
1970	41,320	106,615	0.23	7.0
1971	44,889	178,486	0.24	7.1
1972	47,342	117,577	0.25	7.2
1973	50,221	182,238	0.26	6.5
1974	53,150	150,636	0.29	6.8
1975	55,415	237,409	0.31	6.9
1976	58,855	320,172	0.33	6.8
1977	61,204	201,533	0.35	6.4
1978	64,407	285,646	0.37	6.6
1979	67,161	281,294	0.40	6.3
1980	70,494	302,927	0.43	6.6
1981	74,189	331,228	0.48	6.2
1982	78,234	745,476	0.56	6.1
1983	81,313	511,176	0.60	6.7
1984	85,657	366,039	0.64	5.8
1985	89,164	399,441	0.69	6.1
1986	92,792E	734,167E	0.70E	6.7E
% Change 1965-1986	+214	+556	+233	−13

Year	Average Trans. Plant per Circuit Volt Mile[b]	Period	Incr. Trans. Plant per incr. Circuit Volt Mile[b]	Percent of Transmission Circuit Miles by Voltage[bc]			
				Year	22-50KV	51-131KV	132-800KV
1965	$0.33	1961-1965	$0.50	1965	31.8	42.6	25.6
1970	0.39	1966-1970	0.53	1970	29.7	39.0	31.3
1975	0.47	1971-1975	0.82	1975	29.7	36.3	34.0
1980	0.59	1976-1980	1.30	1980	30.7	33.4	35.9
1985	0.71	1981-1985	1.86	1985	31.0	32.5	36.5
1986	0.74E	1981-1986	2.06E	1986	31.3	32.4	36.3

[a]22KV and over.
[b]Volt-miles defined as miles of transmission × voltage of transmission line.
[c]Total Industry.
Sources: FPC, EIA *Statistics*, EEI *Year Book*. Merrill Lynch estimates.

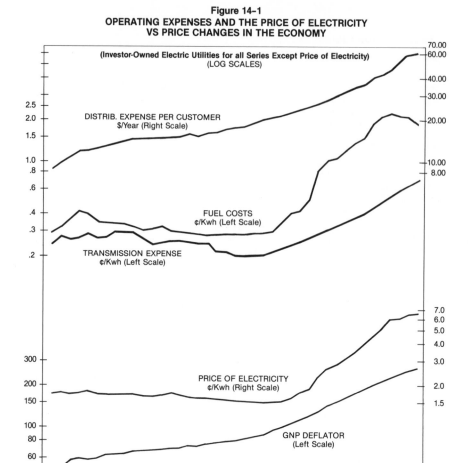

Figure 14-1
OPERATING EXPENSES AND THE PRICE OF ELECTRICITY
VS PRICE CHANGES IN THE ECONOMY

price for fuel rose and was passed on to many customers by means of the fuel adjustment clause, price became a determinant in dampening the demand for electricity. In 1974, sales of electricity dropped from the year-earlier level. That was the first time since 1946 that a year-to-year decline occurred. Furthermore, the pattern of steady, rapid growth ceased. The industry had geared its capital spending and expense budget to automatic sales gains. When those gains did not materialize, the industry faced two severe problems. First, it was caught in a squeeze between high fixed costs and declining base rate revenues that resulted from a drop in sales. Second, the industry was uncertain about what to do with a capital spending program that was based on rapid growth in demand. For a while, managements and regulators viewed the slowdown in demand as an aberration. As a result, managements made commitments to build, and those commitments proved to be not only erroneous but also a financial burden in the succeeding years. Finally, many utilities had inadequate fuel adjustment clauses, and the rapid increase in fuel costs squeezed margins. The industry reeled from the financial consequences of increased costs and reduced sales. More important, however, was that the era of rapid growth in sales had ended, but the industry's reaction was delayed.

3) *Consolidated Edison Omits its Common Stock Dividend in April 1974*— Consolidated Edison ran into a financial bind that culminated in the sale of some of its facilities to an agency of the State of New York and in the omission of its dividend. Con Edison's dividend omission hit the industry with the impact of a wrecking ball. It smashed the keystone of faith for investment in utilities: that the dividend is safe and will be paid. Wall Street firms, at the behest of panic-stricken clients, prepared lists that showed which utilities were in bad shape. In April 1974, the price for the average utility stock fell by 18%. By September, prices for utility stocks had fallen by 36%. That was not the kind of performance expected of utility stocks. The April drop was the greatest since March 1938, and the April-September collapse was the greatest in a calendar year since 1937. In 1974, utility stocks declined to well below book value, thereby making future financing dilutionary. Furthermore, because bond investors began to worry about the risk involved in investing in low quality utilities, selling low quality bonds also became difficult, and the spread between Aaa and Baa rated bonds— almost always between 50 and 100 basis points (100 basis points equals 1%) in the postwar period—rose to more than 200 basis points by the end of 1974. Investors had to accept the possibility of financial risk in utility securities. Managements realized that not only could they not raise money at will, but that money might only be obtained at astronomical rates. Partly because of financial pressures, capital expenditures declined in 1975 for the first time since 1962. It was a new ball game, but some of the players, unfortunately, were still playing by the old rules.

4) *The Nuclear Accident at Three Mile Island on March 28, 1979*—On that day, a cooling system malfunction started the country's first major, well publicized civilian nuclear accident. For days, reports of core meltdown, escape of radiation and potential explosion frightened the population of the Northeast. The reactor finally went out of service after having incurred several hundred million dollars worth of damage. The Three Mile Island accident destroyed the complacency about nuclear power best typified by

the comment often made before the accident: "There never has been a nuclear accident." Anti-nuclear demonstrations attracted thousands. Many investors made it clear that they did not want to own securities in nuclear-oriented electric utilities, probably less because of fear of the health and safety hazards of nuclear power, than because of the financial hazards. Building a nuclear plant involved risking huge sums in a project that could be delayed or halted and that was often bitterly fought against by a determined opposition. The Three Mile Island disaster revealed another risk: if the nuclear plant went out of service, the power company might have to replace the lost nuclear power with far more expensive power purchased from others. If the regulators did not allow the utility to pass on to consumers the increased costs, the utility could suffer serious financial losses. General Public Utilities, the subsidiaries of which owned the Three Mile Island reactor, was forced to omit its dividend and was unable to place securities in the public market after the accident. The utility industry, the public, and the Government had placed their faith in nuclear power as a cheap, safe form of energy that would also reduce our reliance on foreign oil. Escalation of construction costs brought into question its cheapness. The Three Mile Island accident confirmed—in the minds of detractors of nuclear power—the doubts about safety. The Nuclear Regulatory Commission (NRC), severely criticized for its administrative maladroitness, imposed a moratorium on the licensing of nuclear reactors. In the period after the Three Mile Island accident, the electric utility industry, in a weakened financial condition and with excess generating capacity in many areas, cancelled or deferred nuclear projects. Nuclear power began with a dream of electricity sufficiently cheap that it could not be metered, and the electric utility industry embraced the new technology. Construction delays, cost overruns, environmental opposition, the constant need to modify plans to meet changing safety regulations, and uncertainty about Government policies, however, all demonstrated that nuclear power would not bring a golden age to the industry. In the case of some utilities, the strains of constructing huge nuclear plants destroyed their financial standing. For many others, nuclear power had lost its luster before the Three Mile Island accident. After the accident, even proponents of the nuclear effort seemed to be thinking more in terms of finishing what was already under construction than planning for additional facilities.

5) *Cincinnati G&E Reveals Inability to Complete Zimmer Nuclear Station As Planned*—On October 5, 1983, Cincinnati G&E shocked investors by announcing that the Zimmer nuclear station, supposedly 97% complete, would require $2.8-$3.5 billion in additional investment and two to three years of work to be finished. That news was the first of many disastrous nuclear crises that followed. Utilities tottered on the brink of bankruptcy, scrambling for funds to complete troubled projects, or to salvage what they could from huge investments in projects that had to be cancelled despite the billions of

dollars that had been sunk in them. Within twelve months, six utilities cut or omitted dividends, almost $6 billion of construction effort was consigned to oblivion, and the stock prices of the affected utilities fell 60-80% from their 1983 highs. The message was clear. Utilities with serious problems caused by construction failures and extreme cost overruns would not be made whole by regulatory agencies. Investors could not depend on regulators for guaranteed returns or for bailouts. The best they could hope for was a rescue effort that kept the utility afloat.

6) *The Russian Nuclear Reactor at Chernobyl Goes Out of Control*—On April 26, 1986, unauthorized testing at Chernobyl produced a nuclear accident that destroyed the generation station, killed 31 people, forced evacuation of 116,000 nearby residents and loosed a radioactive cloud that floated over Europe. Non-Russian reactors are built differently, so the Chernobyl-type accident probably could not have happened elsewhere, a fact often cited by those who choose to believe that Chernobyl is irrelevant outside the Soviet bloc. Unfortunately, a serious, fatal nuclear accident has moved from a statistical probability to something that has happened. Chernobyl has strengthened the credibility of those people who oppose nuclear power, and has reemphasized the importance of emergency evacuation plans. In the words of Lord Marshall of Goring, chairman of the United Kingdom's Central Electricity Generating Board, "In some countries the shock has been so great that governments have made a formal decision to abandon nuclear power."[32] America's utilities will have to deal with the specter of Chernobyl even if it cannot happen here.

As the 1980s began, the electric utility industry was in a weakened financial condition. The nuclear crises of 1983-1984 pushed a number of utilities close to bankruptcy. Demand for power was unpredictable. Development of nuclear power had been arrested. Many utilities had excessive capacity. The concept of central station power was under attack. New methods of regulation seemed to put a premium on discouraging demand for central station power. As a result, the electric utility industry seemed ready for a new direction.

Many utility executives and government officials concluded that electric utilities must turn to smaller power stations (some owned by non-utilities) and must exchange power from surplus to deficit regions as much as possible. In addition, by the late 1980s, utilities began to emphasize cost cutting, repricing of the product and satisfying the customer. The market was more competitive. Utilities could no longer run as monopolies.

Chapter 15

Summary

Monopoly in the local electric utility industry is so taken for granted that it is almost forgotten that competition ever existed.[33]

Walter J. Primeaux, Jr.

Electric utilities developed along the lines envisioned by Edison and his lieutenants. The electric utility became vertically integrated from generation through transmission to distribution. Central station power moved decisively from supplying about 40% of electricity at the turn of the century to supplying roughly 60% during the World War I period and to 80% during the Great Depression. Perhaps not coincidentally, the industry's penetration of the market grew side by side with regulation. Regulation began at the behest of civic reformers and of important elements in the utility industry.

The holding companies were formed early in the history of electric power, and became monsters that encompassed much of the industry by the 1920s. Financial abuse led to the collapse of many holding companies. The New Deal dismembered the spread-out holding companies as part of a reform of the industry. The New Deal also built permanent, huge Federal power agencies that now dominate the power markets of large areas in the South and Northwest. Today, hundreds of investor owned utilities supply about 75% of the nation's power, with the rest derived from several thousand Government owned (Federal, state, and local) power agencies and from rural cooperatives.

For most of its history, the electric industry was able to take advantage of the economies available from new and increasingly large plants and from increasingly efficient transmission and distribution procedures. The result was that the price for electricity (per kilowatt-hour) fell steadily from 1882 to 1969, despite a generally upward trend in prices throughout the economy. Also during that period usage increased as steadily as prices declined. The 1970s ended that long idyll. New technology seemed incapable of further reducing costs. The rapid rise in fuel costs, combined with a lack of additional efficiencies in production and rampant cost inflation, caused the price for electricity to rise. Consequently sales faltered. The utilities could not—or would not—adjust immediately to the new conditions. The regulators also had a hard time understanding that prices could no longer be lowered but had to be raised. The 1970s was a period of declining profitability, lowered bond ratings, falling stock prices, and an industry in turmoil. With the beginning of the 1980s though, managements, legislators and regulators began to take more effective remedial action.

Those difficulties of the past two decades have caused many to reappraise the structure of the industry and its methods of doing business. In the Pacific Northwest, new generating facilities may be built under an arrangement that calls for the entire region to share the financial risk involved in building the facility. Many utilities are buying electricity from non-utility generators rather than building their own regulated power stations, as a matter of choice. Some utilities have chosen to diversify into other businesses. Others have put into place management techniques that have dramatically improved efficiency and profitability. A number of regulators have reexamined regulatory procedures in order to provide the utilities with greater incentives to innovate and control costs. Even the necessity of regulation is being questioned. The coming decade could be one of major changes in the electric utility industry.

Notes

[1] Henry Adams, *The Education of Henry Adams* (New York: Random House Modern Library, 1931), pp. 380-381. The quotation is from the famous chapter "The Dynamo and the Virgin."

[2] Matthew Josephson, *Edison* (New York: McGraw Hill, 1959), p. 178.

[3] Philip Sporn, *Energy—Its Production, Conversion, and Use in the Service of Man* (New York: Columbia Graduate School of Business, 1963), p. 12.

[4] The questionable nature of the telephone patent is described in Robert Conot's *A Streak of Luck* (New York: Seaview Books, 1979), pp. 81-83.

[5] Conot, *op. cit.*, p. 129.

[6] Josephson, *op. cit.*, p. 185.

[7] Josephson, *op. cit.*, p. 189.

[8] Forrest McDonald, *Insull* (Chicago: The University of Chicago Press, 1962), p. 26.

[9] "Harnessing a Monument," *EPRI Journal*, March 1979, p. 38.

[10] McDonald, *op. cit.*, p. 20.

[11] "The Electric Century," *Electrical World*, June 1, 1974, p. 44.

[12] Harold H. Young, *Forty Years of Public Utility' Finance* (Charlottesville:The University Press of Virginia, 1965), p. 33.

[13] Douglas D. Anderson, *Regulatory Politics and Electric Utilities* (Boston: Auburn House, 1981), p. 56.

[14] Eli Winston Clemens, *Economics and Public Utilities* (New York: Appleton- Century-Crofts, 1950), p. 91.

[15] Clemens, *op. cit.*, p. 13.

[16] J. Maurice Clark, *Studies in the Economics of Overhead Costs* (Chicago: The University of Chicago Press, 1962 impression), p. 11. This point was suggested in Charles D.

Stalon, "Deregulation of the Electric Generating Industry: Some Unsystematic Observations", in *Proceedings: Edison Electric Institute Sixteenth Financial Conference October 4-7, 1981* (Washington, D.C.; Edison Electric Institute, 1982). That analysis seems to question at least one assumption (free entry and exit) of the contestable market theory. See William J. Baumol, "Contestable Markets: An Uprising in the Theory of Industry Structure", American Economic Review, March 1982.

[17]William Z. Ripley, "From Main Street to Wall Street," 1926 essay in *The Atlantic Monthly*, reprinted in *Looking Back at Tomorrow*, Louise Desaulniers, ed. (Boston: *The Atlantic Monthly*, 1978), p. 125.

[18]Arthur M. Schlesinger, Jr., *The Age of Roosevelt: The Crisis of the Old Old Order* (Boston: Houghton Mifflin, 1957), p. 119.

[19]Schlesinger, *op. cit.*, p. 118.

[20]Schlesinger, *op. cit.*, pp. 123-124.

[21]Mary Earhart Dillon, *Wendell Willkie* (Philadelphia and New York: J.B. Lippincott, 1952), p. 42.

[22]Benjamin Graham, David L. Dodd, Sidney Cottle, with Charles Tatham, *Security Analysis* (New York: McGraw-Hill, 1962), p. 570.

[23]For a discussion of Averch-Johnson, see Alfred E. Kahn, *The Economics of Regulation* (New York: John Wiley & Sons, 1970-71), Vol. II, p. 49.

[24]Herbert G. May and Bruce M. Metzger, eds., *The Oxford Annotated Bible* (New York: Oxford University Press, 1962), p. 630.

[25]*The Electric Utility Industry and the Environment, A Report to the Citizens Advisory Committee on Recreation and Natural Beauty by the Electric Utility Task Force on Environment* (Library of Congress Card Catalog Number: 68-57661) provides a view of what concerned the industry at the time.

[26]Edward F. Renshaw, "Commentary," in Walter L. Balk and Jay M. Shafritz, eds., *Public Utility Productivity: Management and Measurement* (Albany: The New York State Department of Public Service, 1975), pp. 72-73.

[27]Lee Metcalf and Vic Reinemer, *Overcharge* (New York: David McKay, 1967), p. 7.

[28]Leonard S. Hyman and Carmine J. Grigoli, "The Credit Standing of Electric Utilities," *Public Utilities Fortnightly,"* Vol. 99, No. 5, March 3, 1977, pp. 24-30.

[29]James C. Bonbright, *Principles of Public Utility Rates* (New York: Columbia University Press, 1961), p. 249.

[30]William Rodgers, *Brown-Out* (New York: Stein and Day, 1972), p. 11.

[31]Rodgers, *op. cit.*, p. 20.

[32]"Chernobyl and Its Legacy," *EPRI Journal*, June 1987, p. 6.

[33]Walter J. Primeaux, Jr., "A Reexamination of the Monopoly Market Structure for Electric Utilities", in A. Phillips, ed., *Promoting Competition in Regulated Markets* (Washington, D.C.: Brookings Institution, 1975), p. 175.

Part Four
Regulation

Chapter **16**

The Development of Public Utility Regulation

The concept of a public utility is essentially a creation of legislation, but social scientists have endeavored to rationalize legislative procedure by identifying the intrinsic common characteristics which our lawmakers have set aside for special 'public utility' treatment. . . .[1]

Joe S. Bain

How can we discuss the development of public utility regulation without first defining a public utility? The answer is that the historical and legal precedents for the regulation of business were established before most of the industries that are commonly called public utilities existed. Perhaps the laws came first, and then economists tried to come up with a package of common, rational industry economic characteristics that presumably made the laws necessary. Or, the laws possibly were a product of antibusiness thinking in the time of the Grangers, trustbusters, and muckrakers, rather than a result of a careful study of natural monopoly, declining cost curves, and all the other supposed characteristics of a public utility.

Historically, governments, including those of Great Britain and the American colonies, have regulated some prices and services. Regulated businesses rarely were monopolies, but provided a service to the public or supplied a product of some importance. Early examples would be ferrymen, bakers, innkeepers, and common carriers. In 1820, Congress gave the City of Washington the right to regulate the price of bread, sweeping chimneys, and wharfage. In 1839, Rhode Island set up a regulatory commission. Other New England states soon followed. The commissions, however, were mainly advisory and dealt with railroads. At the behest of the gas utilities, Massachusetts in 1885 established a board. Congress, in 1887, established the Interstate Commerce Commission, the most important regulatory body of the day. The first state regulatory agencies of the kind that we now know were created in 1907 in New York and Wisconsin. By 1920, two-thirds of the states had utility regulatory agencies.

The regulatory agencies followed concepts established by the courts of the period. Several landmark cases defined what a regulator could or should do. The first major decision in the field was *Munn v. Illinois*.[2]

In 1871, the Illinois legislature passed a law to fix the rates charged by grain elevators. Several Chicago elevator owners went to court to point out that their businesses had been established before the law was enacted. The owners claimed that they had been deprived of their rights under the Fourteenth Amendment ("nor shall any State deprive any person of life, liberty, or property, without due process of law").[3]

Chief Justice Waite wrote the Supreme Court's majority opinion in the case. The Chief Justice delved into the history of price regulation and quoted Britain's Lord Chief Justice Hale (1609-1676). "Looking, then, to the common law, from whence came the right which the Constitution protects, we find that when private property is 'affected with a public interest, it ceases to be *juris privati* only.' "[4] Chief Justice Waite continued:

> Property does come clothed with a public interest when used in a manner to make it of public consequence, and affect the community at large. When, therefore, one devotes his property to a use in which the public has an interest, he, in effect, grants to the public an interest in that use, and must submit to be controlled ... He may withdraw his grant by discontinuing the use. ...

> Common carriers exercise a sort of public office, and have duties to perform in which the public is interested. ...

> Their business is, therefore, "affected with a public interest," within the meaning of the doctrine which Lord Hale has so forcibly stated."[5]

The Court pointed out that grain from seven or eight states had to pass through Chicago, and that the Chicago warehouses were owned by a few people who set rates together, indicating "a 'virtual' monopoly."[6] If the ferryman or innkeeper can be regulated, certainly grain elevators can:

> They stand, to use again the language of their counsel, in the very "gateway of commerce," and take toll from all who pass.

The Court then set forth what can be described as the theory of legislative ratemaking. The plaintiffs argued that the Court should set a return on their property:

> It is insisted, however, that the owner of property is entitled to a reasonable compensation for its use ... and what is reasonable is a judicial and not a legislative question.

> As has already been shown, the practice has been otherwise. In countries where the common law prevails, it has been customary ... for the

legislature to declare what shall be a reasonable compensation ... The controlling fact is the power to regulate at all. If that exists, the right to establish the maximum charge, as one of the means of regulation, is implied. ...

We know that this is a power which may be abused; but that is no argument against the existence. For protection against abuses by legislatures the people must resort to the polls, not to the courts.[7]

The decision in the Munn case upheld the right of the state to regulate the prices charged to the public by a business "affected with a public interest." The decision also proposed a philosophy of regulation that, if adhered to, would have made impossible the development of healthy, privately owned utilities. Price would have been set by the legislatures, with no recourse to the courts. During a period of inflation, businesses would encounter difficulties because of rigidities of price. Justice Field dissented, saying, "If this be sound law all property and all business in the state are at the mercy of a majority of its legislature."[8]

Fortunately, the regulation of price moved beyond the concept set forth in the Munn decision. As early as 1679, an English court held that a common carrier was entitled to a reasonable payment.[9] Determining what is reasonable can turn into more of a theological than economic or legal argument. The Supreme Court tried its hand at that question in 1898, and the result, *Smyth v. Ames*,[10] although in some ways a monument to judicial confusion about finance, revolutionized thinking about regulation[11] and put an end to the absolute right of legislatures to fix rates as they pleased.

Nebraska, in 1893, established a Board of Transportation to fix railroad rates. The railroads challenged the rates set. The issues were rate base and whether the railroads had been deprived of property without due process of law. The railroads had been built during and after the Civil War boom period. Subsequently, prices fell. The railroads wanted their assets to be valued at original cost. The State of Nebraska (represented by the silver-tongued orator of the Platte, William Jennings Bryan) wanted the properties to be valued at reproduction cost (which was lower than original cost).

The Supreme Court quickly affirmed the right of a state to set rates as long as the rates provided "just compensation."[12] The Court then defined "proper compensation":

We hold ... that the basis of all calculations as to the reasonableness of rates ... must be the fair value of the property ... And, in order to ascertain that value, the original cost of construction, the amount expended in permanent improvements, the amount and market value of its bonds and stock, the present as compared with the original cost of construction, the probable earning capacity of the property under par-

ticular rates prescribed by statute, and the same required to meet operating expenses, are all matters for consideration, and are to be given
such weight as may be just and right in each case. We do not say that
there may not be other matters to be regarded in estimating the value
of the property. What the company is entitled to ask is a fair return
upon the value of that which it employs for the public convenience.

On the other hand, what the public is entitled to demand is that no
more be exacted from it for the use of a public highway than the
services rendered by it are reasonably worth.[13]

It is difficult for an observer, more than 80 years later, to comprehend
how that confused judicial laundry list just delineated set ratemaking doc-
trine for more than 40 years. Consider the strange ingredients thrown into
the Mrs. Murphy's chowder called "just compensation." Present costs and
original costs are contradictory terms. The market value of securities depends on earning power, but earning power is what needs to be determined, and the reasoning is therefore circular. The Supreme Court concluded by saying: consider everything. For the next 20 years, regulators and
utilities battled over the choice of rate base: fair value or original cost.

Halfway through the period, Justice Brandeis, with Justice Holmes con-
curring, wrote a scathing denunciation of regulatory practices. That dissent-
ing opinion, written in the 1923 Southwestern Bell decision,[14] was ahead of
its time.

The so-called rule of Smyth v. Ames is . . . legally and economically
unsound. The thing devoted by the investor to the public use is not
specific property, tangible and intangible, but capital embarked in the
enterprise. Upon the capital so invested the federal Constitution guarantees to the utility the opportunity to earn a fair return.

The investor agrees, by embarking capital in a utility, that its charge to
the public shall be reasonable. His company is the substitute for the
state in the performance of the public service, thus becoming a public
servant. The compensation which the Constitution guarantees an opportunity to earn is the reasonable cost of conducting the business. Cost
includes not only operating expenses, but also capital charges. Capital
charges cover the allowance, by way of interest, for the use of the
capital, whatever the nature of the security issues therefor; the allowance for risk incurred; and enough more to attract capital. The reasonable rate to be prescribed by a commission may allow an efficiently
managed utility much more. But a rate is constitutionally compensatory,
if it allows to the utility the opportunity to earn the cost of service as
defined. . . .

The experience of the twenty-five years since Smyth v. Ames was decided has demonstrated that the rule there enunciated is delusive. . . .

The rule of Smyth v. Ames sets the laborious and baffling technique of finding the present value of the utility. It is impossible to find an exchange value of a utility, since utilities, unlike merchandise or land, are not commonly bought and sold in the market. Nor can the present value of the utility be determined by capitalizing its net earnings, since the earnings are determined, in large measure, by the rate which the company will be permitted to charge.

Under the rule of Smyth v. Ames . . . each step in the process of estimating the cost of reproduction involves forming an opinion. . . .

It is true that the decision is usually rested largely upon the records of financial transactions, on statistics and calculations. But . . . "every figure . . . that we have set down with delusive exactness" is speculative.

The conviction is widespread that a sound conclusion as to the actual value of a utility is not to be reached by a meticulous study of conflicting estimates of the cost of reproducing new the congerie of old machinery and equipment, called the plant, and the still more fanciful estimates concerning the value of the intangible elements of an established business. Many commissions . . . have declared . . . that "capital honestly and prudently invested must . . . be taken as the controlling factor in fixing . . . rates."[15]

The Brandeis dissent laid the groundwork for changes in regulation that would take place years later. It did not influence the Supreme Court of the period. The Bluefield decision of 1923[16] set aside a decision in which a company's estimate of reproduction cost was disregarded. Then followed *McCardle v. Indianapolis Water Co.*[17], which was, to quote Wilcox, "the high-water mark of reproduction cost valuation. . . . "[18]

Bluefield is better known to regulators for another reason, a paragraph that sets forth the standards for rate of return:

The return should be reasonably sufficient to assure confidence in the financial soundness of the utility and should be adequate, under efficient and economical management, to maintain and support its credit and enable it to raise the money necessary for the proper discharge of its public duties.[19]

The Roosevelt era's Supreme Court backed away from an insistence on the fair value rate base. The decision in the Hope Natural Gas Co. case of 1944[20] marked the beginning of a new era of regulation. The Federal Power

Commission disregarded estimates of the fair value of Hope's properties in setting a rate of return. Hope appealed the decision. Justice Douglas wrote:

> ... that "fair value" is the end product of the process of ratemaking, not the starting point. ... The heart of the matter is that rates cannot be made to depend on "fair value" when the value of the going enterprise depends on earnings under whatever rates may be anticipated.

> We held ... that the commission was not bound to the use of any single formula ... in determining rates. ... And when the commission's order is challenged in the courts, the question is whether that order "viewed in its entirety" meets the requirements of the act. Under the statutory standard of "just and reasonable" it is the result reached, not the method employed, which is controlling.

> It is not theory, but the impact of the rate order which counts. If the total effect of the rate order cannot be said to be unjust and unreasonable, judicial inquiry ... is at an end. ... Moreover, the commission's order ... is the product of expert judgment which carries a presumption of validity. ...

> From the investor or company point of view it is important that there be enough revenue not only for operating expenses, but also for the capital costs of the business. These include service on the debt and dividends on the stock. By that standard the return to the equity owner should be commensurate with returns on investments in other enterprises having corresponding risks. That return, moreover, should be sufficient to assure confidence in the financial integrity of the enterprise so as to maintain its credit and to attract capital ...[21]

Munn v. Illinois ushered in a period of legislative ratemaking. *Smyth v. Ames*, in a sense, heralded a period of judicial ratemaking (in which lawyers fought before courts over the methodology of the rate case), and *Hope* brought forth the age of the regulatory commission.

Chapter 17

What Is a Public Utility?

As with other important terms . . . a definition is, at best, too general to be useful and, at worst, mere legal pedantry. To say that a public utility is a business affected with a public interest is to include piggeries and mortuary parlors. To say that a public utility supplies a service necessary to our present stage of economic life . . . is to include the United States Steel Corporation. . . . The legalistic descriptions are equivocal. . . . As a practical matter, a public utility . . . is a private enterprise over which the . . . government attempts to determine the prices received for its services rather than to allow the prices to be determined by the free play of economic forces. In the end, economic forces will dominate every situation, but temporarily and through the perspective of a short period of time, and within the myopic intelligence of the politically minded bureaucrats, they can be thwarted or measurably controlled by administrative or judicial decrees. . . .[22]

Arthur Stone Dewing

Electric, gas, telephone, and water companies are public utilities. What distinguishes those regulated industries from the insurance, milk, or stock brokerage industries, all of which are or have been regulated in various ways? The answer to that question leads us to the standard characteristics of and rationalizations for public utility designation—"rationalizations" because it is doubtful how well the standards hold true today and if they ever held true in the textbook sense. Characteristics of a public utility include:

1) *The franchise or the designation of a service area* —In the past, when a utility served only a municipality, it had to seek a franchise for its operations in the area. The franchise gave the public utility privileges such as use of the streets for its facilities. In return, the utility agreed to pay certain taxes, possibly to set rates at particular levels, and to provide a given measure of service. The franchise usually ran for a specific period and often granted the utility a monopoly in the municipality. Eventually service areas were extended beyond municipal limits. Large service areas developed for which boundaries were set by state agencies. In general, a regulatory agency now grants a public utility a monopoly to provide a particular service to the

public within a geographic area. The monopoly is a monopoly only in the legal sense. Competitors can offer alternatives to the utility's service. For example, oil, gas, solar heating, and better insulation are alternatives to electric heating. An industrial firm may choose to generate its own power, rather than buy power from the local utility.

2) *Obligation to serve*—The consumer within a service territory cannot choose between suppliers of a utility service. The utility cannot choose to serve some customers and not others, as long as the company receives a reasonable price for its services. Nor can it discriminate unduly between customers. In an unregulated industry, a customer may be turned away for reasons of poor profitability. In the utility industry, that customer would probably be served. The utility can seek rate relief to cover the additional costs caused by a new customer. The utility may not receive the rate relief requested, but the customer must still be served. Furthermore, taking on the new customer may disadvantage old customers, but they must not receive preferential treatment just as new customers cannot be discriminated against.

3) *Necessity of the service to the public*—The utility provides a service that is necessary, widely used, and for which good substitutes are not available. Those concepts, derived from Bain,[23] do not consider the question of whether an adequate substitute could be developed, if the price for the utility's service was at a sufficiently high level. Arthur Stone Dewing, who was a student of history and who was involved in bankruptcies and reorganizations, did not have any illusions about the permanence of monopoly. Bonbright said, "What must justify public utility regulation . . . is the necessity of the regulation and not merely the necessity of the product."[24]

4) *The service provided is a natural monopoly*—The term "natural monopoly" has been interpreted in many ways. Some experts have argued that a utility exhibits diminishing unit costs as scale increases. If so, customers will be served at a lower cost by one large system of a monopoly than by several smaller, less efficient, competing facilities. Monopoly also prevents needless duplication of plant and equipment. The utility also may provide a nonstorable service that must be supplied at peak periods by expensive plant. High overhead costs could cause competing utilities to cut prices to the level of variable costs to capture market share, and bankruptcies could result. Thus, ruinous competition could impair the industry's ability to serve the customer. Bonbright made two points on the natural monopoly. He said that natural monopoly "is due . . . to the severely localized and hence restricted markets for utility services—markets limited because of the necessarily close connection between the utility plant on the one hand and the consumers' premises on the other."[25] A manufacturing plant can have the whole country or world for its market. A utility distribution system serves a limited area. "Were it compelled to share its limited market with two or more rival plants owning duplicate distribution networks, the total cost of serving the city would be materially higher."[26] Bonbright then declared that

the declining cost characteristic of utilities had been overstressed and was not a prerequisite for a natural monopoly because "even if the unit cost of supplying a given area with a given type of public utility service must increase with an enhanced rate of output, *any specified* required rate of output can be supplied most economically by a single plant or system."[27]

Chapter 18

The Purpose and Drawbacks of Regulation

Regulation was . . . a substitute for competition. Where competition was impossible, its purpose was to bring the benefits that competition would have brought.[28]

Clair Wilcox

Begin with the basic premise: the utility is a monopoly. The monopoly generally is assumed to be permanent, despite historic evidence to the contrary. Electric light replaced gas light. The telephone reduced the value of the telegraph. Refrigerators and air conditioners put the ice house out of business. And, the automobile destroyed the trolley lines. Today, the monopoly status of the telephone company has been challenged. Gas, electric, and oil firms fight to serve heating customers. Cogeneration facilities and the fuel cell may make central station power unnecessary. Soft technologists urge the Government to encourage decentralized energy sources that will diminish the role of the traditional utility. The concept of the utility as a monopoly is static. It is valid only during that period when the utility dominates its market. The temporary nature of the monopoly has important implications for the rate of return and recovery of capital.

In the United States, to monopolize or attempt to monopolize is illegal under the antitrust laws. The standard textbooks tell us that competition breeds efficiency and innovation: competition is a force that weeds out the unfit producer and protects the consumer from exploitation. "The essence of regulation," according to Kahn, "is the explicit replacement of competition with governmental orders as the principal institutional device for assuring good performance."[29] Of course, the question remains whether we mean competition in the textbook or in the real world sense. Perhaps we should say that utilities must compete for capital and for customers in the world of imperfect competition.

Regulators must assure that the customer receives reliable service from the utility because the customer generally has no choice. Regulators must fairly apportion the costs of service so that no group of customers is charged unduly. Finally, regulators must set the overall level of revenues at a point where the utility can earn a return similar to that earned in competitive industries.

Practically, regulators generally do not concern themselves with quality of service unless the quality is obviously bad. The big issues in rate cases are the overall level of revenues and the apportionment of revenue sources among customers.

Regulation has been attacked from all sides. Some believe that the regulators have sold out to the utilities, and others think that the regulators are too politically oriented to treat utilities fairly. Many economists accept the concept of regulation, but quarrel with the methods used by the regulators. The complaints, too numerous to cover fully, include three fundamental objections to regulation.

1) *The public utility's "monopoly status . . . is an illusion"*[30]—An analysis based on the halcyon days of the late 1950s and early 1960s took a view that even if it had a monopoly the utility would not exploit customers because it could increase earnings by lowering rates and thereby increase sales. Therefore regulation was unnecessary, anyway. Furthermore, regulation was not only unnecessary, but actually harmful, because regulation stifled innovation. For example, a regulated company might hesitate to reduce rates on an experimental basis because the company might not be able to raise rates later if the rate reductions did not result in the expected increase in demand. In the 1980s, the circumstances have changed. Competition clearly exists in the telephone industry. Some studies of electrical companies bring the natural monopoly status into question because they indicate that economies of scale no longer exist in some aspects of industry operation, and competition from decentralized power sources is a realistic possibility. Therefore, the possible disappearance of economies of scale and the appearance of competition call into question the supposed natural monopoly status of electric utilities. Before, the utilities would not have exploited customers because it was not in the interest of the utilities to do so. Now, critics might reason, the utility no longer has the ability to exploit the customer.

2) *Cost of service regulation provides little incentive to be efficient*—Some experts believe that under regulation, bad management often is bailed out and good management often receives no reward. In addition, reducing costs might involve the utility in innovation and risk taking. If the measures taken fail, the company might even be penalized by the regulators.

3) *Public utilities supply vital services and, therefore, should not be run on a profit basis, but should be socialized, in which case regulation would be unnecessary*—Whether a government owned utility would be run differently is beyond the scope of our discussion. Nevertheless, although utilities in the United States mainly are privately owned, social welfare considerations such as lifeline rates, rules on cutoff of service, and more liberal customer deposit regulations have crept into the ratemaking and regulatory process. In that sense, industry practices, but not the industry itself, have been socialized.

19

Setting the Rate of Return

The regulatory commissions do not fix rates so as to guarantee that they will yield a rate of return. . . . The commission's function is simply to determine a rate which will have that result of permitting a utility to earn a fair return, if the utility's earning power and other economic circumstances . . . so . . . permit. . . .[31]

Francis X. Welch

Ratemaking in theory is a relatively simple process. To the cost of producing the service furnished is added a reasonable return to the investor. The making of public utility rates requires four basic determinations:

1. what are the enterprise's gross utility revenues under the rate structure examined;

2. what are its operating expenses, including maintenance, depreciation, and all taxes, appropriately incurred to produce those gross revenues;

3. what utility property provides the service for which rates are charged and thus represents the base (rate base) on which a return should be earned; and

4. what percentage figure (rate of return) should be applied to the rate base in order to establish the return (wages of capital) to which investors in the utility enterprise are reasonably entitled. . . .

Simple as this formula sounds, the task of the rate maker is more often than not extremely difficult.[32]

Maine Supreme Judicial Court

Revenues must be set in such a way to allow the utility to cover operating costs and to earn an acceptable level of profit. That profit is usually stated as a given return on investment in utility plant, or as a return on rate base. The system is called "cost of service ratemaking." In a sense, return on the capital invested in the business is one of the costs that must be covered. The regulator examines a utility's results for a test period to determine if the utility is earning a proper return. The regulator uses the following calculations:

	Revenue
less	Operating expenses
less	Taxes
equals	Operating income or income available to provide a return on invested capital

and

$$\frac{\text{Operating Income}}{\text{Rate Base}} = \text{Rate of Return}$$

Regulatory agencies do not necessarily accept company figures. Revenue and operating expense figures are adjusted for abnormal weather conditions and changes in the customer load. The regulators generally want to consider "normal" conditions. Sometimes a regulatory agency bases its decision on estimated results of a future test year on the ground that rates are being set for the future, and, therefore, should respond to projected conditions at the time that the rates will go into effect. When an estimated test year is used, the utility and its opponents may disagree in their estimates of revenue and expenses. The company and the regulators also may differ on estimates of rate base. Small differences add up, as can be seen below.

		Company Projection	Commission Projection
	Revenues	$1,000	$1,010
less	Expenses	500	495
less	Income taxes	250	255
equals	Operating income	250	260
divided by	Rate base	4,000	3,990
equals	Rate of return earned	6.25%	6.52%

With so many figures subject to adjustment, one cannot always determine if the rate order was designed to produce the allowed rate of return or if the revenues and expenses cited in the decision were adjusted to produce a return on paper that will not, in fact, be realized.

Income Taxes

An important step in rate setting is to determine the utility's tax bill, which must be subtracted before the amount of income that is available for the providers of capital can be determined. Two accounting procedures are used: "flow through" and "normalization." The methods address the problem of inter-period allocation of tax savings that result from the use of accelerated depreciation or, in the past, from taking the investment tax credit. Should the tax savings be used to reduce rates in the year in which the savings are received (flow through) or should the savings be spread over the life of the property (normalization)?

Let us consider a simplified situation. A utility uses a tax strategy that will reduce taxes by $50 in the first year, but will cause the utility to pay $50 more in the fifth year. Regulators have set a 10% rate of return for the utility.

Line		Year 1	Year 5
1.	Rate base	$1000	$1000
2.	Pretax income	250	250
3.	Regular income taxes	150	150
4.	Tax (reduction) or increase due to tax strategy	(50)	50
5.	Income taxes paid (3 + 4)	100	200
6.	Net income (2 − 5)	150	50
7.	Rate of return (6 ÷ 1)	15%	5%

In the first year, the utility earns more than its allowed return because of the tax savings. The regulator could require the utility to reduce its prices to bring return down to 10%. In the fifth year, the utility has to pay back the tax savings, so it is not earning the allowed 10% return. Regulators could raise prices to bring return up to the allowed level. If the tax saving is included in income for ratemaking purposes, as shown above, then the savings are said to have "flowed through" to customers.

Other regulators do not want the price of electricity to fluctuate because of temporary tax savings. They require the utility to set aside a reserve for tax savings to be used when taxes must be paid. Because the taxes must be paid eventually, the set aside is called "deferred taxes." Using the same example as before, we have:

Line		Year 1	Year 5
1.	Rate base	$1000	$1000
2.	Pretax income	250	250
3.	Income taxes paid	100	200
4.	Taxes deferred to reserve or (withdrawn) from reserve set aside from savings	50	(50)
5.	Regular income taxes (3 + 4)	150	150

6.	Net income (2 − 5)	100	100
7.	Rate of return (6 ÷ 1)	10%	10%

Note that when tax savings are deferred (or "normalized") the effect of the swing in taxes is averaged out and the taxes shown in the income statement are as if no tax savings had been realized.

Advocates of flow through have made two arguments:

1) Tax savings really do not diminish in the future because new investments by the utility keep generating new tax savings. Therefore, the utility will not reach the point at which the tax savings will have to be paid back, so a reserve is not necessary.

2) If the day of reckoning does come, the utility can always ask the regulator for rate relief to cover the higher taxes. In the meantime, ratepayers could be spared the higher price that results from a set aside for "phantom taxes."

To a great extent, tax law in the 1980s has made the debate academic because new tax benefits cannot be taken if they are flowed through. (Flow through of old tax benefits remains.) For investors, objections to flow through are more pragmatic. As will be explained later in our discussion of utility finance, flow through companies generate less cash flow per dollar of earnings and interest coverage ratios also are lower per dollar of interest expense. Both deficiencies increase the risk of the utility in the eyes of investors, thereby raising cost of capital to the company.

Justification for flow through accounting depends on regular increases in plant and a continuation of current tax laws. Flow through accounting guarantees that the tax benefits from a plant that will serve customers for 30 years will go to those who are customers in the early years of the plant's life, possibly at the expense of customers in later years. Present day regulators say that their successors will give the utility higher rates at the time of the crossover when straight line depreciation becomes greater than accelerated depreciation. That, however, could occur at a time when growth in demand had slackened so that little new plant is being added. The utility could then face a new, highly price elastic demand curve (possibly because of the introduction of new technologies). Consequently, an increase in the price of the service to recoup higher tax charges may not result in additional income. Thus, a utility that uses flow through accounting may never recoup the lost revenue and might have to pay higher taxes at a time when its financial and market position is weakening.[33]

Having determined the tax bill for regulatory purposes and subtracted that amount and the operating expenses from revenues, the remainder is available to compensate the suppliers of capital.

Calculating Return on Rate Base

Some regulators, however, consider income other than operating income when they determine how much income is available to meet capital costs, and make their determination on the basis of what is included in the rate base. For example, if regulators include in the rate base plant that has not yet been put into service (construction work in progress, or CWIP), the regulators may include in income a credit intended to offset capital charges incurred before the plant is put into service (the allowance for funds used during construction).

Many methods are used to determine the rate base. We discuss seven important variants that can be combined in the rate base formula.

1) *Net original cost rate base*—The rate base is determined by the original cost of the properties, less depreciation.

2) *Fair value*—The cost of the plant is adjusted to account for at least some of the additional cost now required to duplicate the plant. Several states claim to be fair value jurisdictions, but most of the rate orders differ little from those of other jurisdictions.

3) *Average rate base*—The test year encompasses the operating results of an entire period. The rate base at one point in that period may not be representative of the investment throughout the test period. Many regulators, as a result, will determine an average of the rate base throughout the year and will use that average in the case.

4) *End of period rate base*—The rate order considers not only experience of the past test year, but also what may occur in the future. If a utility has been adding plant at a rapid pace, the average rate base may not be representative of plant investment at the time the rate order goes into effect. Thus, the utility is unlikely to be able to earn the allowed return on the enlarged rate base. Many regulators attempt to reduce that attrition in return by using an end of period rate base.

5) *Used and useful rate base*—Should current consumers be required to pay a return on plant that is not yet in service? In a number of jurisdictions, the regulators include in rate base only plant that is actually serving customers.

6) *Construction work in progress in rate base and allowance for funds used during construction included in income*—In this approach, the regulators do not distinguish between useful and incomplete plant. Nor do they distinguish between income derived from the sale of a service and income created by a bookkeeping credit in the income statement.

7) *Construction work in progress in rate base*—In this case, the regulator agrees to have the customers bear the current burden of construction work in progress for the following reasons:

a) The plant will, in the main, serve current customers.

b) The plant will be completed in the near term. To hand down a rate order excluding the particular plant would be to regulate for the past rather than for the future. Moreover, the utility would have to file for another rate hike immediately after the new plant is placed in service.

c) The utility has a serious cash flow problem because of the size of its capital expenditure program and cannot finance the completion of the plant additions unless it can generate more cash from operations. Charging the current consumer for the capital costs of the construction program will help cash flow.

d) Making consumers pay in advance for assets that will serve them later sends a price signal about future costs to consumers, who can then begin a process of adjusting their demands to the new price level.

Let us take a simple example of some of the many returns that can be derived from the same set of numbers. In an actual case, rate base also includes some amount for working capital.

Revenues	$ 600
Operating expenses	
and taxes	400
Operating income (OI)	200
Allowance for funds	
used during construction (AFUDC)	10
Income before interest charges (IBIC)	$ 210
Beginning of year net plant in service	$2,000
End of year net plant in service (End NPIS)	2,200
Beginning of year construction work in progress	50
End of year construction work in progress (End CWIP)	100
Working capital in all periods (WC)	50

The above numbers will produce various rates of return, as shown below.

$$1) \text{ Rate of Return} = \frac{OI}{\text{Average NPIS} + WC} = \frac{200}{2,100 + 50} = 9.3\%$$

$$2) \text{ Rate of Return} = \frac{OI}{\text{End NPIS} + WC} = \frac{200}{2,200 + 50} = 8.9\%$$

3) Rate of return on fair value (where fair value equals 150% of the end of period net original cost of plant in service) =

$$\frac{OI}{\text{Fair Value Rate Base} + WC} = \frac{200}{3,300 + 50} = 6.0\%$$

4) Rate of Return $= \dfrac{IBIC}{\text{End NPIS} + \text{End CWIP} + WC} = \dfrac{210}{2,200 + 100 + 50} = 8.9\%$

5) Rate of Return $= \dfrac{OI}{\text{End NPIS} + \text{End CWIP} + WC} = \dfrac{200}{2,200 + 100 + 50} = 8.5\%$

6) Rate of Return on rate base that includes some construction work in progress without an AFUDC offset (assumes half of year end CWIP goes into rate base) and year end plant =

$$\frac{OI}{\text{End NPIS} + 1/2 \text{ End CWIP} + WC} = \frac{200}{2200 + 50 + 50} = 8.7\%$$

7) Rate of Return that includes all CWIP in denominator and only some AFUDC in numerator either by specifying a lower rate for AFUDC or including only part of AFUDC (assumes half of AFUDC) =

$$\frac{OI + 1/2 \text{ AFUDC}}{\text{End NPIS} + \text{End CWIP} + WC} = \frac{200 + 5}{2200 + 100 + 50} = 8.7\%$$

As can be seen in the above examples 1) and 2), rate of return is lower when a year end rate base is used, and the company, as a result, can justify more rate relief.

As can be seen from 2) and 3), the utility may report a low return on a fair value rate base in comparison with that on an original cost rate base. Do not conclude from the examples, however, that a company using fair value can now justify a greater amount of rate relief because of the low return. Most fair value jurisdictions have tended to allow lower returns on the higher fair value rate bases.

Examples 4) and 5) demonstrate that a utility might show better returns by capitalizing credits on construction funds at a higher rate than the company can earn on plant in service, and, unfortunately, that higher returns on paper may not be good substitutes for cash. Examples 6) and 7) give halfway measures that could be used by regulators that do not want to unduly encourage construction, but want to aid cash flow.

AFUDC and CWIP: A Recapitulation

To summarize, when plant is not in service and when the utility is not being allowed a current return on that plant by the regulators, the company will capitalize the financing costs of the facility (allowance for funds used during construction, or AFUDC) and will add those costs to the total cost of the plant. When the plant is completed, the rate base will then include both the actual expenditures on construction and the capitalized financial charges.

The utility depreciates the total cost, including the AFUDC, and earns a return on the total cost. Therefore, the consumer actually pays on the basis of total cost during the life of the plant. When the construction period is long, however, the utility has to advance large sums for financing charges, while it collects no cash from the consumer. That can create a serious cash drain for a utility with a big capital spending program. Therefore, utility investors should be concerned about the treatment of CWIP by the regulators.

The problem can be handled in several ways. (Keep in mind that there are partial solutions, too, such as adding some CWIP to the rate base.)

In some jurisdictions, the plant under construction is included in the rate base, and the current consumer pays a high bill to provide a return on CWIP. In other jurisdictions, CWIP may be included in the rate base, but the rate of return is calculated to include the allowance for funds used during construction (see the following examples). In still other jurisdictions, no CWIP is permitted in the rate base, and the utility capitalizes construction costs by using allowance for funds used during construction (AFUDC). Because AFUDC is a non-cash credit, from a cash flow standpoint including CWIP in the rate base (RB) without the offsetting AFUDC is the preferred conservative method. A simplified example follows.

	Case A	Case B	Case C
	CWIP in RB	CWIP in RB and AFUDC in Allowed Income	No CWIP in RB and No AFUDC in Allowed Income
Line			
1) Operating Income	$ 80	$ 64	$ 64
2) AFUDC (8% rate)	0	16	16
3) Income Before Interest Charges	80	80	80
4) Plant in Service	800	800	800

5) CWlP	200	200	200
6) Total Plant	1,000	1,000	1,000
7) Rate Base—See Line	6	6	4
8) Allowed Income—See Line	1	3	1
9) Rate of Return Formula—See Lines	1/6	3/6	1/4
10) Rate of Return	8%	8%	8%

Note that in Case A, the utility collects $80 from operations, but in Cases B and C, it collects only $64 from operations and the balance of the income before interest charges of $80 is a $16 bookkeeping credit (AFUDC).

In addition, regulators generally include in rate base a sum for working capital. They may not allow a return on an unnecessary facility and may subtract from rate base costs of construction that they consider to be excessive. They may also reduce rate base by the amount that has been financed by cost free income tax deferrals.

Trends in Rate of Return

The final step is to set the proper return to be allowed. In the early days of regulation, when great emphasis was placed on finding the fair value of the rate base, allowed rates of return stayed in a relatively narrow range.

A phrase that was often repeated in a study of rate cases from 1915 on is, "The Commission gave no indication how the rate of return was established."[34] The Arthur Andersen compilation of rate cases from 1915 to 1960 indicates that the current method of determining cost of capital, which was pioneered by the Federal Power Commission, was first used in the Safe Harbor Water Power decision of October 25, 1946.[35] By 1949, several regulatory agencies appear to have adopted the FPC method.

The allowance for rate of return seems to have had four phases. Between 1915 and 1929, regulators granted returns in the 7-to-8% range, perhaps using level of business and interest rates as a basis. In the early years of the Depression, both interest rates and allowed returns drifted down. By the mid-1930s, returns settled in a 5.5-to-6% range and remained there until the mid-1960s. It was this thirty year period that gave many people the idea that a proper rate of return was 6%. Finally, because of strong business conditions, inflation, and sharply rising interest rates that began in the mid-1960s, rate of allowed return began a rise that peaked after interest rates began to fall in the 1980s. (See Figures 19-1 and 19-2.)

The need for substantial amounts of rate relief may have forced regulators to do more than arbitrarily choose a rate of return that was somewhat above interest rates. Greater attention was paid to calculating a utility's overall cost of capital from the cost of each of the components of capital. Tables 19-2, 19-3 and 19-4 show the trends in rates of return, return on equity, and money market costs from 1915 to 1986.

In determining the cost of common equity, regulators must assess both business and financial risk. Regulators may decide that a gas company incurs a greater business risk than an electric company because of the gas company's sensitivity to unpredictable weather conditions and uncertainties about supply. Or regulators may decide that one electric company is at more risk than another because of the characteristics of its service area. Financial risk may also be measured by the size of the utility's borrowings in relation to its total capitalization. Figure 19-3 shows trends in return allowed on equity.

Calculating the Rate of Return

In theory, calculating the cost of capital or the rate of return is simple. For example, a utility borrows $500 at a cost of 8% and raises $500 of common equity. The regulatory agency believes that cost of equity is 13%. Thus, cost of capital is:

Capital Component	$ Amount	Cost	Weighted $ Cost
Debt	$ 500 ×	0.08 =	$ 40
Common Stock	500 ×	0.13 =	65
Total	$1,000		$105

This is a 10.5% rate of return.

Usually, the commission determines the cost of each segment of the capital structure and adds the results to determine the overall cost of capital, or rate of return. Determining the cost of debt and preferred stock is fairly easy because the required interest charges and dividends are fixed. Determining the return on common equity, however, is a long and complicated process. In many states, the commission will allow a utility to earn a high return on equity if the utility has a low equity ratio, on the theory that greater financial risk requires greater compensation. In addition, many commissions consider deferred credits (usually deferred taxes) to be part of the capital structure, but they allow a zero rate of return on that segment of capital because it has no cost to the company. That is, a deferred tax is considered to be the equivalent of an interest free loan from the Government. As a result of new tax laws, however, some deferred tax credits must be allowed a rate of return.

Here are some sample calculations of allowed rates of return:

a) Cost of common equity at 12% but different costs of debt and preferred.

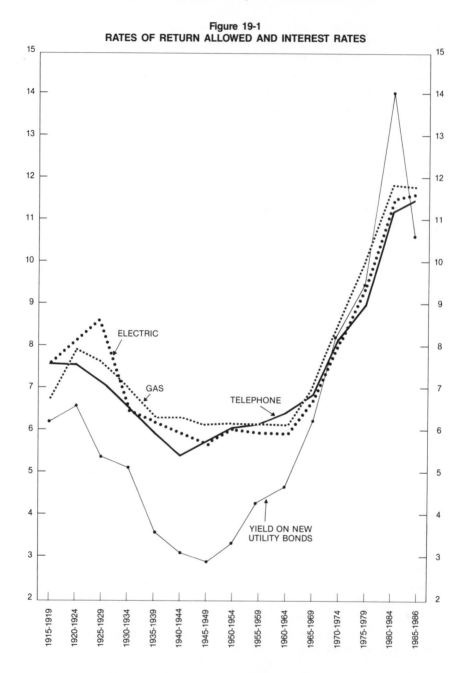

Figure 19-1
RATES OF RETURN ALLOWED AND INTEREST RATES

Figure 19-2
RATES OF RETURN ALLOWED AND INTEREST RATES (1968-1986)

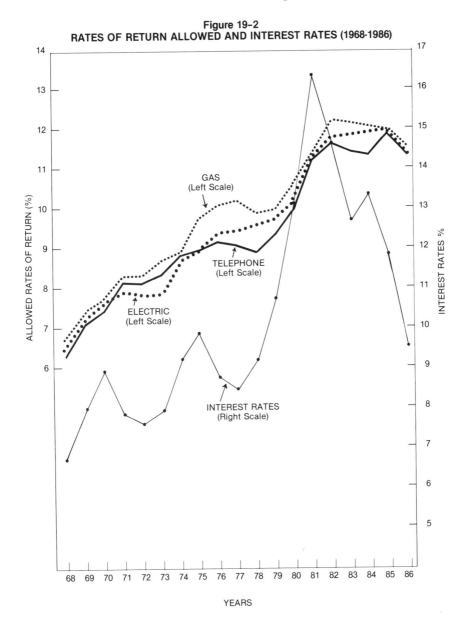

YEARS

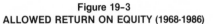

Figure 19-3
ALLOWED RETURN ON EQUITY (1968-1986)

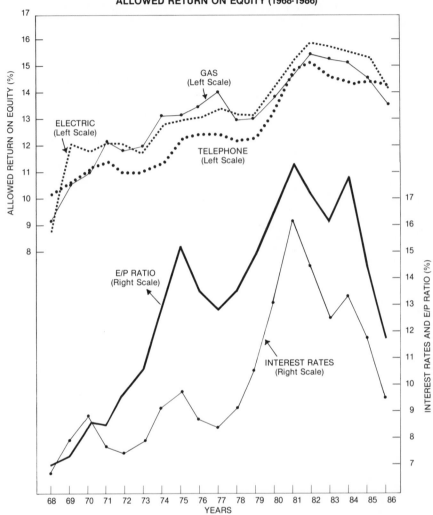

Table 19-1

**Estimated Average Rates of Return Granted in Rate Cases
and Indicators of Costs of Capital (%)**

	1915-1930	1931-1940	1941-1950	1951-1960	1961-1970	1971-1980	1981-1986
Return Granted on Rate Base							
Electric	7.5	6.5	6.2	6.2	6.4	8.9	11.6
Gas	7.4	6.5	5.9	5.9	6.5	9.4	11.9
Telephone	7.2	5.9	5.7	6.1	6.7	8.8	11.4
Return Granted on Equity							
Electric	—	—	—	9.2	11.1	12.9	15.2
Gas	—	—	—	9.1	10.6	13.0	14.8
Telephone	—	—	—	9.6	9.6	11.9	14.6
Indicators of Cost of Capital							
Bond Yields	6.0	4.1	3.0	4.0	5.8	9.2	13.0
Earnings/Price Ratio	—	5.7	8.1	6.7	6.0	13.1	15.9

Sources: Welch. *op. cit.*, pp. 480-481.
 Merrill Lynch Regulatory Data Base.
 Moody's Public Utility Manual (1987).
 Arthur Andersen & Co.

Notes: Bond yields are all for newly issued utility bonds. Earnings price ratio of Moody's Electric
 Utility Average. Simple averages of annual modal values (1915-1961) for returns granted.
 Simple average of unweighted annual means (1962-1986) for returns granted.

Table 19-2

Regulatory Data
1915-1961

	Modal Rate of Return (%) (Andersen)			Cases Reported (Andersen)			Long Term Interest Rates and Earnings Yield (%) (Moody's)	
	Electric	Gas	Telephone	Electric	Gas	Telephone	Newly Issued Utility Bonds	Electric Average Earnings/Price Ratio
	(1)	(2)	(3)	(4)	(5)	(6)	(7)	(8)
1915	7.0	6.0	—	6	1	0	5.80E	—
1916	8.0	7.5	8.0	3	4	2	5.70E	—
1917	7.0	8.0	8.0	3	2	1	6.00E	—
1918	7.5	6.0	6.7	6	4	2	6.65E	—
1919	8.0	6.0	7.4	5	4	2	6.60E	—
1920	8.0	8.0	7.0	6	8	5	7.40E	—
1921	7.5	8.0	8.0	7	13	6	7.31	—
1922	8.0	8.0	7.0	5	7	3	6.02	—
1923	8.0	8.0	7.5	8	9	1	5.98	—
1924	8.0	7.6	8.0	3	4	6	6.03	—
1925	7.5	8.0	8.0	2	7	6	5.61	—
1926	7.7	8.0	7.2	2	6	7	5.50	—
1927	7.0	7.5	7.0	1	3	2	5.26	—
1928	6.0	7.5	6.5	1	5	3	5.20	—
1929	7.5	7.0	7.0	3	1	7	5.21	3.80
1930	—	7.5	7.0	0	3	4	5.20	4.26
1931	7.0	8.0	7.7	3	1	1	4.71	5.43
1932	7.0	7.0	5.7	5	3	2	5.74	6.33
1933	6.0	6.0	6.5	5	7	3	4.98	4.55
1934	6.0	6.5	6.0	8	4	5	4.86	4.39

Table 19-2—Continued

Regulatory Data
1915-1961

	Modal Rate of Return (%) (Andersen)			Cases Reported (Andersen)			Long Term Interest Rates and Earnings Yield (%) (Moody's)	
	Electric	Gas	Telephone	Electric	Gas	Telephone	Newly Issued Utility Bonds	Electric Average Earnings/Price Ratio
	(1)	(2)	(3)	(4)	(5)	(6)	(7)	(8)
1935	6.7	7.0	5.0	8	5	3	3.84	5.65
1936	6.5	6.0	6.0	7	2	5	3.55	5.00
1937	6.0	6.0	—	4	4	0	3.55	6.21
1938	6.0	6.5	5.5	4	2	1	3.46	5.85
1939	6.0	6.2	6.0	6	2	1	3.46	6.49
1940	6.1	6.2	5.2	5	2	3	3.08	7.04
1941	5.5	6.2	5.0	1	2	1	3.07	8.77
1942	—	6.5	6.0	0	6	1	3.26	10.87
1943	6.0	6.5	5.2	3	6	3	3.26	8.20
1944	6.0	6.2	5.8	6	6	1	2.98	8.40
1945	5.5	6.5	5.5	4	5	1	2.85	6.54
1946	5.0	6.0	—	4	4	0	2.73	6.45
1947	6.0	6.0	5.5	3	5	10	2.79	7.30
1948	6.0	6.0	5.5	6	10	10	3.09	8.13
1949	5.7	6.0	6.0	9	9	20	3.07	8.33
1950	6.5	6.0	6.0	4	3	20	2.85	8.40
1951	6.0	6.0	6.0	7	6	26	3.29	7.52
1952	5.7	6.2	6.0	18	14	26	3.38	6.94
1953	6.0	6.2	6.0	13	17	21	3.77	7.35
1954	5.7	6.2	6.0	10	15	19	3.17	6.62

Table 19-2—Continued

Regulatory Data
1915-1961

| | Modal Rate of Return (%) (Andersen) | | | Cases Reported (Andersen) | | | Long Term Interest Rates and Earnings Yield (%) (Moody's) | |
	Electric	Gas	Telephone	Electric	Gas	Telephone	Newly Issued Utility Bonds	Electric Average Earnings/Price Ratio
	(1)	(2)	(3)	(4)	(5)	(6)	(7)	(8)
1955	5.8	6.0	6.0	6	17	18	3.33	6.54
1956	5.8	6.2	6.0	11	10	22	3.86	6.76
1957	6.1	6.0	6.1	10	19	23	4.74	6.90
1958	6.0	6.2	6.1	16	19	29	4.21	6.25
1959	5.8	6.2	6.5	16	16	18	4.97	5.75
1960	6.0	6.0	6.8	14	29	16	4.84	5.92
1961	5.5	6.2	6.3	6	22	5	4.70	4.78

Table 19-3

Regulatory Data
1935-1986

| Year | Average Rates of Return (%) (Welch) | | | Average Rates of Return (%) (Merrill Lynch) | | | Cases Reported (Merrill Lynch) | | | Long Term Interest Rates and Earnings Yield (%) (Moody's) | |
| | Electric | Gas | Telephone | Electric | Gas | Telephone | Electric | Gas | Telephone | Newly Issued Utility Bonds | Electric Average Earnings/Price Ratio |
	(9)	(10)	(11)	(12)	(13)	(14)	(15)	(16)	(17)	(18)	(19)
1935	7.0	6.7	6.0							3.84	5.65
1936	6.0	6.5	6.0							3.55	5.00
1937	6.0	6.0	5.6							3.55	6.21
1938	6.7	6.0	5.4							3.46	5.85
1939	6.2	6.0	5.3							3.46	6.49
1940	6.2	6.2	5.2							3.08	7.04
1941	6.2	5.4	5.0							3.07	8.77
1942	6.5	6.0	5.3							3.26	10.87
1943	6.5	6.0	5.3							3.26	8.20
1944	6.2	6.0	5.7							2.98	8.40
1945	6.4	5.5	5.5							2.85	6.54
1946	6.0	5.4	6.1							2.73	6.45
1947	6.0	6.0	5.6							2.79	7.30
1948	6.0	6.0	5.6							3.09	8.13
1949	6.0	5.8	6.0							3.07	8.33
1950	6.0	6.4	6.0							2.85	8.40
1951	6.0	6.0	6.0							3.29	7.52
1952	6.3	5.8	6.0							3.38	6.94
1953	6.3	6.0	6.0							3.77	7.35

Table 19-3—Continued

Regulatory Data
1935-1986

| Year | Average Rates of Return (%) (Welch) | | | Average Rates of Return (%) (Merrill Lynch) | | | Cases Reported (Merrill Lynch) | | | Long Term Interest Rates and Earnings Yield (%) (Moody's) | |
| | Electric | Gas | Telephone | Electric | Gas | Telephone | Electric | Gas | Telephone | Newly Issued Utility Bonds | Electric Average Earnings/Price Ratio |
	(9)	(10)	(11)	(12)	(13)	(14)	(15)	(16)	(17)	(18)	(19)
1954	6.3	5.8	6.0							3.17	6.62
1955	6.0	5.8	6.0							3.33	6.54
1956	6.3	5.8	6.0							3.86	6.76
1957	6.0	6.2	6.0							4.74	6.90
1958	6.1	6.0	6.1							4.21	6.25
1959	6.2	5.8	6.1							4.97	5.75
1960	6.0	6.0	6.2							4.84	5.92
1961	5.9	6.0	6.2							4.70	4.78
1962	5.8	6.0	6.2							4.44	5.18
1963	5.9	6.1	6.3							4.39	4.85
1964	6.0	6.2	6.4							4.56	4.98
1965	6.2	6.1	6.4	6.00	6.88	6.57	2	5	1	4.68	5.05
1966	6.5	6.6	6.7	6.43	6.50	6.38	2	1	1	5.61	6.13
1967				—	—	7.25	0	0	1	6.01	6.54
1968				6.44	6.67	6.19	4	10	10	6.72	6.76
1969				7.24	7.43	7.23	6	8	13	7.99	7.30
1970				7.53	7.54	7.44	29	31	17	8.85	8.70
1971				7.81	8.20	8.10	42	40	26	7.71	8.47

Table 19-3—Continued

Regulatory Data

1935-1986

Year	Average Rates of Return (%) (Welch)			Average Rates of Return (%) (Merrill Lynch)			Cases Reported (Merrill Lynch)			Long Term Interest Rates and Earnings Yield (%) (Moody's)	
	Electric	Gas	Telephone	Electric	Gas	Telephone	Electric	Gas	Telephone	Newly Issued Utility Bonds	Electric Average Earnings/Price Ratio
	(9)	(10)	(11)	(12)	(13)	(14)	(15)	(16)	(17)	(18)	(19)
1972				7.77	8.27	8.08	84	48	59	7.46	9.62
1973				7.82	8.58	8.25	69	54	50	7.88	10.64
1974				8.55	8.82	8.80	106	58	45	9.21	15.87
1975				8.88	9.61	8.85	133	67	64	9.76	15.15
1976				9.32	10.03	9.10	112	47	55	8.80	13.51
1977				9.33	10.10	8.98	100	41	56	8.38	12.82
1978				9.47	9.81	8.82	94	67	33	9.22	13.52
1979				9.58	9.90	9.31	84	44	27	10.64	14.85
1980				10.24	10.47	9.90	114	36	53	13.09	16.38
1981				11.06	11.16	11.14	137	39	68	16.30	18.33
1982				11.73	12.10	11.63	123	80	65	14.56	17.15
1983				11.71	12.31	11.44	105	46	81	12.53	16.05
1984				11.83	12.22	11.32	79	32	42	13.33	17.80
1985				11.99	11.94	11.81	54	24	43	11.78	14.39
1986				11.22	11.37	11.21	44	18	18	9.45	11.82

Table 19-4
Regulatory Data
1965-1986

Year	Average Return on Equity (%) (Merrill Lynch)			Cases Reported (Merrill Lynch)			Long Term Interest Rates and Earnings Yield (%)	
	Electric	Gas	Telephone	Electric	Gas	Telephone	Newly Issued Utility Bonds (Moody's)	Electric Average Earnings/Price Ratio (Moody's)
	(20)	(21)	(22)	(23)	(24)	(25)	(26)	(27)
1965	11.31%	—%	8.57%	1	0	1	4.68%	5.05%
1966	11.27	11.70	—	2	1	0	5.61	6.13
1967	—	—	9.00	0	0	1	6.01	6.54
1968	8.85	9.10	10.09	1	4	6	6.72	6.76
1969	12.00	10.51	10.52	4	4	11	7.99	7.30
1970	11.89	11.02	10.78	23	24	13	8.85	8.70
1971	12.07	12.15	11.39	33	35	20	7.71	8.47
1972	12.08	11.89	10.91	78	42	45	7.46	9.62
1973	11.80	11.96	10.85	56	48	35	7.88	10.64
1974	12.69	13.09	11.33	97	50	36	9.21	15.87
1975	12.95	13.10	12.14	128	65	56	9.76	15.15
1976	13.21	13.44	12.26	109	40	51	8.80	13.51
1977	13.41	13.96	12.34	104	44	57	8.38	12.82
1978	13.26	13.08	12.18	93	58	28	9.22	13.52
1979	13.34	13.23	12.34	92	37	25	10.64	14.85
1980	14.08	13.78	13.07	117	32	50	13.09	16.38
1981	15.13	14.74	14.65	139	37	79	16.30	18.33
1982	15.76	15.53	15.06	125	70	61	14.56	17.15
1983	15.46	15.26	14.77	106	48	87	12.53	16.05
1984	15.37	15.22	14.49	82	36	48	13.33	17.80
1985	15.16	14.70	14.64	59	22	43	11.78	14.39
1986	14.09	13.56	14.22	45	16	13	9.45	11.82

Table 19-4—Continued

Sources for Tables 19-2, 19-3 and 19-4

Columns 1-6
Numbers estimated from charts in:

Arthur Andersen & Co., *Return Allowed in Public Utility Rate Cases* (1960 Edition) and *Return Allowed in Public Utility Rate Cases* (Vol. I 1915-1954 and Vol. II 1955-1961). No date or place of publication. Fair value and original cost returns are not distinguished for the series.

Column 7
All newly issued utility bonds. Moody's *Public Utilities Manual 1987*. (New York: Moody's Investors Service, 1987). 1915-1920 estimated from high grade utility bond yields.

Column 8
$$\left(\frac{1}{\text{P/E Ratio}}\right) \times 100 \text{ for Moody's Electric Utility Average, from: Moody's } \textit{Public Utilities Manual}, 1987.$$

Column 9-11
Derived from figure on p. 481 of Welch, *op. cit.* Shows mean rates of return for cases published in *Public Utilities Reports*.

Columns 12-17
Unweighted averages, all on original cost basis. Fair value translated to an original cost basis or omitted. Merrill Lynch Regulatory Data Base.

Column 18
See Column 7.

Column 19
See Column 8.

Columns 20-25
Unweighted averages, all on original cost basis. Fair value translated to an original cost basis or omitted. Merrill Lynch Regulatory Data Base.

Column 26
See Column 7.

Column 27
See Column 8.

	— Company X —			— Company Y —	
	Amount	Cost		Amount	Cost
Debt @ 5%	$ 50	$2.50	Debt @ 6%	$ 50	$3.00
Preferred @ 5%	10	0.50	Preferred @ 6%	10	0.60
Common @ 12%	30	3.60	Common @ 12%	30	3.60
Deferred					
credits @ 0%	10	0.00			
Total	$100	$6.60	Total	$100	$7.20
		or a 6.6% return			or a 7.2% return

b) Costs of debt and preferred are the same, but return on equity is different because of differences in equity ratios. (Actually, the cost of debt and preferred might be higher in the leveraged company.)

	— Company X —			— Company Y —	
	Amount	Cost		Amount	Cost
Debt @ 5%	$ 40	$2.00	Debt @ 5%	$ 50	$2.50
Preferred @ 5%	10	0.50	Preferred @ 5%	10	0.50
Common @ 11%	40	4.40	Common @ 12%	30	3.60
Deferred			Deferred		
credits @ 0%	10	0.00	credits @ 0%	10	0.00
Total	$100	$6.90	Total	$100	$6.60
		or a 6.9% return			or a 6.6% return

c) Same assumptions as in example b) above for Company X but a 7.67% rate of return allowed on deferred credits. (The 7.67% is the weighted cost of all components of capital other than deferred credits.) Note that if the return on the deferred credits is added to the return on equity, the order, in effect, raises the return on equity, as is shown below in the recalculation on the right.

				Return on Deferred Credits is Added to Return on Common Equity		
Company X		Amount	Cost		Amount	Cost
Debt @ 5%		$40	$2.00	Debt @ 5.0%	$ 40	$2.00
Preferred @ 5%		10	0.50	Preferred @ 5.0%	10	0.50
Common @ 11%		40	4.40	Common @ 12.925%	40	5.17
Deferred				Deferred		
credits @ 7.67%		10	0.77	credits @ 0%	10	0.00
		$100	$7.67		$100	$7.67
			or a 7.67% return			or a 7.67% return

The utility's cost of capital does not remain static. For instance, Company A, which maintains its capitalization ratios, has to borrow additional funds at a higher rate than the rate previously paid in order to build new plant. The regulators consider the cost of equity to be unchanged at 12%.

Utility A Expands
Capitalization and Cost of Capital
Before Expansion

	Amount	Cost
Debt	$500 @ 5%	$25
Common Equity	500 @ 12%	60
Total	$1,000	$ 85
		or 8.5% cost of capital

Securities Offered to
Finance Expansion

	Amount	Cost
Debt	$ 500 @ 8%	$ 40
Common Equity	500 @ 12%	60
Total	$1,000	$100
		or 10.0% cost of new capital

Capitalization and Cost of
Capital After Expansion

	Amount	Cost
Old Debt	$ 500 @ 5%	$ 25
New Debt	500 @ 8%	40
Common Equity	1,000 @ 12%	120
Total	$2,000	$185
		or a 9.25% cost of capital

In another example, Utility B already has borrowed a great deal of money at a high interest rate, and the company wants to make its financial situation safer by calling in some of the debt and replacing the debt with common stockholders' equity. After the recapitalization, the regulators believe that the common stockholders are not taking as much risk as before and, therefore, should be satisfied with a lower return on their equity investment.

Utility B Recapitalizes and Allowed Return is Reduced

Capitalization and Allowed Rate of Return before Recapitalization

	Ratio	Amount		Cost
Debt	70%	$ 700 @ 6%		$ 42
Common Equity	30%	300 @ 14%		42
Total	100%	$1,000		$ 84
			or an 8.4% rate of return	

Capitalization and Allowed Rate of Return after Recapitalization

	Ratio	Amount		Cost
Debt	50%	$ 500 @ 6%		$ 30
Common Equity	50%	500 @ 10%		50
Total	100%	$1,000		$ 80
			or an 8.0% rate of return	

Capitalization

One would not expect the capitalization used in the rate case to be a problem. After all, the regulators need only look at the balance sheet. Life, though, is not that easy. Regulators may believe that the capitalization is not optimal and may substitute a hypothetical capitalization ratio for the real one. For example, should a company that has only common equity in a state in which regulators generally grant a 12% return on equity be allowed a 12% rate of return? The company cannot be forced to sell debt, but the consumer should not have to pay the cost of the excessive conservatism. The regulators derive a rate of return by using a hypothetical capitalization ratio of 50% debt (at an 8% cost) and 50% equity (at a 12% cost). Although the rate order states that the utility is entitled to a 12% return on equity, the company can earn only 10% in actual equity because a hypothetical capitalization is used in the order.

Rate of Return Determined by Using Hypothetical Capitalization

	Ratio	Amount		Cost
Debt	50%	$ 500 @ 8%		$ 40
Common Equity	50%	500 @ 12%		60
Total	100%	$1,000		$100
			or a 10% rate of return	

Determining the capitalization for the rate case might be a problem if the company plans to do financing after the close of hearings and requests that the regulators base their findings on a projected capitalization. The regulators might not be willing to accept the projections because the financing might not be made according to plan.

Determining capitalization (and cost of capital) when the operating utility is owned by a holding company is complicated. Many methods are used. A few of them, in a simplified form, follow.

All common stock of Operating Company (OC) is owned by Parent Company (PC). Operating Company sells its debt in the public markets. Parent Company has no other utility subsidiaries. All of its money, raised by selling debt and common stock, is used to invest in the equity in Operating Company. Debt of both the Operating Company and the Parent were sold at a cost of 6%.

	OC		PC		Consolidated	
	$	Ratio	$	Ratio	$	Ratio
Debt	$ 300	30%	$ 490	70%	$ 790	79%
Common Equity	700	70	210	30	210	21
	$1,000	100%	$700	100%	$1,000	100%

How can rate of return for Operating Company be calculated? The first method would be to ignore the parent-subsidiary relationship. The regulators consider OC's capitalization ratios. They might conclude that the common stockholders of OC are not exposed to much risk because of the small amount of debt outstanding. The regulators might decide upon a 10% return on equity. Rate of return is 8.8%, calculated as follows:

	Fraction of Capitalization		Cost %		Weighted Cost of Capital (%)
Debt	0.30	×	6.0%	=	1.80
Common Equity	0.70	×	10.0	=	7.00
	1.00				8.80%

Some regulatory agencies use one of several variants of the double leverage method of calculation. The regulator wants to trace the subsidiary's equity capital to its source. In our example, the source is $490 of parent company debt and $210 of parent company equity. The regulator rearranges OC's capitalization as follows.

	Reported Capitalization of OC	%		Double Leverage Capitalization	%
Debt	$ 300	30	Debt of OC	$ 300	30
Common Equity	700	70	Debt of PC used to purchase equity in OC	490	49
	$1,000	100	Common Equity of PC used to purchase equity in OC	210	21
				$1,000	100%

Both debt components have a 6% cost. The common stockholders, however, receive a return higher than 10% because they are exposed to greater risk because of the large amount of debt that has a prior call on earnings and asset. The regulators therefore allow 19.33% on equity. Rate of return remains 8.80%.

	Fraction of Capitalization		Cost		Weighted Cost of capital (%)
Debt of OC	0.30	×	6.00	=	1.80
Debt of PC	0.49	×	6.00	=	2.94
Common Equity	0.21	×	19.33	=	4.06
	1.00				8.80

Utilities oppose double leverage. The procedure assumes that cost of capital is determined by its source, not by return on alternative investments of similar risk levels. In addition, despite the wide differences in the capitalization ratio, the regulator may not be willing to adjust return allowed on equity beyond a limited range. In the previous case, the regulators might not go above a 1.5% return on equity, with the result that the overall rate of return drops to 7.89% and return on OC's equity drops to 8.70%.

Double Leverage Calculation

	Fraction of Capitalization		Cost		Weighted Cost of Capital (%)
Debt of OC	0.30	×	6.00	=	1.80
Debt of PC	0.49	×	6.00	=	2.94
Common Equity	0.21	×	15.00	=	3.15
	1.00				7.89%

OC Return

	Fraction of Capitalization		Cost		Weighted cost of capital (%)
Debt	0.30	×	6.00 =		1.80
Common Equity	0.70	×	8.70 =		6.09
	1.00				7.89%

The third method uses consolidated figures on the theory that the holding company and its units are financed and run as a system. That method was often used in Bell Telephone rate cases, before the split-up of AT&T. The debt and preferred costs used are usually averages for the consolidated system, and cost of common is set in the usual fashion.

Return on Common Equity

The most difficult question is how does the regulator discover the proper return on the common stock equity? No contractual relationship exists. The companies and regulators have resorted to pseudoscientific methodologies that purport to discover stockholders' needs on the basis of returns shown on other investments or from studies of capital market data. A number of methods are popular.

1) *The comparable earnings method*—In the Hope case, the Supreme Court said that "the return to the equity owner should be commensurate with returns on investments in other enterprises having corresponding risks."[36] Many rate of return experts have interpreted that as meaning that the point of reference should be the reported returns on the book equity of comparable enterprises. What is a comparable enterprise? Some practitioners have taken the terms literally—a utility should earn a return on book equity that is close to the return being earned by similar utilities. That approach solves the problem of finding comparable enterprises, but creates another one. To some extent, the return earned by the utility is a function of the return allowed in the company's last rate case. If every regulatory agency followed the policy of allowing the same return as every other regulator, the process would become circular. The criticism goes a step further. Why should we believe that the return earned by other utilities (especially under the trying conditions of the past two decades) is the return expected by investors? Most regulatory agencies grant higher returns than those actually earned by utilities. Rate of return allowed represents the regulatory agency's judgment about the return required by investors. Return desired by investors cannot

be determined by examining return earned on the book equity of comparable utilities.

The difficulties of a utility-to-utility comparison are avoidable. The solution is to examine the returns earned on the book equity of industrial corporations that have characteristics similar to those of utilities. A more perplexing question then arises: how are industrial corporations that are comparable to utilities to be chosen? What are the characteristics of utilities? The commonly cited characteristics include the following:

a) Utilities must raise huge amounts of capital.

b) Utilities show steady sales patterns, are relatively insensitive to economic cycles, and their stock prices are relatively stable.

c) Utilities are capital intensive and often require $4 of plant to produce $1 of revenue.

d) Utilities employ small amounts of working capital.

e) In general, utilities hold monopolies on the provision of a particular service in a given area.

f) Utilities are capitalized to take advantage of financial leverage and borrow far more per dollar of assets than most industrial corporations.

g) Prices charged by utilities are regulated by governmental agencies.

Finding industrial companies that are comparable to utilities is difficult. Even if possible, there are additional problems.[37] For example:

a) Industrial companies having earnings and stock price stability like that of utilities can be found mainly in monopolistic or oligopolistic industries. The returns of those companies can be attributed to monopoly power. Few would argue that a utility is entitled to a monopolistic rate of return.

b) Accounting procedures do not allow true comparisons. An industrial corporation's balance sheet may include assets purchased at a price other than original cost. The plant may have been purchased long ago, so that the balance sheet does not accurately indicate the plant's current value, but revenues are on a current value basis. Depreciation rates of industrial firms have not been set by regulators at unrealistically low levels. Fluctuations in foreign currencies also add to the accounting complications.

One can attempt to circumvent problems of determining comparability by eliminating from the sample obviously oligopolistic firms, by avoiding companies with large foreign operations, by concentrating on industrial corporations that need to raise capital externally, and by using analyses of the risk of investing in individual securities.[38]

Unfortunately, inflation has made income statements and balance sheets of firms unreliable indicators of desired returns. The reported income may be overstated—in real terms—because of the inadequacy of depreciation allowances. Depreciation on the historical cost of fixed assets will not provide enough funds to replace the fixed assets at current prices. When replacement becomes necessary, the firm must use supposed profits to make the payment. On the other hand, fixed assets might be sold for far more than book value, as a result of the revaluation caused by inflation. In the capital markets, securities—to some extent—may be priced to indicate current value of assets and an inflation-adjusted earning power.

As an extreme example, Firm X is comparable to a particular utility. Its stock sells for $10 a share, has book value per share of $100, and earns $3 a share. The plant is obsolete and inefficient. The cost of replacement is $200 per share. The company's depreciation rate is 3%. Can we say that the investor desires a 3% return, which is the return on book value? If the regulator granted a 3% return on equity to the utility, the stock price would plummet. Can we say that the correct return is 30%—the earnings return on the market value of the stock, That percentage is not really what investors expect, because they know that part of it is a return of capital resulting from inadequate depreciation rates. If the utility were to be granted a 30% return on book equity, the stock price would rise up far above book value, indicating that the allowed return is excessive.

The comparable earnings approach meets the requirement that "the return to the equity owner should be commensurate with returns on investments in other enterprises having comparable risks" (Hope Natural Gas). The comparable earnings approach is based on the audited books of large corporations rather than on attempts to read the minds of investors. The Hope decision, though. was written before the steady postwar inflation. (Wholesale prices in 1944 were no higher than they had been in 1864. Prices in 1864 were little higher than those in 1814. In 1944, there was little reason to expect the country to break out of a pattern of widely swinging price cycles about a barely rising trend line.) The distortions introduced into financial statements by inflation make comparisons difficult. The problem with the comparable earnings approach is that investors cannot always make investments that realize the returns shown on the books of the corporation. The investor seeking to place new funds must settle for the return currently available in the marketplace, or the return from the purchase of assets at current prices.

2) *The discounted cash flow technique*—For many years, regulators hesitated to use comparable earnings approach, ostensibly because of the difficulty of coming up with an acceptable sample of comparable companies. Witnesses using that approach had a tendency to be selective in their choice of comparable firms. Regulators objected that the witnesses had selected companies that would produce a desired answer. Given the adversary nature of the regulatory process, that objection was reasonable.

Rate of return experts developed alternative methods of finding a fair return on equity. Those methods "purport to give the objective judgment of the market place as to what is the cost of capital."[39] The discounted cash flow (DCF) technique is the most popular of those currently in use.

Discounted cash flow analysis accepts that the price of a common share equals the present value of the sum of all future income to be received from the share.[40] Assuming that the dividend payout ratio, earnings price ratio, and growth rate remain constant, in perpetuity, then (all numbers in decimals):

$$k = \frac{d}{p} + g$$

where:

k = expected return on investment in stock
d = dividend per share
p = price of stock
g = expected annual growth in dividend or market price of stock

To complete the analysis:

$$g = br$$

where:

b = the earnings retention rate (1 − payout ratio)
r = expected return on book equity.

The formulas are similar to those used by many investors. Unfortunately, the stated assumptions present practical problems, and the assumption that the stock price must remain at book value could invalidate the calculations. The basic formula also is circular. "The variable g . . . is affected by r and in some cases by the expected ratio of market value to book value. The term r is the result of regulatory action and the market-to-book ratio is influenced by regulatory action. This results in independent variable g being dependent on dependent variable k of the formula, which is circular."[41] The market to book ratio affects the calculation in several ways. For example, when the market to book ratio is more than 100%, and the utility must sell stock for financing, the stock's growth in earnings and dividends per share (g) will be faster than if the stock sold at or below book value. Thus, if the market to book ratio differs for two utilities, the same k applied to the two stocks will produce different realized returns. To further complicate matters, the application to the book value of a return derived from the market value when book value differs from market value may be invalid.

The following examples show the effect of price on growth in earnings per share. Three utilities, with stock selling at 90%, 100%, and 110% of book value, must increase common equity by 10% to finance expansion. Each company sells stock at the market value at the end of the previous year. Each company earns 10% on equity.

Company A (90% of Book Value)	Year 1	Year 2
Common equity	$1,000.00	$1,100.00
Number of shares	100	111.1
Book value per share	$10.00	$9.90
Price per share (year-end)	9.00	—
Earnings	100.00	110.00
Earnings per share	$1.00	$0.99
% change in EPS	—	−1%

Company B (100% of Book Value)	Year 1	Year 2
Common Equity	$1,000.00	$1,100.00
Number of shares	100	110
Book value per share	$10.00	$10.00
Price per share (year-end)	10.00	—
Earnings	100.00	110.00
Earnings per share	1.00	1.00
% change in EPS	—	0%

Company C (110% of Book Value)	Year 1	Year 2
Common equity	$1,000.00	$1,100.00
Number of shares	100	109.1
Book value per share	$10.00	$10.10
Price per share (year-end)	11.00	—
Earnings	100.00	110.00
Earnings per share	1.00	$1.01
% change in EPS	—	+1%

The percentage change in the rate of growth caused by the market/book differential can be formulated as:

$$\frac{o}{e} \times \left[\left(\frac{m}{b} \times 100 \right) - 100 \right]$$

where: o = dollar value of new stock offering
         e = common equity before offering
         m = market value of shares
         b = book value of shares

Now let us attempt to determine k (expected return on investment in stock), ignoring the problem of circularity, while including and excluding the effect on growth of the market-book differential. Each of three utilities pays a 60¢ dividend. The expert witnesses have determined (based on past experience) that investors expect 4% growth from each utility.

	Company A	Company B	Company C
Dividend	$ 0.60	$ 0.60	$ 0.60
Price	9.00	10.00	11.00
D/P	6.66%	6.00%	5.45%
g	4.00	4.00	4.00
k	10.66	10.00	9.45

Does it make sense to say that investors will pay a higher price for a stock from which they expect a lower return? If the return on book equity to C were reduced to 9.45%, the stock would probably not remain at $11.00. Investors would (showing that regulators had misjudged their expectations) sell the stock until it fell to a price commensurate with the new, lower return on book equity. Investors base their expectations of return on the price of the stock, not on the underlying book value.

Growth differentials are caused by selling stock at different prices. The differentials are −1% for A, 0% for B, and +1% for C. The g and k of the formula again change, adding to the confusion:

	Company A	Company B	Company C
g	3.00%	4.00%	5.00%
k	9.66	10.00	10.45

What is the correct k to use in the rate case? The formula for k looks objective but is as subjective as the choice of comparable companies in the comparable earnings approach. Should stock price and dividend used in the formula be that of one date, or an average? If the latter, how long a period should be averaged? If the former, at what date? What selection would be representative? The answer of the expert witness is to pick the period that gives the desired result. The next step is to determine g. Should one use a past growth rate and, if so, which period should be chosen? Or should an estimate of future growth be based on investor expectations as divined by Wall Street security analysts? Some regulators have used growth in book value as in a past period as a proxy, for investor expectations for g.

In a 1978 decision, one commission wrote that the witness "was more pessimistic in his evaluation of investors' expectations of future dividend growth. In light of the company's poor past performance, he was of the opinion that investors anticipated a low rate of growth and were looking to the high dividend yield for the bulk of their return requirement."[42] That statement seems to say that if a company showed bad results in the past, investors expect nothing but a repetition of bad results, and deserve nothing better. And let us not forget that the witnesses in the case can pick the past period to produce the desired results. In another decision, a commission relied on the projections of "anticipated rate of growth in dividends per share" made by *Value Line,* a leading investment advisory service. The commission thought that the staff witness should have used a mean estimate for several similar companies, but said that "we believe that the DCF approach . . . provides the best estimate of a utility's cost of equity. We continued to be troubled, however, by the problem of deriving the growth term of the DCF model . . . we realize that the projections of a widely circulated investment survey such as *Value Line,* regardless of their accuracy, may provide a reliable estimate of investor expectations simply because of their influence on investor expectations. We therefore accept the anticipated growth in dividends per share projected by *Value Line* as the growth term in the DCF formula."[43] In effect, the return on equity set by the commission was really determined by the *Value Line* analyst. The commissioners showed little appreciation of the real problem of the DCF method. Investors' expectations are determined, to a great extent, by what they expect regulators to do. Regulators, in turn, make their decisions based on what investors expect. Perhaps the best way to get a generous rate order is to launch an investor relations campaign to convince stockholders that a great order is on the way. On the other hand, consumer groups could run a campaign to convince investors that a poor order is on the way.

3) *The capital asset pricing model (CAPM)*[44]—This approach to determining the proper return on equity is an offshoot of modern portfolio theory (MPT). Return on investment consists of two parts—a risk free return (such as that available from Treasury bills) and an additional return for risk. Risk is measured by comparing the volatility of return on a particular security with return in the market as a whole. That risk is measured by use of the familiar beta (B) of MPT. Thus:

$$R = R_f + B (R_m - R_f)$$

where:

R   = the return expected from a security
R_f = the return on risk free securities
R_m = the market rate of return

Note that beta, as used above, does not simply show the price movements of particular stock as a multiple of the price movements of the market as a whole.

Investors have the choice of a risk free investment, and they will demand a higher return if they invest at a higher risk level. Whether beta is the proper measure of return, and whether the many assumptions underlying CAPM are realistic are matters for scholarly tomes. Is CAPM workable when applied to solving a problem: what return should be granted in a rate case? CAPM uses only past data to determine what the investor might expect in the future. Capital markets are extraordinarily unstable. A period in the recent past can be chosen to prove any predetermined hypothesis. Is there any correct past period or is the choice of period subjective? There is nothing wrong with subjectivity, but the use of a supposedly scientific CAPM formula wraps this subjectivity in specious objectivity.

Has the beta for a particular security been stable, and will it remain stable in the future? It may well be that beta has greater predictive value when applied to a portfolio than to a single security. Industries and companies have life cycles. At one time or another, electric utilities have been exciting, speculative vehicles, bankrupts, growth stocks, deteriorating income vehicles, near bankrupts, and pure income vehicles.

Does CAPM have predictive value? We are trying to determine investor expectations (the investors' predictions of their future returns). We want to know what investors expect to happen, not what already has happened. There is no reason to think that investors know in advance what will happen in a given future period. Nor can we be certain that what happened in the immediate past is what the investor expects in the immediate future. If that were the case, in fact, stocks would only go in one direction. Furthermore, there is no reason to believe that investor return is stable from period to period. In fact, the evidence is to the contrary, which provides another reason to be hesitant about applying to the future the return from a particular period in the past.

Another problem, how confident one can be about the statistical validity of the risk/return relationship at a given level of risk, may affect the results for a particular company or industry more than the results for an entire portfolio. For instance, what if the risk return relationship in a past period looks like that of Figure 19-4?

The formula risk/return relationship is shown by the straight line. But the points are not uniformly distributed about the line for its entire length.

Figure 19-4
MARKET RISK AND MARKET RETURN
BY INDUSTRY GROUP

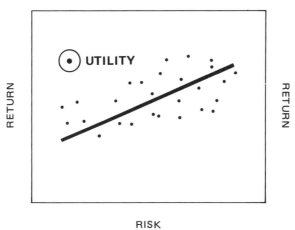

RISK

The point representing the utility industry (circled in the figure) had a low risk level, but provided a market return substantially higher than would have been estimated from the risk/return line. In fact, note that all the low risk stocks yielded returns greater than would have been expected. Vandell and Malernee claim that low beta stocks actually do earn higher returns than they theoretically should.[45] If true, a CAPM formula consistently would understate the proper return for those groups.

In short, the CAPM approach attempts to determine investors' expectations of future return from the past performance of a group of stocks chosen because the stocks have risk characteristics similar to those of the security in question. Some regulators already see it as the revealed truth. CAPM, though, may be no more scientific or useful than the comparable earnings or DCF approaches.

4) *Ad hoc or financial integrity approaches*—During the difficult last few years, utilities and regulators have had to fashion special approaches to meet specific problems, especially for plummeting interest coverage ratios and the fall of stock prices to levels below book value. Three approaches have been taken:

a) Set a return to produce a necessary interest coverage ratio. It may be necessary to ignore normal standards of return if a utility is to be able to obtain financing under certain conditions. Consider the following example. For simplicity, assume a zero income tax rate.

Rate base		$1,000
Pretax operating income		60
Operating income		60
Rate of return		60/1000 = 6.0%

	Capital	Return on Capital		Earnings
Debt	$ 500 ×	8%	=	$ 40
Equity	500 ×	4	=	20
Total Capital	$1,000 ×	6%	=	$ 60
Interest Coverage Ratio		$60/$40	=	1.5×

The company obviously needs rate relief because of the low return being earned on equity. The regulators have given a 10% return on equity to other companies. Can the regulators be persuaded to offer a higher return? The regulators might be told that the company must have a coverage ratio of 2.5 times total interest expenses of $40 if it is to be able to sell debt in the future. If we start with an interest coverage of 2.5 times and work backward, the result would be:

Rate base		$1,000
Pretax operating income		100
Operating income		100
Rate of return		10%

	Capital	Return on Capital	Earnings
Debt	$ 500 ×	8% =	$ 40
Equity	500 ×	12 =	60
Total Capital	$1,000 ×	10 =	$100
Interest Coverage Ratio		$100/$40 =	2.5 ×

That approach has been used for utilities that get into tight financial positions. Regulators have not been sympathetic to its use when a utility simply desires high coverage, which would produce an extremely high return on equity.

b) The second approach is to provide equity with a return set at a fixed amount above current debt costs. In 1965-1973, interest rates rose while return earned on utilities' equity remained stable. When interest rates rose sharply in 1974 and 1975, many utilities had to pay higher interest rates on new debt than the rates earned on common equity. In short, the protected creditor was able to make a higher return on investment than the risk taking equity holder. In addition, for years, the return differential for higher risk of equity investment had been diminishing, despite the increasing risk of investment caused by the industry's many problems. The declining risk differential may have contributed to the poor relative performance of utility stocks in much of the time since 1965. With many of the stocks selling below book value and with utility investors demoralized, the conventional methods of determining return were not working well. Some experts suggested that the proper return on equity should be set at a specific number of percentage points above long term bond yields. The approach is still used to some extent. (Recently, some rate case witnesses have argued that debt is a riskier investment than equity, and it should, therefore, produce a higher return than equity. That view seems to be based on some bad years in the bond market during conditions of severe inflation. It ignores the priority that debt has over equity in both current income and recovery of investment and confuses investors' expectations with actual results in the marketplace.)

c) A third approach is to provide a return on equity designed to keep the common stock price at or slightly above book value. According to the Hope decision, the proper rate of return must be high enough to maintain confidence in the utility's credit and to allow the company to attract capital. Despite a deterioration in credit standing, a utility may be able to attract capital (at least for a while), but possibly at a cost that would be damaging to the organization for the long term. A utility cannot be expected to maintain financial stability if each security offering is at a cost that makes the next offering more difficult. For example, a regulatory agency insists on a 6% rate of return, despite rising interest costs caused in part by falling bond quality. Each year, interest coverage declines as does the bond rating. Eventually the debt offerings cannot be sold. We assume an income tax rate of zero, and half of capital needs coming from the sale of debt.

	Years			
	1	2	3	4
Rate base (capital spending $200 per year)	$1,000	$1,200	$1,400	$1,600
Operating income (6% of rate base)	60	72	84	96
Debt sold (half of capital spending)	—	100	100	100
Cost of debt sold	—	6%	8%	10%
Total debt outstanding	$ 500	$ 600	$ 700	$ 800
Interest costs (total)	$ 25	$ 31	$ 39	$ 49
Interest coverage $\left(\dfrac{\text{Operating Income}}{\text{Interest Costs}}\right)$	2.4×	2.32×	2.15×	196×

The regulator, through the above policy, has put investors on notice that no attempt will be made to protect the integrity of the debt. Past investors must suffer the loss of market value. Future investors must demand a current return high enough to compensate them for additional future risk. Eventually, the market dries up or the cost of financing becomes too high, and the utility can no longer attract capital at a reasonable price.

A common stockholder can act in the same manner as a bondholder. If investors consider a utility's prospects bad, or if the regulator does not realize that equity costs have risen, then investors will not buy until the price falls and provides a proper return on the market value of the shares. This raises the cost of capital to the utility. Furthermore, investors will demand a price that compensates them for any future devaluations that might result from unfavorable regulation. For example, regulators set a 10% return on equity, and the company pays out all earnings (so that return is the same as the dividend).

	Years[a]			
	1	2	3	4
Common equity	$1,000	$1,100.1	$1,200.1	$1,300.1
Number of shares	$ 100	111.1	123.5	37.3
Book value/share (b)	$ 10	$ 9.90	$ 9.72	$ 9.47
Earnings on common equity (10%)	$ 100	$ 110	$ 120	$ 130
Dividends and earnings per share	$ 1.00	$ 0.99	$ 0.97	$ 0.94
Return on common demanded in marketplace (c)	10%	11%	12%	13%
Market value/share	$ 10.00	$ 9.00	$ 8.08	$ 7.23
Market/book ratio	100%	91%	83%	76%

Notes:
(a) All numbers have been rounded.
(b) Book value per share is common equity/number of shares.
(c) Return on common demanded in the marketplace is the return demanded on market value, i.e., earnings per share/market value per share.

Another example shows that the market/book ratio is of vital importance to electric utilities that sell common stock. Assume that a company is allowed to earn 10% on common equity and that the company must sell $1 million of stock to meet financing needs in the year.

	Previous Year
Common equity	$10,000,000
Net income	$ 1,000,000
Shares outstanding	1,000,000
EPS	$ 1.00
Book value per share	$10.00

	This Year — After *$1 Million of* *New Common is Sold*

A. Stock sells at 2 times book value, or $20.

Common equity	$11,000,000
Net income	$ 1,100,000
Shares outstanding	1,050,000
EPS	$ 1.05

B. Stock sells at book value, or $10.

Common equity	$11,000,000
Net income	$ 1,100,000
Shares outstanding	1,100,000
EPS	$ 1.00

C. Stock sells at 90% of book value, or $9.

Common equity	$11,000,000
Net income	$ 1,100,000
Shares outstanding	1,111,111
EPS	$ 0.99

In case A, each new share at $20 contributes $2 to earnings, i.e., 10% of $20. Accordingly, earnings per share are helped by the sale. In case B, each new share at $10 earns $1 and has no effect on earnings. In case C, each new share at $9 brings in only 90¢, thereby diluting per share earnings.

Because of the dilutionary effect on current holdings of selling stock below book value, many regulators believe that earnings should be high enough to keep the stock at or slightly above book value. Because a positive correlation exists between return on equity and the market/book ratio, regulators often try to set a return on equity that will keep the stock selling near book value. Too high a market/book ratio, though, indicates to those regulators that the utility is overearning. Therefore, when the market/book ratio is low, selling new shares may be dilutive, but the regulators may have plenty of room to improve earnings if they so desire. When the market/book ratio is high, selling new shares could benefit earnings per share, but regulators could decide that the company is earning too much money.

Welch wrote:

> ... The final test that any utility enterprise has to meet, if it is to continue in business, is whether it can sell its securities on the investment market. According to the Federal Power Commission, if the return allowed cannot meet this test—if it has to sell stocks at a discount or bonds at a price giving higher yield than normally prevails in the market—that company is faced with financial difficulties . . .[46]

Bonbright discusses the sale of common stock at a price below book value in terms of "impairing the integrity"[47] of the investment made by previous stockholders. Clearly, sales at prices below book value erode the earnings potential of previously issued shares. If such sales are expected to continue for a long period, purchasers of new shares may intensify their demands for a higher return to offset the expected attrition, and thereby further increase the cost of capital.

In theory, when the return allowed on book equity is greater than the rate of return desired in the marketplace, the stock moves above book value. When return allowed on equity is below the return desired in the marketplace, the stock falls below book value.[48] Most regulators would like utility stocks to sell at a price enough above book value so that new shares could be marketed at book value. (The stock must sell above book value to provide a cushion for marketing costs.)

Some analysts have argued that a relation exists between return earned on book equity and the market/book ratio.[49] The relation varies with the level of the market, the extent of investors' willingness to pay for a higher return on equity, and even an investor's preference for current income (a high payout ratio) or growth (greater reinvestment of earnings). The following figures illustrate those differences.

In Figure 19-5 the relationships are shown at different points in the market cycle. The A line is for a period of high stock prices, the B line for the low point in the market. The utility must earn a higher return on equity (b) for its stock to sell at book value during the low point in the market cycle, than the return needed at the high point (a) of the market cycle.

Figure 19-5
MARKET/BOOK RATIO AT HIGH AND LOW POINTS
IN MARKET CYCLE

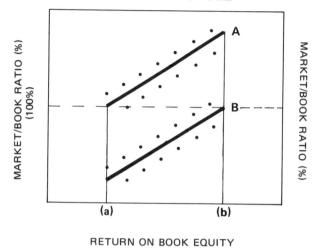

RETURN ON BOOK EQUITY

Figure 19-6
SLOPE OF MARKET/BOOK TO RETURN ON EQUITY RELATIONSHIP

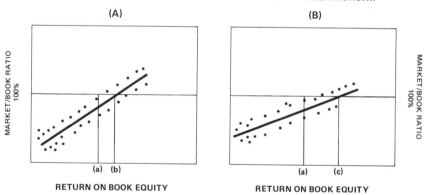

Figure 19-6 shows that the slope of the regression line can change, even if the mean point for the group remains the same. In both cases, the average company earns return (a) and sells at slightly below book value. In Figure 19-6A, the company need earn only a bit more (b) to reach book value. In Figure 19-6B, the utility must earn far more (c) to reach book value. In case A, the market highly values the additional return and is willing to pay for small increments of return. In case B, the market differentiates little between high and low returns, and a substantial rise in return is necessary to push up the market/book ratio.

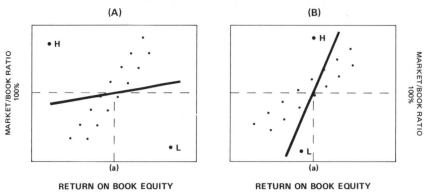

Figure 19-7
DISTORTION CAUSED BY HIGH OR LOW PAYOUT RATIOS

In Figure 19-7, the regression lines are distorted by outlying points which will pull the lines away from the trends set by most of the points. The distortion is caused by another phenomenon of the market—utility investors sometimes prefer current dividends to future growth and will pay more for a stock that has a higher dividend payout ratio. Occasionally, either for reasons of policy or because earnings were higher or lower than expected, a utility's payout ratio will differ greatly from the industry norm. The stock may then sell well above or below the market/book ratio that might be expected, given the return on book equity.

The distortion of the regression line causes the same problems as in the previous set of figures. But still another, more serious problem exists. Take the two high payout companies (H). Each sells far above its expected market book ratio. From the high market/book ratio, a regulator might conclude that the company is overearning and that return on equity should be reduced. The companies (H) probably are overpaying rather than overearning. On the other hand, the two companies with low payout ratios (L) may be underpaying, rather than underearning. A number of utilities have raised dividends to push up their market/book ratios at the risk of having regulators at some future time cite the higher market/book ratios as evidence that rate relief is not needed.

In summary, the market/book ratio provides an indication of whether or not the utility is earning a satisfactory return, and whether or not the current return is fair to existing shareholders as well as to new ones. Unfortunately, the method suffers from distortions, especially when a specific utility has unusual features.

Validity of Methods

Ambrose Bierce, an expert on the subject, defined a cynic as "A blackguard whose faulty vision sees things as they are, not as they ought to be. . . ."[50]

Few wish to be included in such company, but apparently the adversary, litigious nature of rate cases makes necessary a host of seemingly scientific methods to prove the case. Each method has its faults. New methods arise and old ones are declared unsatisfactory by those who have just had the truth revealed to them. Bonbright, discussing the cost of equity capital to any company, concluded:

> ... that the only such cost that can be determined with confidence is a *minimum* or *partial cost*. That is to say, the analyst ... may be able to reach a credible conclusion that the cost of common stock capital comes to *at least* some specified percent; but the extent of the probable deficiency is necessarily a matter of surmise. Hence, if the minimum estimated cost is to be used in the determination of a computed "overall cost of capital," the resulting computation should be subject to a material, "judgment-reached" enhancement in order to give reasonable assurance of full-cost coverage.[51]

When you add to that the point that in the past decade most utilities have not even come close to earning their allowed returns, it becomes clear that the formula returns do need to be modified if they are to produce realistic results.

Chapter 20

The Rate Structure and Utility Economics

A rate system is primarily governed by practical considerations. If added use costs the consumer more than it costs the company, there is probable failure to develop services which would be worth their cost. If added use costs the consumer less than it costs the company, there is a stimulus to wasteful use.[52]

J. M. Clark

Until now, we have concerned ourselves with how the regulator determines the amount of revenue that the utility should collect to earn the allowed rate of return on the rate base. We have considered pricing in the aggregate sense. Pricing, in this case, does not necessarily serve the purpose that economists assign to pricing.

What purpose does utility pricing serve? For the regulator, the formula of price times volume less expenses provides the return that the utility is allowed to earn. Whether that price sends the right signals to consumers or promotes economic efficiency is a question that regulators often ignore. If prices should be higher to promote economic efficiency, the utility could earn too high a rate of return. If prices should be lower, the utility could earn a return that would be considered confiscatory, or it could go bankrupt because of failure to cover high fixed costs. Under present regulatory structure, some economists believe that the problem cannot be solved without a taxation-subsidy scheme. That is, the Government would tax away excess profits when rates need to be higher to promote economic efficiency and would pay the utility a subsidy when rates need to be lower. The alternative to the taxation-subsidy arrangement would be to put the utilities under Government ownership, with pricing to promote economic efficiency rather than profit.

Orthodox microeconomic theory holds that society will efficiently allocate economic resources when those resources are priced at the margin. Jules Joskow defined "marginal cost as the cost of society's scarce resources which must be used to produce one additional unit of some commodity or the value of resources that would be saved by producing one less unit of that commodity."[53] The consumer who purchases the product priced at the margin will do so only if the product is worthwhile enough for him to forgo the purchase of still another product priced at the margin. Through marginal cost pricing, the consumer knows how much it costs society to produce that last unit, and what costs can be avoided by not producing that unit.

Bonbright refers to:

> the consumer-rationing function of public utility rates. In support of this function, rates should be made just high enough to deter potential customers from demanding services of types and in amounts for which they are unwilling to defray the costs of rendition.[54]

A few examples can illustrate how use of marginal pricing would curb some of the inefficiencies caused by our energy and utility pricing structure.

If it costs $15 to produce a new barrel of oil, and oil is priced at $10 (because some oil, found a long time ago, can be produced at $5, which reduces the average production cost to $10), oil buyers are less constrained by price. They then use more oil than they would at $15. Every barrel that they buy at $10, however, costs $15 to replace.

In another example, parallel to what is happening in the telecommunications field, a utility can offer a special service because its plant is not fully utilized. The incremental cost of adding on the special service is $5 a unit. If part of the plant is allocated to the special service for regulatory purposes (despite the fact that the plant is already built and costs will not go up due to new customers), the service will not earn what the regulators consider to be a high enough return. The regulators might conclude that, because the new service is not earning a high enough return, the customers of other utility services must be subsidizing the service. For example, if another company announces that it will build a utility plant that will only provide a specialized service, then the specialized service must carry the entire cost of the plant. The company can offer the service at a cost of $15, which would include a proper rate of return. Is society better off if its assets are spent to build a new plant to provide a service for which the cost will be $15 a unit, or should the first utility be authorized to offer the service at incremental cost?

Or consider the case of a utility with 10 customers whose average costs and charge per customer is $250. Adding an eleventh customer will cost $400. The customer has an alternative to utility service: a solar cell that costs $300 for equivalent service. The utility, however, follows its previous policy of averaging costs, and now charges each of the eleven customers $264. The new customer forgoes the solar cell. Was that the right decision for the economy as a whole? Should $400 of scarce resources have been expended when $300 would have done the job?

To summarize the problem of the regulator: if a utility sets rates to cover marginal or incremental costs, consumers would be encouraged to promote economic efficiency. Depending on whether incremental costs were higher or lower than total costs, the utility might lose money, earn a return too low by legal regulatory standards, or earn too high a return. The present regulatory system may be keeping price too low for economic efficiency and may thereby be encouraging demand, or the system may be keeping price too high for economic efficiency.

Marginal or Incremental Costs

Let us briefly review the meaning of marginal and incremental costs to utilities. The short term cost curve of an ordinary business might look like that of Figure 20-1:

Units of Output	Fixed Costs	Variable Costs	Total Costs
0	$1.00	$0.00	$1.00
1	1.00	0.50	1.50
2	1.00	0.90	1.90
3	1.00	1.20	2.20
4	1.00	1.60	2.60
5	1.00	2.10	3.10
6	1.00	2.80	3.80

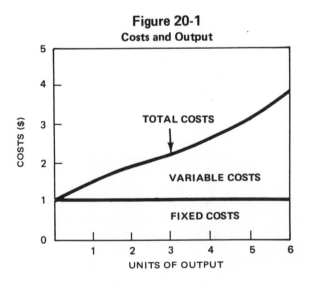

Figure 20-1
Costs and Output

On a per-unit basis, the curves would be (Figure 20-2):

Units of Output	Total Costs	Average Cost	Marginal Cost
0	$1.00	—	—
1	1.50	1.50	0.50
2	1.90	0.95	0.40
3	2.20	0.733	0.30
4	2.60	0.65	0.40
5	3.10	0.62	0.50
6	3.80	0.633	0.70

Figure 20-2
Average and Marginal Costs

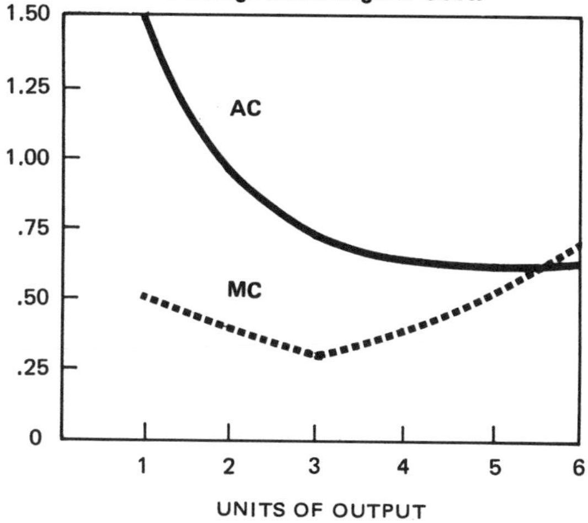

After a certain point marginal cost (MC) rises above average cost (AC). If the product can be sold for marginal cost at a point where MC is greater than AC, the company makes a profit as can be seen in Figure 20-2.

The cost curve to a utility for which most short run costs are fixed (the utility must spend money to maintain the huge plant whether the plant is used or not) might be as shown in Figure 20-3.

Units of Output	Fixed Costs	Variable Costs	Total Costs
0	$5.00	$0.00	$5.00
1	5.00	0.40	5.40
2	5.00	0.70	5.70
3	5.00	0.90	5.90
4	5.00	1.10	6.10
5	5.00	1.30	6.30
6	5.00	1.50	6.50

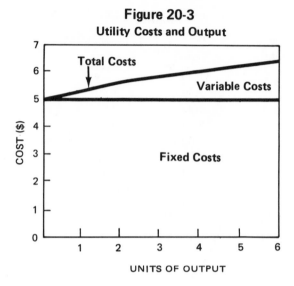

Figure 20-3
Utility Costs and Output

On a per unit basis, the curves would be:

Units of Output	Total Costs	Average Costs	Marginal Costs
0	$5.00	—	—
1	5.40	$5.40	$0.40
2	5.70	2.85	0.30
3	5.90	1.967	0.20
4	6.10	1.525	0.20
5	6.30	1.26	0.20
6	6.50	1.083	0.20

Clark, in his study of overhead costs, made the point that a utility cannot cover its expenses if it charges marginal costs when the average cost curve is declining. Figure 20-4 illustrates that problem.[55] For a strict marginalist the solution would be to charge marginal cost, and let the loss be made up indirectly by a Government subsidy to the private company, or directly by means of socializing the utility.

Marginalists currently active in the utility arena take a more practical view. Rates cannot be frequently changed. Customers cannot make long term plans (put into service new machines, air conditioners, build structures with a different design, determine work shifts, or decide on a plant site) when the only price signals they receive are short term fluctuations. Rather than worrying about short run marginal costs, say the new marginalists, long run incremental costs should be examined. How much new plant will be required to meet the growth in demand expected for the next few years? How much will it cost to produce the output of those plants? Are current

Figure 20-4
Utility Costs Per Unit and Output

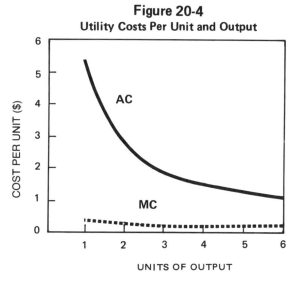

UNITS OF OUTPUT

rates sufficiently high to cover those new costs? If not, should rates be raised to cover those new costs, so that users understand what they will have to pay for service if they continue to increase usage? One could argue that part or all of the increase in demand is attributable to new customers. Why should old customers pay the higher costs? The answer is that the current customer does not own the utility plant and has no proprietary right to its output over the right of new customers to service.

Incremental cost analysis is being used to develop some rate structures. It has not been welcomed by some utilities, customers who would lose by its introduction, regulators, or competitors of utilities. Incremental cost analysis brings problems as well as benefits:

1) Incremental costs may be difficult to measure, especially costs for a particular class of customer. (Probably true.)

2) It may be extremely expensive to install the meters necessary to measure usage in a way that is useful for incremental costs analysis. (True, but mass production would reduce costs.)

3) Competitors may object to incremental cost pricing if the utility's long run incremental costs are below the price charged by the competitor. (Protecting a competitor should not be a reason to delay action.)

4) Certain classes of customers would be inconvenienced or disadvantaged by incremental cost pricing. (On the other hand, certain customers would benefit. Should the decision be based on which group is most vocal?)

5) Marginal pricing of one product in an imperfect economy in which many other products are not priced at the margin may not bring about efficient allocation of resources. This is the problem associated with

the theory of second best. (At the same time, lack of perfection does not mean that better pricing is not superior to the present system.)

In short, marginal or incremental pricing is not problem free in the real world. If incremental costs are below average costs, even on a long term basis, who will pay the subsidy needed to keep the utility in business? If not, who should keep the extra profit if incremental is above average cost and pricing is based on incremental costs?

The Rate Structure

Service charges depend on the kind of utility, time of day, season, and kind of customer. In general, a utility seeks to cover three different kinds of costs: costs that change with the number of customers, fixed charges associated with the utility plant (which must be covered whether customers are buying a lot of service or not), and variable costs that are incurred by providing a certain quantity of service. In the case of gas and electric utilities, the charge for variable costs usually includes a surcharge for changes in fuel and purchased gas expenses. The tariff schedule does not always spell out the three parts of the charge although the rates have been developed on a three part basis. Often the customer and fixed charge are combined.

The charge for customer costs covers the expense of billing, meter reading, and accounting, as well as the capital costs associated with investments in meters, service connections and some distribution facilities. The capacity or demand charge pays the fixed costs of the utility plant, including those operating expenses that do not vary with production of power. Customers may not always be using the utility plant, but they want that plant to be available to serve them at any time and, therefore, pay for that availability. Deciding how much plant should be allocated to a particular customer or group of customers is not simple. Generally, the key to allocation is the customer group's maximum demand on the plant at a particular time. For instance, all four of the electric company's generators are in use for the full day, two of them supplying residential customers and two supplying industrial customers. Half the capacity charges can be charged to the industrial customers and half to the residential. But what if plant is not utilized evenly all day? Perhaps the industrial customers need two of the generators only during the night, at a time when the residential customers are not taking any electricity. During the day, residential customers require all four generators. One could argue that none of the plant had to be built to meet industrial demand, and all of it had to be built to meet residential demand. Therefore, all capacity costs should be borne by the residential customers. So far, few regulatory agencies have accepted that kind of analysis. They might argue that the industrial customers receive benefits from the plant and should pay some of the capacity costs. Conceivably, the plant would not have been built at all if it could only serve the industrial load.

That kind of analysis is applied when constructing time-of-day, peak load, or long run incremental cost tariff schedules. Consider the case of a utility that has two classes of customers. One takes the same amount of service throughout the day. The second class takes the same amount of service for most of the day, except during peak hours when it takes a substantial amount of extra service. The utility serves the steady demand with efficient, base load plants. It serves the peak demand with another kind of plant. Both total capacity and demand at peak are 4KW, as seen in Figure 20-5.

Figure 20-5
PEAK LOAD AND CAPACITY

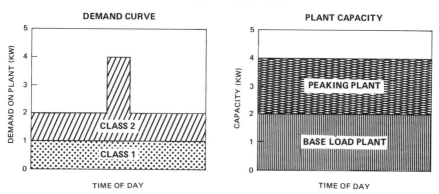

Because both classes equally share the base load plant, each class should pay the utility for that plant. Who should pay the utility for the peaking plant? The obvious answer would be the Class 2 customer, who is responsible for the peak. But is that really what should be done? If the Class 1 customer reduced usage at the peak hour, less peaking plant would be required.

Keep in mind that a lot of confusion exists about the purpose of pricing that attempts to assign costs based on peak load responsibilities. The purpose is not necessarily to reduce demand during peak periods (although the pricing may have that effect), but to allocate costs so that those responsible for the peak demand pay the costs associated with it. In long run incremental cost pricing, capacity charges might be set on the basis of estimates of the costs of planned capacity additions.

Some utilities have allocated capacity charges on the basis of noncoincident maximum demand. For instance, five customers (A, B, C, D, E) take 3,1,6,3, and 2 units of demand at their respective maximum times of usage. The utility's capacity costs are $15. If costs are apportioned by maximum non-coincident demand, the customers would pay $3, $1, $6, $3 and $2. What if the demand pattern and capacity were as shown in Figure 20-6?

Figure 20-6
NONCOINCIDENTAL DEMAND AND CAPACITY

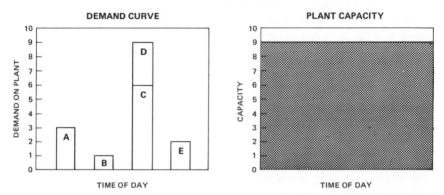

Clearly, most of the plant had to be built to meet the needs of customers C and D. The others are off-peak customers. The entire plant would have been built to meet the needs of C and D and those two customers should bear most (some would argue all) of the capacity costs, not just 9/15 of the costs. In short, the noncoincident maximum load method is of dubious value in allocating capacity costs.

The third method looks at average and excess demand. Part of the fixed costs are allocated by the average loads of customers. The balance of the fixed costs are allocated by how much capacity over the average is required by the customer.

Variable Costs

Variable costs associated with usage are easier to measure if the utility produces a physical output such as a kilowatt-hour of electricity or a thousand cubic feet of gas. For instance, a certain amount of fuel must be burned to produce a kilowatt-hour. After a certain number of hours of production, the generator must be taken down for maintenance and repairs. A certain number of employees are required to keep the generator running. Admittedly, every cost cannot be quantified precisely, but some vary directly with production and some do not. In addition, costs vary with the time and conditions of production. Off-peak power might be produced by the utility's low cost nuclear power station, which is kept running all the time. Power demanded at 3:00 pm on a hot summer day, when the utility's capacity is taxed to its limit, might be produced, in part, by inefficient standby generators and expensively fueled peaking units. That difference in cost might be reflected in rates. A utility may attempt to charge the customer for those differences in costs either by means of generalized rates (such as seasonal ones) or by the actual metering of the time of usage.

The fuel adjustment clause add-on also varies with use. Its purpose is to protect the utility from sudden changes in fuel costs. Because fuel prices can change quickly and drastically, the utility could suffer if it had to wait for a general rate increase to recover the higher costs. Without a fuel adjustment clause, a utility might be requesting rate changes almost monthly. Recently, some regulators have argued that the automatic nature of the fuel clause pass-on provides utility managements with little incentive to control fuel costs. The concept of the fuel adjustment clause is under scrutiny, and a few regulatory agencies have made incentive arrangements to encourage efficient operating procedures.

The Rate Schedule

A utility must add all expenses and then determine a set of rates for a customer class. The schedules specify rates by time of year, sometimes by time of day, and may include special prices for customers that qualify for conservation, volume usage, or other discounts.

A large midwestern utility has this simple schedule for its residential customers:

Facilities charge —	$10.00 per month
Energy charge —	9.45¢ per kwh in summer season
	5.00¢ per kwh in balance of year
Fuel cost adjustment —	Energy charge is adjusted for
	changes in fuel cost to utility

A southern utility has a more complicated residential bill:

Basic facilities charge —	$7.54 per month
Energy charge —	
First 350 kwh per month	6.54¢ per kwh
Next 950 kwh per month	7.33¢ per kwh
All usage over 1300	
kwh per month	7.18¢ per kwh (July-Oct.)
	6.62¢ per kwh (Nov.-June)

The fuel adjustment rider is included in the energy charge. Furthermore, customers with a qualifying electric water heater pay only 7.19¢ for energy in the second price block (next 950 kwh per month).

Another southern utility has these rates for residential customers:

Basic customer charge —	$6.25 per month
Kwh charge —	
First 800 kwh	5.26¢ per kwh
Excess over 800 kwh	6.09¢ per kwh (June-Sept.)
	3.73¢ per kwh (Oct.-May)
Fuel charge rider —	1.47¢ per kwh

The fuel charge rider varies with the cost of fuel to the utility.

Commercial and small industrial customers may pay on a different basis. The tariff will specify voltage, type of motors allowed and other technical matters. The tariff determines the electric bill by measuring demand in kilowatts (usually the maximum demand in the past 12 months) and consumption in kilowatt-hours. The monthly schedule for one utility is:

Basic facilities charge —	$10.00
Demand charge —	
First 30 kw	No charge
Over 30 kw	$3.30 per kw
Energy charge for first 125 kwh per kw billing demand per month —	
First 3,000 kwh	9.12¢ per kwh
Next 87,000 kwh	4.67¢ per kwh
All consumption over 90,000 kwh	3.74¢ per kwh
Energy charge for next 275 kwh per kw billing demand per month —	
First 6,000 kwh	6.36¢ per kwh
Next 95,000 kwh	4.76¢ per kwh
All consumption over 101,000 kwh	4.61¢ per kwh
Energy charge for over 400 kwh per kw billing demand per month —	
All kwh	4.28¢ per kwh

In addition, the company adds or subtracts a fuel adjustment charge. For the tariff, if demand is 1,000 kw and consumption is 100,000 kwh, the bill will be:

Facilities charge	$ 10.00
Demand charge	3201.00*
Energy charge	7921.50**

* (1,000 kw - 30 kw) × $3.30
** Calculated at the first schedule because
   customer takes less than 125 kwh per kw.

3,000 kwh @ 9.12¢	$ 273.60
87,000 kwh @ 4.67¢	4062.90
10,000 kwh @ 3.74¢	374.00
Total energy charge	7921.50

Rate schedules for industrial customers are complex. The utility must keep in service large amounts of plant to meet the needs of the industrial customer. The customer must pay the fixed charges on that plant, and that rate schedule should encourage the customers to maintain a high load factor (the relationship of average to peak demand). The schedule usually specifies the voltage at which the service is taken, too. One utility has the following industrial tariff:

Facilities charge per month
based on customer's delivery
voltage of —

Below 2.4 kv	$ 50.00
2.4 kv to 12.47 kv	200.00
Above 12.47 kv	600.00

Monthly demand charge per kw of maximum on-peak demand	Delivery 138, 69 and 34.5	Voltage (kv) 12.47 and below
Summer	$15.41/kw	$18.86/kw
Up to 50% of customer contract capacity (winter)	5.50	5.50
In excess of 50% of customer contract capacity (winter)	3.00	3.00
Energy charges for all kwh	4.00¢	4.10¢

In addition, the utility's tariff has a 1.30¢ per kwh energy credit for kwh taken during designated off peak periods.

In the industrial tariff schedules that follow, demand is measured in kilovolt amperes (KVA), a measure of apparent power, or in KW, but the basic idea behind the monthly tariff is the same.

	Nominal Service Voltage—Kilovolts			
	4.16-12.47	23-34.5	69	138
Demand Charge (per KVA):				
First 1,000 KVA	$6.65	$6.55	$6.40	$6.15
Next 29,000 KVA	$6.55	$6.45	$6.35	$6.00
Additional KVA	$5.60	$5.30	$5.10	$4.90
Energy Charge (per KWH):				
First 300 KWH/KVA				
Demand	1.275¢	1.187¢	1.187¢	1.154¢
Additional KWH (per KWH)	.670¢	.600¢	.600¢	.575¢
Customer Charge:	$200	$500	$1,500	$2,500

The demand charge is usually based on the customer's peak demand. In the above schedule, in the first voltage category, let us assume that the peak demand is 1,000 KVA and the 1,000 KVA equals 1,000 KW, for simplicity. The demand charge will be 1,000 × $6.65 or $6,650. Usage will be 350,000 KWH in the month. The first energy block will be 300,000 KWH (300 hours of usage times 1,000 KW) which will cost 300,000 × $0.01275 or $3,825. The balance, or 50,000 KWH, will cost 50,000 × $0.00670 or $335. In addition, the customer will pay a $200 customer charge plus the fuel adjustment charge.

Another major utility finally reformed its monthly industrial power tariff to simplify it as follows (based on service at 138 KV):

Customer Charge	$4,757 per month
Demand Charge	$6.15 per KVA at customer's peak
Energy Charge	$0.0037 per KWH
Fuel Adjustment Surcharge	$0.017749 per KWH

The fuel surcharge is shown as of a particular month and it will change from month to month. In this instance, the customer also shows a 1,000 KVA peak (which we will let equal 1,000 KW) and takes 350,000 KWH in the month. The customer charge is $4,757 and the demand charge is $6,150, the energy charge is $1,295 and the fuel surcharge is $6,212.15.

Price Differentials

The price of energy and other vital utility services is rising. Presumably many consumers need those services, but have difficulty paying for even a small amount of service. Some regulators have changed the rate structure so that the consumer can buy a limited (lifeline) amount of service at a low price. Once usage exceeds the lifeline amount, the price rises. That is, rates per unit go up rather than down with greater usage. When lifeline rates are applied to all customers, wealthy apartment dwellers and owners of occasionally used ski lodges as well as the poor can benefit. The loss of revenue from the low initial cost of service must be made up either by higher rates to big residential users or by higher rates to industrial customers.

As a final point about rates to different classes of customers, the key question is not how much the customer group pays per unit of output, but rather what rate of return the customer group's business provides to the utility. It may be that as a result of the time or kind of usage, industrial business brings in a 9% return when the price averages 2¢ for each unit taken, and the residential customer provides only a 6% return when his price is 4¢ a unit. Leveling the price differentials between industrial and residential customers might eliminate the supposed unfairness of a situation in which two groups pay different prices for the same product. But that attitude considers only one dimension of demand: quantity. It does not consider that what is really demanded is capacity and quantity at particular times. Residential and industrial customers do not get the same service even if they take the same number of units of service (in terms of kilowatt-hours, thousands of cubic feet, or number of phone calls). Price leveling might be more discriminatory than the present system and might also bring about misallocation of economic resources.

Conclusion

Once the total revenue has been decided, a rate structure of prices to customer groups must be designed to produce the required amount of revenue. Doing so is a complicated matter and will become more complicated with the introduction of new economic and social theories.

Chapter 21

Summary

Private enterprise, free from the interference of the sovereign power, never existed within the range of recorded history—not in ancient times, not in the medieval ages, nor in Puritan New England, nor in the California vigilante days.[56]

Arthur Stone Dewing

The concept of the regulated business preceded the formation of the industries that are currently classified as utilities. An industry does not have to be a natural monopoly to be regulated. The idea of the natural monopoly is both static and dubious. As technology changes, what may have been a monopoly at one time becomes subject to competition. If an industry that was regulated to protect the consumer continues to be rigidly regulated after the onset of competition, the regulation may end up protecting the competitor because the former monopolist is controlled by a regulatory strait jacket that prevents response to the new situation. Even without considering technological change, the consumer can find some substitutes for some of the natural monopoly's services: oil and gas vs. electric heating, installation of insulation vs. purchase of more fuel, self generation vs. central station power, telephone vs. telegraph or mail. If pricing of utility services better reflected costs, more competitors might enter the field.

In theory, the regulatory process protects the consumer from the natural monopoly by simulating the results of a competitive environment. The price control system that has resulted does not seem to have achieved that goal. Usually, prices are set on the basis of average historical costs. In the late 1950s and early 1960s, regulators may have allowed returns to rise above the cost of capital. Since 1965 regulators may have been unwilling to allow companies to earn their costs of capital.

The rate case, in which costs are set, serves financial, legal, economic, and political purposes. Despite the elaborate nature of the testimony, and the length of some decisions, handing down a rate of return is not a scientific process. The investor in utilities (and the consumer) must rely on the intelligence and the good will of the regulators.

Finally, the rate structure may be designed to ration services, to bring about redistribution of wealth, to promote economic efficiency, to serve social policies, or just to assure that each customer group provides a certain rate of return.

One could argue that public utility regulation, in its current form, keeps down the cost of service to certain groups of customers, prevents utilities from actually earning a fair return, encourages the wasteful use of energy, misallocates economic resources, discourages technological innovation and reduces incentives to managerial efficiency.

In short, public utility regulation has a hodgepodge of goals and some unfortunate side effects. Regulation could be better. Sometimes it is a wonder that regulation works at all.

Notes

[1]Joe S. Bain, *Industrial Organization* (New York: John Wiley & Sons, Inc., 1959), p. 589.

[2]94 US 113 (1877).

[3]Henry Steele Commager, ed., *Documents of American History* (N.Y.: Appleton-Century-Crofts, Inc., 1949), p. 147.

[4]Francis X. Welch, *Cases and Text on Public Utility Regulation, Revised Edition* (Washington, D.C.: Public Utilities Reports, Inc., 1968), p. 6.

[5]Welch, *op. cit.*, p. 7.

[6]Welch, *op. cit.*, p. 8.

[7]Welch, *op. cit.*, pp. 10-11.

[8]Welch, *op. cit.*, p. 11.

[9]Bastard v Bastard, Kings Bench, 2 Shower, 82. Cited in Welch, *op. cit.*, p. 242.

[10]169 US 466.

[11]In an 1886 decision, *Stone v Farmers' Loan and Trust Co.* (116 US 307), the Supreme Court moved away from Munn, asserting that the courts could review rates set by a legislature. It was not until *Smyth v Ames*, though, that the court laid out standards of reasonableness for fixing rates.

[12]Welch, *op. cit.*, p. 279.

[13]*Ibid.*

[14]*Missouri ex rel. Southwestern Bell Telephone Co. v Missouri Public Service Commission*, 262 US 276.

[15]Welch, *op. cit.*, pp. 285-292.

[16]*Bluefield Water Works & Improv. Co. v West Va. Public Service Commission*, 262 US 679.

[17]272 US 400.

[18]Clair Wilcox, *Public Policies Toward Business, Revised Edition* (Homewood, Ill.: Richard D. Irwin, Inc., 1960), p. 570.

[19] 262 US 679, 693.

[20]*Federal Power Commission v Hope Natural Gas Co.*, 320 US 591.

[21]Welch, *op. cit.*, pp. 301-302.

[22]Arthur Stone Dewing, *The Financial Policy of Corporations* (New York: The Ronald Press Co., 1953), pp. 309-310.

[23]Bain, *op. cit.*, p. 590.

[24]James C. Bonbright, *Principles of Public Utility Rates* (New York: Columbia University Press, 1961), p. 9.

[25]Bonbright, *op. cit.*, p. 13.

[26]*Ibid.*

[27]Bonbright, *op. cit.*, pp. 14-15.

[28]Clair Wilcox, *op. cit.*, p. 540.

[29]Alfred E. Kahn, *The Economics of Regulation: Principles and Institutions* (New York: John Wiley & Sons, Inc., 1970). Volume I, p. 20.

[30]Bonbright, *op. cit.*, p. 18.

[31]Welch, *op. cit.*, p. 478.

[32]*New England Telephone and Telegraph Company v Maine Public Utilities Commission* (390 A 2d 8, June 28, 1978).

[33]This situation is similar to that of a company seeking a higher depreciation rate. The regulators do not want to impose unnecessarily high costs on current customers and ignore the possibility that future customers might have to pay more for service because current customers did not pay their fair share of depreciation expenses. In a recent case, the Federal Energy Regulatory Commission took such an approach: "For nuclear production plant, the company requested a negative 10% salvage factor. . . . Since the widespread growth of nuclear generating facilities is a relatively recent occurrence, there is little hard evidence on which to establish a proper salvage rate. . . . Pending further developments . . . we shall . . . base the depreciation, expense . . . on a zero salvage factor, without prejudice to a redetermination of this item when information becomes available." (Federal Energy Regulatory Commission, *Re Carolina Power & Light Co.*, Opinion No. 19, Docket No. ER 76-495, August 2, 1978. *Public Utilities Reports*, 26 PUR4th—No. 1, January 5, 1979, p. 78.) Presumably, the FERC planned to wait until the plant is decommissioned, at which time there should be hard evidence. Can we believe that future customers will willingly pay the costs derived from our use of power? It is more realistic to expect unrecovered current costs to be borne by the company than by future consumers.

[34]Arthur Andersen & Co., *Return Allowed in Public Utility Rate Cases 1960 Edition*, first page of 1929 cases, no page number.

[35]66 PUR (NS) 212.

[36]Welch, *op. cit.*, p. 301.

[37]Richard H. Adelaar and Leonard S. Hyman. "The Comparable Earnings Approach as a Useful Tool in Utility Regulation." *Public Utilities Fortnightly*, Vol. 87, No. 5, March 4, 1971.

[38]In Adelaar and Hyman, *op. cit.*, the authors eliminated from the sample regulated industries, industries with high concentration ratios, and two other small industries. The remaining sample consisted of 32 S&P industry groups comprising 191 major firms. The authors found that rate of growth in sales was an important determinant of rate of return. Because the company's demand for capital is growing faster than capital markets as a whole, the company must pay more for capital to induce portfolio managers to take the added risk of having a large percentage of their portfolios in a single security. The article also argued that to compete successfully in capital markets faster-growing utilities must be allowed higher returns than slower-growing utilities. In another article (Leonard S. Hyman, "Utility Stocks in 1967-72: A Tale of Woe," *Public Utilities Fortnightly*, Vol. 93, No. 5, Feb. 28, 1974), the author indicated that the total return on a utility stock investment might have been reduced when the utility's need for new equity capital was high.

[39]Adelaar and Hyman, *op. cit.*, p. 31.

[40]The analysis is based on Adelaar and Hyman, *op. cit.* That analysis, in turn, is derived from "Capital Equipment Analysis: The Required Rate of Profit" by Myron J. Gordon and Eli Shapiro, in Ezra Solomon (ed.), *The Management of Corporate Capital* (New York: The Free Press of Glencoe, 1959), pp. 114-145.

[41]Adelaar and Hyman, *op. cit.*, p. 33.

[42]Rhode Island Public Utilities Commission, Re *Blackstone Valley Electric Company*, Docket No. 1289, February 17, 1978. *Public Utilities Reports*, September 15, 1978, p. 318.

[43]Arkansas Public Service Commission, *In the matter of the application of Southwestern Electric Power Company for a general rate increase*, Docket No. U-2793, February 3, 1978.

[44]For two easy-to-read (and unsympathetic) analyses of CAPM, see Robert F. Vandell and James K. Malernee, "The Capital Asset Pricing Model and Utility Equity Returns", *Public Utilities Fortnightly*, July 6, 1978, and Gerald J. Glassman, "Discounted Cash Flow versus the Capital Asset Pricing Model (Is g Better Than b?)", *Public Utilities Fortnightly*, September 14, 1978.

[45]Vandell and Malernee, *op. cit.*, p. 27.

[46]Welch, *op. cit.*, p. 486.

[47]Bonbright, *op. cit.*, p. 249.

[48]Kahn, *op. cit.*, pp. 49-50, Vol. I.

[49]Leonard S. Hyman, "Utility Stocks in 1967-72: A Tale of Woe," *Public Utilities Fortnightly*, February 28, 1974; "Market to Book Ratio: Statistical Confirmation or Aberration?," *Public Utilities Fortnightly*, December 19, 1979.

[50]Ambrose Bierce, *The Devil's Dictionary* (New York: Dover Publications, Inc., 1958), p. 27.

[51]Bonbright, *op. cit.*, p. 254.

[52]J. Maurice Clark, *Studies in the Economics of Overhead Costs* (Chicago: University of Chicago Press, 1923, twelfth impression, 1962), p. 324.

[53]Paul Rodgers, J. Edward Smith, Jr. and Russell J. Profozich, *Current Issues in Electric Utility Rate Setting* (Washington, D.C.: National Association of Regulatory Utility Commissioners, 1976) p. A-67.

[54]Bonbright, *op. cit.*, pp. 76-77.

[55]J. M. Clark, *op. cit.* The analysis, of course, is far more complicated than that outlined above.

[56]Arthur Stone Dewing, *op. cit.*, p. 312, footnote e.

Part Five
Financial Structure

Chapter 22

The Basics

Regulation of rates requires accounting information, and sound regulation requires sound accounting. . . .[1]

Haskins & Sells

The financial structure of the electric utility industry is based on certain fundamental tenets, which are:

1) The electric utility industry is capital intensive.

2) The industry is a natural monopoly.

3) The business risk to shareholders in the competitive industry should be replaced by financial risk to shareholders in the regulated monopoly.

Capital Intensity

Everyone knows that the industry is capital intensive, that it takes three or four dollars of plant to produce one dollar of revenue. Because the customer should not be expected to pay for that much capital equipment in a short time, the cost of the plant is written off over many years. All of that is accepted as natural. Unfortunately, the naturalness is not that clear, and may be, in part, a result of the history of the industry and how people made money in it.

When the industry began, it was controlled by the manufacturing companies. The real money was made from the sale, engineering and financing of equipment, not from the sale of electricity. The industry's formative years were spent developing massive investments. Policy toward investment was basically unchanged until the late 1970s.

The regulatory process also affects capital intensity. After all, we are looking at a ratio determined by dividing capital by revenue. Therefore, if revenue can be lowered, the ratio rises. Most regulators see their job as that of keeping down the revenue that the company receives. On the other hand, the utility gets paid a return on capital invested. Therefore, according to some academics[2], the management has every reason to expand the capital invested in the business, because the more capital that is invested, the higher the income of the utility. That argument is of dubious validity nowadays, when incremental cost of capital may be greater than incremental return on investment, but it could explain some management decisions of the past. In other words, managements may have tried to enlarge the numerator and the regulators to decrease the denominator, thereby raising the capital intensity of the business.

The belief that the industry is capital intensive also derives from financing policies of the past, when operating utilities were sold at inflated prices to holding companies. Because holding companies had to earn a profitable return on those inflated investments, the amount needed to run an electric company became even higher. Just as the original builders of electric utilities made their profits from selling equipment, many of the organizers that followed made their money from the engineering fees charged to captive companies and from the sale of the utility's securities. Fees and commissions both escalated with the need to build and to raise money.

The low cost of money that prevailed for much of this century also encouraged capital intensive solutions. If the company could borrow cheaply to build a big machine, why not do so? And, it should be added, the big machine often was much more efficient than the smaller one. If money costs were low, it might be worthwhile to build a machine much larger than was actually required, because the large machine could operate so efficiently that the resulting savings offset the extra cost of borrowing more money than would have been needed to build a smaller unit. Thus, a combination of economies of scale and low cost of capital may have encouraged electric utilities to add more investment than was required.

Finally, one might argue that the industry overbuilt to produce operating economies that would prevent others from entering the business and that would drive out non-central station power.

The point of the discussion is not to deny that the industry requires a great deal of capital to produce a dollar of revenue, but to assert that the industry's capital intensity should not be accepted as completely natural.

Capital intensity results, in part, from regulation, monetary policies, economies of scale, greed of promoters, and other factors. Inertia probably carried the day for years after capital intensity ceased to be a virtue. Now that money costs are high, however, and new equipment may not be providing economies of scale, the industry is trying to reduce the need for capital in the business. Both investors and consumers may be beneficiaries.

Financial Risk

Standard theory holds that the business of the utility as a natural monopoly is not as risky as the business of a company in a competitive industry. Therefore, the utility can take greater financial risks (i.e., borrow more money) than the average industrial firm.[3] Again we can ask whether that statement developed from self-evident characteristics of the industry, or as a rationalization for other practices. For example, in the early days of the industry, operating utilities were not especially profitable. They did not have cash to spare. Consequently, some promoters and vendors of equipment accepted company bonds in lieu of cash, thereby increasing the amount of debt in the capitalization. In the days of the holding companies, managements attempted to assure their control by means of ownership of a large percentage of the stock of the parent holding company. To minimize the amount of investment needed to control the holding company empire, the constituent companies financed their capital needs as much as possible by sale of debt. Another possibility is that because the utility industry tended not to be highly profitable, capital was leveraged to bring return on equity up to acceptable levels. Whatever the origins of the practice, the electric utility industry raises almost two-thirds of its capital by the sale of senior securities (debt and preferred stock). Even more remarkable, those financing practices have not changed for decades, although upheavals in the capital markets have diminished the advantages of those financial policies.

Natural Monopoly

Few persons believe that electric utilities have an impregnable monopoly in the energy market. After all, natural gas, oil, wind, and the sun perform some of the same functions as electricity. Furthermore, large users of electricity can produce some or all of their own power when the price of the utility's power rises excessively. Although we seldom speak of competition among utilities, competition exists in the sense that new customers for whom the cost of energy is important might locate in the service territory of a utility with favorable rates.

In discussing the financial position and the ability of a utility to increase or to reduce debt, analysts generally assume that the utility industry will remain a monopoly: that customers can always be forced to pay whatever price is necessary to provide the utility with the revenues to meet financial obligations. If a utility is not collecting sufficient revenue to set aside an adequate reserve for depreciation, future rate payers can be forced to make up the deficiency. The same comment applies to taxes whose payments are deferred. Moreover, if money is not set aside to assure the repayment of debt at maturity, the utility can sell new debt to pay off a maturing issue. The assumption is that the utility will have no difficulty borrowing to meet its needs, because a natural monopoly that provides an essential service will always be able to borrow money.

That line of argument is not necessarily correct. At some time in the future, alternatives to central station power could develop. When that happens, electric utilities will be unable to charge more than the price of the alternative energy source. The price set may be below the amount that the electric utility needs to cover depreciation charges on plant that has not been fully written off, or may be below the price needed to provide the utility with sufficient revenue to pay its debts or to pay deferred income taxes. If such a situation were to occur, the utility would no longer be a monopoly. With every rate increase, customers could be lost to alternative energy sources. The potential for competition may or may not develop in the immediate future. Regulators, however, do not even seem to consider the possibility and, as a result, companies find themselves financing and accounting as if nothing could disturb their monopoly.

How to Evaluate the Finances of the Industry

We will examine the industry's finances by means of three financial statements: the balance sheet, the statement of income and retained earnings, and the statement of sources and use of funds. Then, we will examine the reaction of the financial markets to the state of the industry and will consider whether past trends indicate the future.

Chapter 23

The Statement of Income and Retained Earnings

Many investors prefer companies showing a growth rate at least equal to the industry trend. However, such growth is valueless unless it can be translated into increasing investment and earnings per share.[4]

Badger, Torgerson and Guthmann

The income statement covers a specific period and shows the amount of money that customers have been charged for services within that period (revenues) and the costs that have been incurred by the firm to provide those services (expenses). The difference between revenue and expense is the profit or net income that is left for the owners of the business. Some of the income is paid to owners in the form of dividends. The rest is kept by the firm for use in the business (retained earnings). Although that sounds simple, how to calculate both revenues and expenses can be a matter for disputes. Accounting procedures that tend to understate revenues or to overstate expenses are "conservative." Procedures that tend to overstate revenues and to understate expenses are "liberal." In addition to annual statements, most companies provide income statements on a quarterly basis, and some even publish monthly statements of income.

The following is an example of a standard income statement for an industrial concern:

Sales (revenues)	$1,000
Cost of sales (expenses directly associated with production of product)	500
Depreciation (wear and tear on machinery)	100
Interest (on borrowed money)	100
Total Expenses	700
Pretax income	300
Income taxes	150
Net income (profit)	$ 150

Income statements for utilities have been recast for regulatory purposes as follows:

Revenues	$1,000
Operating Expenses:	
Production, maintenance, etc.	500
Depreciation	100
Income Taxes	150
Total operating expenses	750
Operating income	250
Interest expense	100
Net income	$ 150

The difference exists because the utility regulator is concerned with the return on capital—the interest paid to creditors of the firm and the profits available to stockholders. In our simplified statement, operating income, which is after deduction of taxes but before interest expense, represents the income available to pay the owners of the capital that has been invested in the business.

The actual income statement is more complicated, as can be seen in the following example:

Statement of Income

(thousands of dollars)

			Year Ended December 31,	
Line			1987	1988
1.	*Operating Revenue*		$500,000	$550,000
2.	*Operating Expenses*			
3.	Operation:			
4.		Fuel	200,000	280,000
5.		Purchased & interchanged power	40,000	(25,000)
6.		Other	50,000	60,000
7.		Total Operation	290,000	315,000
8.		Maintenance	40,000	50,000
9.		Depreciation	35,000	40,000

Statement of Income—Continued

(thousands of dollars)

Line		Year Ended December 31, 1987	1988
10.	Income taxes—		
10a.	Current	25,000	25,000
10b.	Deferred	20,000	20,000
11.	Other taxes	30,000	31,000
12.	Total Operating Expenses	$440,000	$481,000
13.	*Operating Income*	60,000	69,000
14.	Other Income	1,000	1,000
15.	Allowance for other funds used during construction	3,000	4,000
16.	*Income Before Interest Charges*	64,000	74,000
17.	*Interest Charges*		
18.	Interest on long-term debt	23,000	28,000
19.	Other interest	4,000	4,000
20.	Allowance for borrowed funds used during construction	(5,000)	(6,000)
21.	Net interest charges	22,000	26,000
22.	*Net Income*	42,000	48,000
23.	Preferred Dividends	8,000	8,000
24.	Balance Available for Common Stock	34,000	40,000
25.	Average Shares Outstanding During Year	9,000	10,000
26.	Earnings Per Average Common Shares Outstanding	$3.78	$4.00
	Statement of Retained Earnings		
27.	Balance, Beginning of Year	138,000	150,000
	Add:		
28.	Net Income after dividends on Preferred Stock	34,000	40,000
29.	Total	172,000	190,000
	Deduct:		
30.	Cash dividends on Common Stock	22,000	24,000
31.	Balance, End of Year	$150,000	$166,000

The utility sells a certain amount of electricity in the year at particular prices. Receipts from customers produce *Operating Revenue* (line 1).

The costs of paying employees, suppliers, and taxes—expenses involved in producing the electricity—are called *Operating Expenses* (line 2). Expenses shown, under the title *Operation* (line 3), are outlays directly related to producing and transmitting the electricity. The major item is almost always *Fuel* (line 4) that is burned in the boiler to generate the electricity. Sometimes a utility buys power from other utilities, because it does not have a generator in operation or because the power produced by the other utility is cheaper. That power is *Purchased and Interchanged Power* (line 5). At times, the utility sells power to other electric companies. Such interchange power is shown (in parentheses) as a subtraction from expenses. *Other* expenses associated with operations (line 6) includes salaries and miscellaneous items. Total operating expenses are shown on line 7.

Maintenance Expenses (small repairs and regular overhauls of equipment) are shown on line 8. Plant and equipment wears out over time or becomes obsolete and eventually must be replaced by more modern and efficient equipment. The company estimates how long the equipment is expected to last and spreads the cost of the purchase over the productive life of the asset. For example, if a machine costs $100,000 and will last for 20 years, the company will show an expense of $5,000 (one-twentieth of the purchase price) each year. That expense is called *Depreciation* (line 9). Unlike other expenses, depreciation does not entail paying out money. On the contrary, money is collected and set aside, either to pay for a new machine when the old one wears out, or to pay off debts incurred when the machine was purchased, or even to buy new assets.

Income Taxes (line 10) are paid to Federal, state and local governments by the corporation. The tax figure does not always represent taxes actually paid in the year. *Current* taxes (line 10a) are those that are to be paid quickly. Often, the utility sets aside money for taxes to be paid at a future date and includes those *Deferred* taxes (line 10b) in the total of income taxes. Like depreciation, deferred taxes do not represent a cash outlay.

Other Taxes (line 11) includes taxes on real estate and on the company's revenues and are generally levied by state and local governments.

The total of all operating expenses (line 12) is subtracted from revenue, leaving *Operating Income* (line 13).

Other Income (line 14) includes the income from various subsidiary companies, interest earned on investments, income tax credits and a variety of other items.

The allowance for funds used during construction (AFUDC) is split into two parts: *Allowance for Other Funds Used During Construction* (line 15) and *Allowance for Borrowed Funds Used During Construction* (line 20). Let us start by understanding the concept behind AFUDC.

A utility may have a substantial amount of money tied up for years in a facility under construction. That money had to be raised by means of borrowing or by sale of stock. The utility pays interest on borrowed money, and stockholders also expect a return on their investment even though the plant is not yet operating. How can the utility recover those costs involved in raising money to build the power plant? The answer, in many cases, is to add the cost of the money to the cost of the power plant. Once the plant is completed, the utility earns a return on the money used to pay suppliers of machinery, bricks, and construction services, plus a return on the money paid to the suppliers of capital. Furthermore, the utility will recover, by means of depreciation, all the costs of the plant, including the cost of capital.

AFUDC is a mechanism whereby the cost of money is added to the plant account on the balance sheet. The cost of money raised to build the power plant (AFUDC) is added to company income and thus increases the stockholders' equity shown on the right side of the balance sheet. Because the balance sheet must balance, under the double entry system, a similar sum is added to the plant account on the assets side of the balance sheet.

Money is raised either from stockholders or from creditors (lenders). The Federal Energy Regulatory Commission (FERC) has decided that the two sources should be separated. Therefore, the utility calculates the cost of money that has been borrowed to finance the project, the *Allowance for Borrowed Funds Used During Construction* (line 20). Then, if the project is not funded entirely by means of borrowing, the utility assigns a cost to the equity money that has been raised, usually basing the cost on the return on equity that was allowed in the last rate case. The cost of equity funds is the *Allowance for Other Funds Used During Construction* (line 15).

Accordingly, AFUDC serves two purposes. It allows the utility to recover costs of plant (by means of depreciation) and to earn a return on capital costs incurred while a facility is under construction. In addition, AFUDC removes from the income statement the effects of expenses that have nothing to do with operations for the current year.

The sum of Operating Income, Other Income, and Allowance for Other Funds Used During Construction is called *Income Before Interest Charges* (line 16) and is the income available to pay the owners of capital.

Interest Charges (line 17) are usually divided into *Interest on Long-Term Debt* (line 18) and *Other Interest* (line 19). The latter is usually interest on bank loans and on commercial paper.

After interest charges have been subtracted, *Net Income* (line 22) remains and the money is left for the owners of the business. All owners, however, are not equal. The owners of preferred stock must be paid fixed *Preferred Dividends* (line 23) before common stockholders are paid.

The *Balance Available for Common Stock* (line 24) is a residual. To calculate the income available per share of common stock, we must know how many shares are outstanding. The number of shares outstanding changes during the year as shares are repurchased or new shares are issued. Standard practice is to use *Average Shares Outstanding During the Year* (line 25) to calculate per share data.

When income available for all common stock is divided by the average number of shares of common outstanding during the year, *Earnings Per Average Common Share Outstanding* (line 26) results.

What happens to the income left after common stockholders have been paid? The *Net Income After Dividends on Preferred Stock* (line 28) is added to the *Balance of Retained Earnings at the Beginning of the Year* (line 27). From the total (shown on line 29), *Cash Dividends on Common Stock* (line 30) must be subtracted, leaving the *Balance at the End of the Year* (line 31).

In a number of recent rate orders, regulators decided not to implement the full amount of rate relief needed to cover the costs of a new facility, but rather to phase in the new facility. Part of the rate increase would be deferred to a future date, thereby reducing the increase needed in the first year. In the second year, a smaller part of the necessary revenue would be deferred, and the deferral would decline year by year until the revenues reached the required level. Then rates would be increased again to cover the revenues that should have been collected in the early years of the phase-in, but which were deferred to a later date. The usual income statement shows the expenses associated with the plant but revenues would not take into account the fact that some revenues due in the year are being put off into the future. Therefore, accountants needed to devise a new method of accounting, but the method might differ from company to company because few phase-ins are identical. Generally, the income statement will be adjusted through special items that add to income the value of the deferred revenues. That adjustment should be noted carefully, because it represents income that ought to be collected in the future, but might not be if circumstances turn against the utility.

Chapter 24

The Balance Sheet

Creditor, n. One of a tribe of savages dwelling beyond the Financial Straits and dreaded for their desolating incursions.[5]

Ambrose Bierce

The balance sheet shows the property and cash owned by a firm and the amounts owed to it (assets). The money that a firm owes and the source of the money used to purchase those assets (liabilities and capital) are also shown. Data are given as of the end of business on a given day—usually the end of the year or the end of an accounting period.

The balance sheet of an electric utility is similar to that of an industrial company except that industrial companies generally put current assets and liabilities at the top of the balance sheet.

Assets owned by the utility are shown on the left side (or top half) of the balance sheet.

Balance Sheet

Assets

	December 31,	
Line	1987	1988
	(Thousands)	
1. *Utility Plant*		
2. In service	$1,000,000	$1,160,000
3. Less depreciation	250,000	290,000
4. Net plant in service	750,000	870,000
5. Construction work in progress	100,000	120,000

6.	Net plant	850,000	990,000
7.	Other property, & investments	10,000	10,000
8.	*Current Assets*		
9.	Cash & temporary investments	5,000	6,000
10.	Accounts receivable	25,000	28,000
11.	Materials & supplies	50,000	55,000
12.	Total current assets	80,000	89,000
13.	Deferred Charges	20,000	20,000
14.	Total assets	$960,000	$1,109,000

Liabilities and Capital

		December 31,	
		1987	*1988*
15.	*Capitalization*		
16.	Common stock	115,000	171,000
17.	Retained earnings	150,000	166,000
18.	Preferred Stock	90,000	90,000
19.	Long term debt	400,000	480,000
20.	Total capitalization	755,000	907,000
21.	*Current Liabilities*		
22.	Accounts payable	25,000	20,000
23.	Accrued expenses	10,000	12,000
24.	Bank loans & commercial paper	40,000	20,000
25.	Long term debt payable in one year	30,000	30,000
26.	Total current liabilities	105,000	82,000
27.	Deferred Credits	100,000	120,000
28.	Total liabilities and Capitalization	$960,000	$1,109,000

The asset side of the balance sheet shows the cost of what the company owns plus what is owed to it by others plus the value of some money that the company has already paid for future expenses.

The major items on a utility's balance sheet usually represent physical plant (machinery, buildings, and land) that is being or will be used to serve the customer. *Utility Plant* (line 1) is usually divided into several categories. The first is the cost of plant that has been completed and is *In Service* (line 2). That cost includes not only the money paid to the manufacturers of building products and machinery and to construction workers but also the return that was paid to those who supplied the money.

Physical plant wears out over time or machinery may lose value because it is obsolete. Every year the firm reduces the value of a piece of machinery to reflect the aging process by adding to a reserve for *Depreciation* (line 3). *Net Plant in Service* (line 4) represents the original cost of the plant less the depreciation reserve.

Most utility companies have plant under construction to meet the growing demands of their customers. Machinery, buildings, and equipment that are part of an incomplete project are called *Construction Work in Progress* or CWIP (line 5). The sum of all the money invested in plant, less depreciation, is called *Net Plant* (line 6).

Many utilities have invested in other businesses. Those investments are shown under *Other Property and Investments* (line 7).

The company's plant account is often called fixed assets because the property cannot be easily moved and cannot be converted quickly into cash. *Current Assets* (line 8), on the other hand, includes cash, items that can be quickly converted into cash, and accounts that will be paid to the company within 12 months.

The utility maintains *Cash and Temporary Investments* (line 9) to pay expenses. It charges the customers for electricity used and, until the bills have been paid, the money owed to the company represents *Accounts Receivable* (line 10). The utility keeps an inventory of spare parts, office supplies, emergency materials, and a supply of fuel for its power plants, all of which are included in *Materials and Supplies* (line 11). The total of those items makes up *Total Current Assets* (line 12).

Deferred Charges (line 13) represent money that has already been paid for something that applies, at least in part, to some future period. For example, the utility paid an underwriter (investment banker) to market some bonds. The money received from the sale of the bonds will be used by the utility for a 20 year period. The expense should, therefore, be spread over the 20 years. Accordingly, the total underwriting expense becomes a deferred charge. Each year, one twentieth of the total is shown as an expense while the deferred expense item on the balance sheet is reduced by an equal amount. In another example, the company incurs some major expense because of a storm or because of the scrapping of some big project. The regulators might want that expense to be spread over several years so that consumers do not have to pay sharply higher rates in a single year to offset the total charge. The regulator tells the utility to defer the charge and to write it off (that is to reduce the total by a specific amount) over several years. The amount of the writeoff becomes part of each year's expenses. Utilities also tend to defer fuel expenses. Most utilities have fuel adjustment clauses included in their rates whereby changes in fuel costs are passed on to customers. Fuel costs, however, may rise in a particular month, but be passed along to customers several months later. The utility could defer the additional fuel expense until the cost can be passed along.

The *Total Assets* (line 14) are the sum of the preceding items.

The *Liabilities and Capital* portion of the balance sheet shows the amounts that owners invested in the business and the amounts the business owes to its creditors.

The utility accounts usually begin with a statement of *Capitalization* (line 15), which shows the amount that has been invested in the business for the long term. Money that cannot be taken out of the business before an appointed time (usually more than one year from the date of the balance sheet) is included in this section.

Common Stock (line 16) is the value assigned to the shares. Some common stock has a nominal or par value ($1 a share, for example), which is a holdover from the early days of corporate organization. When such shares are sold to the public, the price paid is usually well above par value. The difference between par value and the price for the stock is called paid-in surplus. For example, if stockholders purchasing 1,000 shares had invested $6,000 for a stock with a $1 a share par value, the common stock account would look like this:

Common stock ($1 par value, 1,000 shares outstanding)	$1,000
Paid-in surplus	5,000

Usually, part of the year's income is paid to stockholders as dividends and part is retained for future use. The portion not distributed is *Retained Earnings* (line 17).

The sum of retained earnings, paid-in capital, and par value, or the sum of common stock and retained earnings, is called common stockholders' equity. In other words, the money that common stockholders have invested in the business plus the income that could have been paid to common shareholders but was retained instead is their contribution to the capital of the enterprise.

Purchasers of *Preferred Stock* (line 18) receive a fixed dividend that must be paid before common stockholders can receive a dividend. If the company goes out of business, preferred stockholders must be paid in full before holders of the common stock are paid. In those ways, preferred stock is similar to debt. But the rights of preferred shareholders are junior to those of debt holders, and in that way, preferred stock is similar to common stock.

Long Term Debt (line 19) is money borrowed for more than one year (usually 10-to-30 years). Most long term debt is sold in the form of first mortgage bonds. Those are securities that are paid interest, generally twice a year, and that are secured by the property of the corporation.

The sum of common equity, preferred stock, and long term debt is the permanent capital or *Total Capitalization* (line 20) of the utility.

The company has obligations that must be paid within 12 months of the date of the balance sheet. Those obligations are *Current Liabilities* (line 21).

Accounts Payable (line 22) consist of bills that the company must pay within the year (usually sooner). Such bills could be for supplies and other services.

Accrued Expenses (line 23) are known expenses that the company must pay in the near term, although bills have not yet been received. For example, a utility may show money owed to employees for work already performed as an accrued expense before the paychecks are actually written. Taxes may also be treated in that way.

Utilities generally raise money by selling long term securities. The utility often borrows from banks or sells short term commercial paper until it becomes convenient to repay those loans by selling long term securities. *Bank Loans and Commercial Paper* (line 24) can vary greatly from period to period, depending on when long term offerings are planned.

Long Term Debt Payable in One Year (line 25) represents a bond issue that will be due for payment within 12 months of the date of the balance sheet. Some of that debt bears extremely low interest rates and must be paid by selling debt securities carrying the far higher rates now prevailing.

The total of the items in *Total Current Liabilities* (line 26) should be compared with total current assets to determine whether current liabilities are covered by current assets. The difference between current assets and current liabilities is called working capital.

Deferred Credits (line 27), which could be deferred income, are similar to the deferred charges on the assets side of the balance sheet. For example, customers may pay for something in advance. The company collects the cash from the customers, but does not show the income from the transaction until the service is performed. Commonly, deferred credits are deferred income taxes, which are tax savings derived from the use of accelerated depreciation or are the investment tax credit that will be added back to income over the life of the plant the construction of which created the savings. For example, the utility installs a machine that will last for 10 years. The utility receives a tax credit that represents a savings of $1,000 in taxes in the year of installation. The utility does not show the tax saving in the income statement for the year. Instead the savings will be spread over the life of the machine. Therefore, the utility shows a deferred income tax expense in the income statement and creates a deferred income tax credit on the balance sheet. Each year, one-tenth ($100) of the tax savings is added to income, and one-tenth of the deferred income tax credit is subtracted from that account.

Total Liabilities and Capitalization (line 28) must, of course, equal total assets.

As a final note, companies that are phasing in power stations may show an additional asset, representing income deferred for future collection.

Chapter 25

The Statement of Sources and Uses and Funds

*An extremely important characteristic of utilities is that they are "capital intensive"
... High plant investment requirements (to replace equipment ... and meet the
continued growth in the industry) impose heavy and frequent financing requirements. Accordingly, it is important that utilities be well regarded in the investment
community.*[6]

Haskins & Sells

The balance sheet tells what the company owns and owes at a point in time.
The income statement helps to determine how profitable the operations of
the firm were for a given period. The statement of sources and uses of
funds analyzes the cash received and disbursed in a given period. There are
two kinds of statements: the statement of change in financial position and
the statement of source of funds used for construction.

Let us start with a simplified example. The company collects $1,000 in
cash profits from its business operations during the year and pays a $500
dividend to stockholders. Cash in the bank at the beginning of the year is
$3,000. Stock worth $3,000 is sold to raise money. The company has to buy
a new machine costing $6,000. No money is owed on a current basis. (Cur-
rent assets consisted of $3,000 cash in the bank. There are no current
liabilities. Working capital is $3,000 at the beginning of the year.) Here is
how the two statements should appear.

Statement of Changes in Financial Position

Sources of Funds
  Profit $1,000
  Sale of stock 3,000

    Total Sources of Funds $4,000

Statement of Changes in Financial Position—Continued

Uses of Funds
    Purchase of machine $6,000
    Dividend   500

      Total   6,500

Increase (decrease) in working capital   (2,500)

     Total Uses of Funds $4,000

Statement of Sources of Funds Used for Construction

Sources of Funds
    Profits $1,000
    less dividend   500

      Earnings retained in the business   500
    Sale of Stock   3,000
    Decrease in working capital   2,500

Funds Used For Construction $6,000

Other variations are possible. Some companies subtract dividends directly and only show earnings retained in the business as a source of funds. All companies include an analysis of the change in working capital (net current assets or the difference between current assets and current liabilities). Most companies distinguish between funds derived from operations (internal sources of funds) and those derived from financing (external sources) and other sources. In the above example, profits (less dividends) represent the cash derived from operations, receipts from sale of stock represent financing, and cash taken from the bank account (decrease in working capital) belongs in the "other" category. A more realistic set of statements follows.

Statement of Sources and Uses of Funds

	Sources of Funds	1987	1988
1.	Funds derived from operations		
2.	Net income	$42,000	$48,000
3.	Depreciation	35,000	40,000

Statement of Sources and Uses of Funds—Continued

4.	Other	2,000	0
5.	Deferred taxes	20,000	20,000
6.	Allowance for funds used during construction (AFUDC)	(8,000)	(10,000)
7.	Total funds from operations	91,000	98,000
8.	Funds derived from financing		
9.	Sale of common stock	24,000	56,000
10.	Sale of preferred stock	5,000	0
11.	Sale of long term debt	80,000	110,000
12.	Total sources of funds	$200,000	$264,000

Uses of Funds

13.	Construction (less AFUDC)	$140,000	$170,000
14.	Dividends	30,000	32,000
15.	Redemption of long term debt	30,000	30,000
16.	Other	3,000	0
17.	Increase (decrease) in working capital	(3,000)	32,000
18.	Total uses of funds	$200,000	$264,000

Analysis of Change in Working Capital

		1987	*1988*
19.	Increase (decrease) in current assets:		
20.	Cash and temporary investments	$(1,000)	$ 1,000
21.	Accounts receivable	2,000	3,000
22.	Material and supplies	3,000	5,000
23.	Total increase (decrease) in current assets	$4,000	$9000
24.	Decrease (increase) in current liabilities:		
25.	Accounts payable	(8,000)	5,000
26.	Accrued expenses	0	(2,000)
27.	Bank loans and commercial paper	0	20,000
28.	Long term debt payable in one year	1,000	0
29.	Total decrease (increase) in current liabilities	$(7,000)	$23,000
30.	Increase (decrease) in working capital	$(3,000)	$32,000

Funds Derived From Operations (line 1) is the cash that the company collects from its business during the year, less the cash that is spent to maintain operations. The first item listed under operations is *Net Income* (line 2), which is reported before adjusting for any items that do not result in cash. Expenses that do not require the expenditure of cash are listed next. *Depreciation* (line 3) is usually the largest such item. *Other* (line 4) sources could include miscellaneous non-cash expenses, such as amortization of nuclear fuel costs. (Enough nuclear fuel is purchased to last for a considerable period. The fuel is paid for when purchased, but is burned gradually. Therefore, the expense shown is an estimate of the portion of the total cost attributable to the period. It is as if the fuel is being depreciated.) *Deferred Taxes* (line 5) represents the reduction in income taxes for the year (from the use of certain tax rules) that may have to be paid to the IRS in future years. The cash saved in the current year is used for other purposes. Part of the income—*Allowance for Funds Used During Construction* (line 6)—is not cash income, but is a bookkeeping credit. Therefore, the amount is subtracted from the source of funds derived from operations. Utilities do vary in the treatment of AFUDC in the funds statement. Some subtract only part of the allowance. Line 7 shows *Total Funds Derived from Operations*. The rest of the money must come from *Funds Derived from Financing* (line 8), which has three basic sources: *Sale of Common Stock* (line 9), *Sale of Preferred Stock* (line 10), and *Sale of Long Term Debt* (line 11). *Total Sources of Funds* (line 12) includes operating (internal) and financing (external) sources. *Construction* expenditures (line 13) constitute the largest use of funds. Because we have subtracted AFUDC from sources of funds, we also subtract AFUDC from uses of funds. *Dividends* (line 14) are other disbursements and are shown for both preferred and common stock. Bond issues are due at maturity and must be paid off. Redemptions are listed under *Redemption of Long Term Debt* (line 15). *Other* (line 16) uses of funds include such items as investment in non-utility ventures. The final source of funds is the *Increase (Decrease) in Working Capital* (line 17). If cash was needed, for example, the company took it out of the bank account or negotiated short term loans. If more cash was produced by the business than was needed, the company added to its bank account, paid off short term loans, and paid off bills.

The *Total Uses of Funds* (line 18) is always equal to the *Total Sources of Funds*.

We know the amount by which working capital increased or decreased. The change in each component of current assets and current liabilities is presented in the *Analysis of Changes in Working Capital*. We begin with the *Increase (Decrease) in Current Assets* (line 19). That change is the sum of changes in *Cash and Temporary Investments* (line 20), *Accounts Receivable* (line 21), and *Materials and Supplies* (line 22). To that sum, which is the *Increase (Decrease) in Current Assets* (line 23), we add the *Decrease (Increase) in Current Liabilities* (line 24). Remember that an increase in current assets or a decrease in current liabilities increases working capital. On the other side, a decrease in current assets and an increase in current liabilities decreases working capital. The changes in *Accounts Payable* (line 25), *Accrued Expenses* (line 26), *Bank Loans and Commercial Paper* (line 27), and *Long Term Debt Payable in One Year* (line 28) add up to the total *Decrease (Increase) in Current Liabilities* (line 29). The sum of the increase (decrease) in current assets and the decrease (increase) in current liabilities adds up to the *Increase (Decrease) in Working Capital* (line 30).

Incidentally, additional adjustments might have to be made for utilities that are phasing investment into rate base, because those companies include in their income revenue that is not being collected from customers in cash. Such income should be subtracted from internal sources of funds. Or, as an alternative, the deferred item could be considered a use of funds, because the company has to pay all the current costs of the investment without receiving compensating revenue. In either case, the reader should be careful in using funds statements when phase-in deferrals are present.

Chapter 26

Ratio Analysis

The objectives of security analysis are twofold. First it seeks to present the important facts in a manner most informing and useful. . . . Second, it seeks to reach dependable conclusions . . . as to the safety and attractiveness of a given security. . . .[7]

Graham, Dodd and Cottle

The balance sheet, income statement and funds statement provide the raw material needed to analyze the finances of the corporation.

The Balance Sheet

The plant account is the most important section on the asset side of the balance sheet and should be examined to determine how much plant is actually in service and how much is under construction. In some jurisdictions, the regulator will not allow the company to earn a return on plant that has not been put into service, that is, a return on construction work in progress. If a large part of the utility's assets are in CWIP, and the construction program is behind schedule, the utility might be put under financial pressure while trying to finance the project.

For that matter, if the CWIP is not included in the rate base (i.e., is not earning a return), the utility might need a large rate increase—possibly too large for the regulators to grant all at once—upon completion of the plant. We also want to compare the proposed spending program with the plant already in place. A huge spending program in relation to present facilities means that the rate base will grow rapidly, probably faster than operating income will grow unaided by rate relief. That means that rate of return on rate base will drop unless the utility gets substantial amounts of rate relief, which is often difficult to obtain all at once. For a quick analysis, compare the capital spending program on utility plant (including AFUDC and expenditures for nuclear fuel) with the gross plant of the utility (the sum of plant in service, nuclear fuel and construction work in progress before depreciation and nuclear fuel amortization) at the beginning of the period.

That ratio should then be compared with those for other utilities. The higher the ratio of spending to plant, the more likely it is that the utility will require substantial amounts of outside financing to complete the capital expenditure effort and large rate hikes to offset the costs of the new capital. A high ratio, in short, could indicate future financial strains and regulatory problems. Here is an example:

1.	Utility plant at original cost (gross plant in service)	$1,000
2.	Less depreciation	200
3.	Net utility plant in service	800
4.	Construction work in progress	300
5.	Nuclear fuel	50
6.	less amortization	20
7.	Net nuclear fuel	30
8.	Net utility plant	$1,130

Gross plant = line 1+ line 4 + line 5 = $1,350
CWIP as % of net plant = line 4 divided by line 8 = 26%

Construction program for three years:

9.	Capital expenditures	$ 400
10.	Nuclear fuel	100
11.	AFUDC	100
12.	Total	$ 600

Construction program as % of beginning of period gross plant:

$$\frac{\$ 600}{\$1,350} = 45\%$$

The capitalization also deserves attention, for both financial and regulatory reasons. When a large proportion of the capital is provided by debt, the company is said to be leveraged. In general, the covenants or indentures that govern the company's borrowing put limits on how much debt can be sold. Many companies borrow large amounts of short term debt. Some have a permanent layer of short term debt and thus always owe money to banks or to other short term lenders. Short term debt has a different call on assets (if something goes wrong) than does long term debt, but the obligation is still there.

Some companies exclude short term debt from their calculations of capitalization ratios. Doing so can be misleading. Here is an example of how inclusion or exclusion of a large amount of short term debt can change capitalization ratios.

		Capitalization Ratio or % of Total
Common equity	$ 500	41.7%
Preferred stock	100	8.3
Long term debt	400	33.3
Short term debt	200	16.7
	$1,200	100.0%
Common equity	$ 500	50.0%
Preferred Stock	100	10.0
Long term debt	400	40.0
	$1000	100.0%

The final question that deserves attention is: are current assets sufficient to pay current liabilities? In an emergency, selling properties could take a long time, but current liabilities would still have to be paid when due. Current assets include cash or can be converted quickly into cash. Therefore, the greater the ratio of current assets to current liabilities, the easier it would be for the utility to meet its obligations. Analysts of the electric utility industry have had a tendency to ignore the relation between current assets and current liabilities on the ground that a utility can easily sell securities to raise the cash necessary to pay current obligations. That was the case a number of years ago. Now, however, a combination of chaotic capital markets and the declining quality of utility securities has made the ability to sell securities at will less definite.

The ratio of current assets to current liabilities is called the *current ratio*. The difference between current assets and current liabilities is *working capital*.

Current assets	$5,000
Current liabilities	2,000

$$\text{Current ratio} = \frac{\$5,000}{\$2,000} = \qquad 2.5 \text{ to } 1$$

Working capital = $5,000 − $2,000 = $3,000

A large amount of short term debt may create additional risk for the utility. Because short term interest rates are unstable, the company's income could be affected by the rise and fall of interest costs. A large amount of short term debt also creates financing inflexibility. To pay its debts, the utility might be forced to offer long term securities at an unfavorable time, and might not even be able to raise sufficient funds.

Capitalization plays a role in regulation. Regulators want the utility to raise money in the least expensive fashion to keep down the rates charged to customers. Regulators believe that debt financing is cheaper than equity financing, because creditors have protected position and therefore settle for lower profits than stockholders, who take the risks. Interest charges, moreover, reduce income taxes, so part of the cost of debt can be offset through lower taxes. Here are costs of capital for two capitalizations:

Example A: Low Leverage

		% Cost	Cost Excluding Tax Savings	Cost to Customers Taking into Account Income Tax Savings (50% Rate)
Debt	$ 300 ×	10% =	$ 30	$ 15
Equity	700 ×	15% =	105	105
	$1,000		$135	$120

Example B: High Leverage

Debt	$ 700 ×	10% =	$ 70	$ 35
Equity	300 ×	15% =	$ 45	45
	$1,000		$115	$ 80
Ratio of A to B			117%	150%

The preceding examples reveal a conflict of interest. The regulator wants the utility to finance by means of debt to keep down the cost of capital. On the other hand, the utility may want to keep down the use of debt because too much debt increases the risk and may increase debt rates enough to offset savings derived from the lower equity ratio. For example, assume that two utilities have $1,000 of capitalization, one borrowed $300 and the other $700, a storm wipes out $200 of each company's assets, and the companies must go out of business. Before stockholders receive anything, owners of debt must be paid in full. What would be left for stockholders?

	Low Leverage	High Leverage
Original assets	$1,000	$1,000
less: Storm damage	200	200
Assets available for distribution	800	800
less: Payment of debt	300	700
Assets available for distribution to stockholders	500	100
Original stockholder	$ 700	$ 300
Loss on investment	200	200
Loss as % of investment	29%	67%

The Income Statement

Balance sheets change slowly, but income statements change rapidly. Those changes can tell a great deal about the utility and the direction in which it is going.

In some ways revenue, the largest number in the income statement, is one of the least meaningful, as are the ratios developed from revenue. The reason is that revenue includes base revenue and fuel adjustment clause revenue. Let there be two companies of equal size. Company A's fuel costs are the same in the first and second year of operations. Company B's fuel costs are $50 higher in the second year and are immediately passed on to customers by means of the fuel adjustment clause.

	Company A		Company B	
	1st year	*2nd year*	*1st year*	*2nd year*
Base revenue	500	500	500	500
Fuel adj. revenue	0	0	0	50
Total	500	500	500	550

The income statement shows just the total revenue. Did Company B really have a better second year than Company A? We can carry that question a step further. Many people do ratio analysis using total revenue. Here are additional examples:

	Company A		Company B	
	1st year	*2nd year*	*1st year*	*2nd year*
Base revenue	500	500	500	500
Fuel clause revenue	0	0	0	50
Total revenue	500	500	500	550
Fuel expenses	300	300	300	350
Other expenses	50	50	50	50
Total expenses	350	350	350	400
Net operating income	150	150	150	150
Ratio of net income to total revenue	30%	30%	30%	27%

A standard ratio analysis would indicate that Company B was less efficient in the second year than in the first because income represented only 27% of revenue instead of 30% as in the preceding year. Actually, income was the same percentage of base revenue in both years. Thus, the standard ratio analysis of the income statement tends to be misleading and is not especially useful.

Despite the homogeneity of the industry, utilities engage in highly varied accounting practices. Although one kilowatt-hour is always one kilowatt-hour no matter where the utility is situated, $1 of earnings per share in Texas is not necessarily the same as $11 of earnings in California. Analysts refer to the differences in accounting procedures and cash flow behind the reported figures as "quality of earnings."

Whether income tax savings attributed to the investment tax credit and accelerated depreciation are deferred (normalized) or are used to reduce taxes for regulatory purposes (flowed through) can have an important effect.

Normalization refers to a method of allocating tax costs for book purposes by spreading tax savings over the life of the property. For example, assume that income tax payments have been reduced by the use of the investment tax credit. Rather than show the entire tax saving in the income statement for the current year (*flow through*), a deferred tax item is put into the income statement, and the tax saving is added back to earnings over the life of the property, or for some other arbitrary period. Income tax savings generated by the use of accelerated depreciation for tax purposes can be treated the same way. Rather than show the effect of the tax reduction in earnings for the duration of the period in which accelerated depreciation is greater than straight line (flow through), the utility sets up a deferred tax account and adds back the tax savings to earnings when use of accelerated depreciation has reduced the tax depreciation rate below the book rate.

Regulation requires that the utility rate structure must cover all costs of providing service, including income taxes. Yet the income tax on the tax books differs from that reported to shareholders and to commissions. For example, a utility uses accelerated depreciation for tax purposes and straight line depreciation for book purposes. In our example, accelerated depreciation results in a higher depreciation expense in early years than the straight line method. Current taxes are being reduced. At some future time, however, accelerated depreciation will be lower than straight line, and current taxes will be increased:

Accelerated Depreciation

(Tax Reporting)

	Year 1	Year 5	Year 10
Revenues	$100	$100	$100
Operating expenses	30	30	30

(Tax Reporting)

	Year 1	Year 5	Year 10
Depreciation	20	10	0
Pretax income	$ 50	$ 60	$ 70
Income taxes (50% tax rate)	25	30	35
Net Income	$ 25	$ 30	$ 35

Straight Line Depreciation

(Tax Reporting)

	Year 1	Year 5	Year 10
Revenues	$ 100	$ 100	$ 100
Operating expenses	30	30	30
Depreciation	10	10	10
Pretax income	$ 60	$ 60	$ 60
Income taxes (50% tax rate)	30	30	30
Net Income	$ 30	$ 30	$ 30

The utility uses accelerated depreciation for tax purposes, thereby reducing taxes, but uses straight line depreciation for book and regulatory purposes. In Year 1, the utility actually paid $25 in income taxes. In time, however, the company's taxes will rise (so long as plant subject to depreciation does not increase also). Proper accounting procedure calls for the company to report taxes on the books as if straight line depreciation had also been used for tax purposes. The difference between the $25 actually paid and the $30 that would have been paid represents deferred taxes, which will be paid some time in the future when accelerated depreciation drops below straight line depreciation.

Some utility commissions take the position that cost of service includes taxes actually paid, not taxes that might be paid in the future. Present customers are expected to pay for current costs only. Future customers can pay for future costs. Furthermore, so long as the plant account increases fast enough (thus increasing depreciation), the utility is unlikely to reach the point at which accelerated depreciation declines below straight line depreciation. If that is so, deferred taxes may never be paid. Therefore, why set aside any deferred taxes?

Let us consider the example of a growing utility that writes off $40 of original plant during a five year period, uses accelerated depreciation for tax purposes, and adds $20 to its plant account for five years. In the following statement, the depreciation on additional plant is shown separately. The example is simplified, and does not necessarily show the exact pattern of actual tax depreciation, but rather indicates how tax depreciation is higher than book depreciation in early years and lower in later years of the life of the plant.

Accelerated Depreciation
(Tax Reporting)

	Year 1	Year 2	Year 3	Year 4	Year 5
Revenues	$ 100	$ 125	$ 156	$ 196	$ 245
Operating expenses	30	38	47	59	74
Depreciation of plant in service in					
Year 1	16	10	6	4	4
Year 2	0	8	5	3	2
Year 3	0	0	8	5	3
Year 4	0	0	0	8	5
Year 5	0	0	0	0	8
Total Depreciation	16	18	19	20	22
Pretax income	54	69	90	117	149
Income taxes (50% rate)	27	34.5	45	58.5	74.5
Net income	27	34.5	45	58.5	74.5

Note that depreciation for tax purposes does not decline, because new plant is being added and that additional depreciation on the new plant offsets the fall-off of depreciation on the older plant.

Using straight line depreciation, the income statement would appear as follows:

Straight Line Depreciation

(Tax Reporting)

	Year 1	Year 2	Year 3	Year 4	Year 5
Revenues	$100	$125	$156	$196	$245
Operating expenses	30	38	47	59	74
Depreciation of plant placed on service in					
Year 1	8	8	8	8	8
Year 2	0	4	4	4	4
Year 3	0	0	4	4	4
Year 4	0	0	0	4	4
Year 5	0	0	0	0	4
Total Depreciation	8	12	16	20	24
Pretax income	62	75	93	117	147
Income taxes (50% rate)	31	37.5	46.5	58.5	73.5
Net income	31	37.5	46.5	58.5	73.5

The use of flow through (vs. normalization) accounting can produce a higher reported net income with no improvement in cash flow. Note in the following example that both the flow through and normalized companies show the straight line depreciation on their books. The normalized utility, however, shows a deferred tax expense consistent with the use of straight line depreciation while the flow through company does not.

Accounts When Accelerated Exceeds Straight Line Depreciation

	Flow Through	Normalization	Tax Accounts of both
Revenues	$ 100	$ 100	$ 100
Operating expenses	30	30	30
Depreciation	10	10	20

Accounts When Accelerated Exceeds Straight Line Depreciation — Continued

	Flow Through	Normalization	Tax Accounts of both
Pretax income	$ 60	$ 60	$ 50
Income taxes			
Current	25	25	25
Deferred	0	5	0
Net Income	$ 35	$ 30	$ 25
Cash flow (net income, depreciation and deferred taxes)	$ 45	$ 45	$ 45

Whether a utility uses normalization or flow through tax accounting is usually decided by the regulatory agency. Deferred taxes are legitimate expenses from a regulatory standpoint in normalized jurisdictions and must be covered by revenues.

Although normalization does not increase net income, it does (as noted above) add to cash flow. Therefore, the company that normalizes has more cash flow per dollar of net income than the company that flows through and is bound to be in better financial shape, other things being equal.

Now, let us look at how flow through accounting can be used to reduce revenue requirements (that is, the rates charged customers) in the years when tax depreciation is greater than book depreciation. In the example on p. 224, regulators consider a 12% return on equity to be the allowed return. The company has $250 in equity. Using normalized accounting, the company earns 12%. Using flow through accounting, however, the company earns 14%. Rates must be reduced by $10 to bring return on equity to 12%. Note that by doing so, the regulatory agency reduces the cash flow and the interest coverage ratio of the company, although reported net income remains the same. (Cash flow, here, equals net income plus depreciation plus deferred taxes.)

Some items associated with the construction program are expensed for tax purposes but are capitalized for book purposes. For example, certain state and local taxes have to be paid on plant under construction. Those local taxes are legitimate deductible expenses for income tax purposes and are used by the utility to reduce its Federal income tax payments. By lowering income taxes, the reported operating income of the utility has been increased, as has the rate of return. The question remains whether that is a proper way to match expenses with revenues. The deductible state and local taxes are not shown in the income statement because they are associated with construction of plant and, therefore, are capitalized. Why should the

income tax saving be included in income, for the benefit of current ratepayers who are not contributing to the upkeep of the plant under construction?
The solution is to put off tax savings by means of a deferred tax expense
item in the income statement.

Income tax savings are also derived from interest charges attributable to
borrowing made to support construction work in progress. The logic is
identical to that used in the preceding example. If ratepayers do not bear
any of the burden of supporting construction work, why should they gain
from the tax savings generated? The solution is to set up a deferred tax
account as an operating expense to offset the tax savings. An offsetting tax
credit is included in other income, because operating income had to be
reduced by deferred taxes for regulatory purposes, but there was no reason
to change net income. Note, that in the following example, without the tax
deferral, the rate of return would increase, perhaps to a level that would
require a reduction. To reduce rates and to give current ratepayers a break
may seem to be unfair, especially if those consumers are not paying any of
the costs for construction because the costs are not included in the rate
base. If current ratepayers are not responsible for future needs, they should
not receive the benefits of construction designed to meet those needs.

The example on p. 225 concerns an increase in taxes because of
construction. The example could just as easily be applied to higher interest
costs attributable to borrowing for construction purposes.

Each new tax law changes the rules for depreciation, and the Tax Reform Act of 1986 made many changes in the definition of taxable income
and also eliminated the investment tax credit. At present, tax normalization
is the order of the day, although regulators must face still another issue.
The utilities set aside deferred tax accounts on the assumption that future
taxes would have to be paid at the tax rates that prevailed at the time that
the reserve was set up. Since then, the tax rate has declined, so it appears
that many utilities have tax reserves in excess of what will be needed to pay
the taxes. Those reserves were collected from customers in the price of
electricity. Should they be returned to customers? If so, how?

The various tax laws have created formulas for depreciation. One method
uses double-declining-balance or sum-of-the-years-digits for tax purposes.
The other method depreciates property for tax purposes over fewer years
than for regulatory purposes, for instance a utility can depreciate a nuclear
plant over a 20 year period for tax purposes, while using a 30 year period
for regulatory purposes. The company can either normalize (defer) or flow
through the resultant tax savings derived from using a shorter life for
depreciation on the tax return than is used for rate setting. The company
that normalizes has more cash flow per dollar of net income than the
company that flows through the tax savings. On the whole, the new tax laws
have encouraged or required normalization accounting, so the flow through
component of earnings has declined.

Because of the capital intensive nature of the utility business, deprecia-

Flow Through Used to Reduce Revenue Requirements

	Original Tax Books	Normal- ization	Flow through Before Rate Reduction	Tax Books After Rate Reduction	Flow through After Rate Reduction
Revenues	$100	$100	$100	$90	$90
Operating expenses	20	20	20	20	20
Depreciation	20	10	10	20	10
Pretax operating income	60	70	70	50	60
Interest expenses	10	10	10	10	10
Pretax net income	50	60	60	40	50
Current income taxes	25	25	25	20	20
Deferred income taxes	0	5	0	0	0
Net income	$25	$30	$35	$20	$30
Cash flow	$45	$45	$45	$40	$40
Return on equity	10%	12%	14%	8%	12%
Interest coverage ratio	6×	7×	7×	5×	6×

Impact of Taxes for Construction

	Income Statement Before Construction Begins	Income Statement After Construction Begins (no deferred taxes)	Income Statement After Construction Begins (deferred taxes)
Revenues	$1,000	$1,000	$1,000
Operating expenses	500	500	500
Other taxes	100	100[b]	100
Income taxes (deferred)	0	0	50[d]
Income taxes (current)	100	50[c]	50
Total expenses	$ 700	$ 650	$ 700
Operating income	300	350	300
Other income (inc. tax cr.)	0	0	50[e]
Income before interest charges	$ 300	$ 350	$ 350
Interest charges	200	200	200
Net income	$ 100	$ 150	$ 150
Plant in service	4,000	4,000	4,000
Plant under construction	0	1,000	1,000
Rate of Return[a]	7.5%	8.75%	7.5%

[a] On plant in service. Defined as operating income/plant in service.

[b] Other taxes increase to $200, but the additional $100 is capitalized for book purposes because it is a tax on plant under construction.

[c] Reduced from $100 to $50 because taxable net income has declined by $100 because of taxes on plant under construction.

[d] Deferred taxes to offset income tax savings attributable to plant under construction.

[e] Income tax credit to offset deferred taxes.

tion is a major item on both the income and the cash flow statements. The composite *book depreciation* rate is the rate of depreciation of plant in service as shown on the books of the corporation, as opposed to the usually higher rate used for tax purposes. The book depreciation rate is a straight line rate for most utility companies. Furthermore—and this is a key point—the rate of depreciation usually must be approved by the regulatory agency that has jurisdiction over the company. Depreciation is a cost of doing business that must be offset by revenues. The higher the depreciation rate, the more the customer must pay in current utility bills. At the same time, a higher depreciation rate increases cash flow, thereby allowing the utility to finance internally more of its expansion and to have less dependence on the capital markets.

Different kinds of utility plants require different depreciation rates. A typical telephone company might use 6%, an electric company, 4%, a gas distribution company, 3%, and a water company might use an even lower rate.

Even within an industry, the appropriate rate will vary. A hydroelectric company depreciates a dam more slowly than another company depreciates a coal burning plant. Similar utilities, however, often have different book depreciation rates. A higher rate is favorable for investors, because it creates a greater cash flow.

Whether utilities should *defer fuel costs* or should book *unbilled revenues* is subject to controversy. Most electric utilities have fuel adjustment clauses whereby changes in fuel costs are passed on directly to customers. Most fuel adjustment clauses entail some lag. If the utility's fuel costs were to rise now, for example, the increase might not be passed on to customers until next month. As a consequence, the utility's earnings are reduced for the month in which the fuel price rise occurs. Many companies have solved that problem by deferring the fuel costs on their books until the month in which they are collected from the customer. As a result, the fuel clause lag is eliminated from the statement of earnings. Unfortunately, the lag still represents a cash flow problem because the company has to pay the increased cost for fuel before the increase can be collected from the customer. The extent of the problem can be judged from the deferred fuel costs item on the balance sheet. Moreover, if fuel costs continue to rise, the company might never catch up. From an investor's standpoint, earnings are stronger when fuel costs are not deferred. When the fuel adjustment clause is based on a projection of future fuel costs, however, the company can be assured of full collection. For example, the utility expects fuel costs to rise by $50 in the next six months. The company charges customers an additional $50 during that six month period. Should fuel costs rise by $100 instead, the company defers the extra $50 not collected until the next six month period, when it will collect that $50 shortfall, plus (possibly) interest on the $50, plus whatever fuel adjustment revenue has been estimated for the second six month period. On the other hand, if the utility has overcollected during the period, the company will pay the excess (plus interest) to customers in the subsequent period. Thus, fuel costs are deferred, but the recovery of uncollected fuel cost is guaranteed. Guaranteed recovery is not a characteristic of all fuel clauses. For ratio analysis purposes, most analysts do not make allowance for various kinds of fuel cost accounting. Perhaps, the accounting method used should be considered in making judgments.

An electric company generates power in the period when power is required and books the expenses of generation as they are incurred (except if fuel costs are deferred). The company may not read meters and may not bill customers, however, until some time later. To better match revenues and expenses, a number of utilities book revenues on the basis of production or meter readings, rather than on collections. Investors might prefer the earnings of companies that do not engage in such practices. Although the accounting logic of booking unbilled revenues and deferring fuel costs may be correct, those procedures have been criticized for other reasons. For example, they have been used to improve the financial appearance of a utility's income and to reduce the apparent need for rate relief, although financing and cash flow actually have not improved. Even without adjusting ratios for that accounting difference, those changes must be taken into account in the investment decision process.

Neither tax nor fuel accounting is as controversial a subject as the *allowance for funds used during construction* (AFUDC), which is a credit item in the income statement and is intended to be an offset to capital charges incurred before plant is placed in service. Those capitalized charges are added to the cost of the plant when it goes into service. The utility can then earn a return on the cost of the physical plant plus the capital costs incurred in building the plant. Sometimes the AFUDC rate is higher than the rate of return the utility can earn on the property once it is in service. In that situation, reported earnings are higher during construction than during operation. Unlike the sale of electricity (or of other services) AFUDC results in no cash flow. Distortions of earnings and cash flow problems are likely to be most severe for utilities that capitalize construction costs at a high rate. Several utilities use a complicated method in which a higher gross rate is used, but deferred tax offsets bring the net rate down close to the average.

In 1977, the Federal Power Commission revised the procedure for calculating AFUDC, although the results are almost the same as before. Basically, AFUDC is split into two parts: the portion resulting from raising debt money to finance the construction and the portion allocated to equity funding. Simplified versions of the old and new formats follow:

	Old	*New*
Operating Income	$ 400	$ 400
Other income		
AFUDC	50	30*
Other	10	10

Total Other Income	60	40
Income before interest charges	460	440
Interest		
Interest expense	100	100
AFUDC	—	(20)**
Net interest expense	100	80
Net income	360	360

*Derived from raising equity money.
**Derived from raising debt money.

AFUDC suffers from two problems: it assumes that income spread over a period of years (the return on the AFUDC capitalized into the rate base) is as good as the return collected on CWIP in the current year and that a bookkeeping credit is as good as cash.

Owners of debt and preferred stock examine the income statement to determine the safety of their investments. *Pretax interest coverage*—how much money is available from earnings to pay interest charges—is one of the standards used to determine the strength of a debt security. Although many persons think of a corporation's assets as protection for debtholders, what would the assets be worth if they could not generate income? Pretax income is used because interest charges must be met before any income taxes can be paid.

For purposes of analysis, the income accounts should be restated to combine all AFUDC into the other income section and all interest into one line. The standard format and the analytical format are show below:

	Standard	Analytical
Revenue	1,000	1,000
Operating expenses except income taxes	500	500
Income taxes	200	200
Operating income	300	300
Other income:		
Allowance for other funds used during construction	10	30
Income tax credits	4	4
Miscellaneous	1	1
Income before interest charges	315	335
Interest on long term debt	30	30
Other interest	20	20
Allowance for borrowed funds used during construction	(20)	
Net interest charges	30	50
Net income	285	285

The restatement represents a reversion to the earlier method of stating AFUDC. Similar items are lumped together to prevent the possible error of calculating coverages by using net interest charges in the denominator of the coverage ratio. Unfortunately, the analytical format is better suited to equity analysis than to debt analysis and is inadequate for calculating interest coverages because it does not give figures on a pretax basis. A format for interest coverage analysis would be:

Revenue	$1,000
Operating expenses except income taxes	500
Pretax operating income	500
Interest charges	50
Pretax income (excluding other income)	450
Income taxes (net of income tax credits of $4)	196
Net income before AFUDC and miscellaneous income	254
AFUDC	30
Miscellaneous income	1
Net income	$ 285

The following example restates an income statement and the numbers are then used to calculate some standard coverage ratios for interest charges.

	Line	Analytical (Equity)	Line by Line Formula
1.	Revenues	$1,000	
	Operating expenses		
2.	Fuel and operations*	400	
3.	Depreciation	100	
4.	Income taxes	100	
5.	Total operating expenses	600	2 + 3 + 4
6.	Operating Income	400	1 − 5
	Other income		
7.	AFUDC**	80	
8.	Income tax credits	15	
9.	Miscellaneous	5	
10.	Total other income	100	7 + 8 + 9

Line		Analytical (Equity)	Line by Line Formula
11.	Income before interest charges	500	6 + 10
12.	Interest charges	300	
13.	Net income	200	11 − 12
14.	Preferred dividends	50	
15.	Net available to common stock	150	13 − 14
16.	Average shares of common stock	100	
17.	Earnings per average share	$ 1.50	15 ÷ 16

*Includes rentals, the interest component of which is $10.

**Allowances for Funds Used During Construction from both sources.

		Analytical (Debt)	Line by Line Formula
1.	Revenues	$ 1,000	
	Operating expenses except income taxes		
2.	Fuel and operations*	400	
3.	Depreciation	100	
4.	Total operating expenses except income taxes	500	2 + 3
5.	Pretax operating income	500	1 − 4
6.	Total interest charges	300	
7.	Pretax income (excluding other income)	200	5 − 6
8.	Income taxes	100	
9.	Net income (before other income)	100	7 − 8
10.	AFUDC**	80	
11.	Income tax credits	15	
12.	Miscellaneous	5	
13.	Total other income	100	10 + 11 + 12
14.	Net income	200	9 + 13
15.	Preferred dividends	50	
16.	Net available to common stock	150	14 − 15

*Includes rentals, the interest component of which is $10.
**Allowance for Funds Used During Construction from both sources.

Pretax income before interest charges (income before interest charges plus income taxes) is the same as revenues less operating expenses other than income taxes.

1) The formula for *SEC coverage* (used in bond prospectuses approved by the Securities and Exchange Commission) produces the following:

$$\frac{\text{Pretax Op. Inc.} + \text{AFUDC} + \text{Misc. Income} + \text{Interest Component of Rentals}}{\text{Interest charges} + \text{Interest component of rentals}} =$$

$$\frac{\$500 + \$ 80 + \$ 5 + \$10}{\$ 300 + \$10} = \frac{\$595}{\$310} = 1.92 \times$$

2) *Coverage Based on Pretax Income Before Interest Charges:* This ratio is an easily calculated substitute for the SEC coverage, especially when rentals are unavailable or are insignificant:

$$\frac{\text{Pretax Operating Income} + \text{AFUDC} + \text{Misc. Income}}{\text{Interest Charges}} = \frac{500 + 80 + 5}{300} = 1.95 \times$$

3) *Interest Coverage Based on Pretax Operating Income:* This provides a measure of the pretax income from operations that is available to meet fixed charges. The calculation excludes the allowance for funds used during construction (a non-cash item) and other income (which may be highly variable). For our purposes, income taxes include all current and deferred income taxes shown in operating expenses.

The formula for operating income coverage is:

$$\frac{\text{Pretax operating income}}{\text{Interest charges}}$$

Operating income coverage should be viewed as a conservative way of measuring a utility's standing.

Let us return to the example. We are interested only in operating income and intend to ignore the interest component of rentals. Thus, the calculation becomes:

$$\frac{\$500}{\$300} = 1.67 \times$$

4) *Cash Income Coverage:* Depreciation practices differ among utilities. Because depreciation is one of the utility's major non-cash expense items, we include depreciation in the ratio shown below. AFUDC, which is one of the major non-cash credits in the income statement, should be omitted from a conservative coverage ratio. This ratio is calculated according to the formula:

$$\frac{\text{Pretax operating income + Depreciation}}{\text{Total interest charges}}$$

In our example, the coverage would be:

$$\frac{\$500 + \$100}{\$300} = \frac{\$600}{\$300} = 2.00 \times$$

Even that ratio may fail to include some cash coming in, especially that derived from the amortization of nuclear fuel (which is akin to depreciation of the investment in nuclear fuel as the fuel is burned).

5) *Preferred Dividend Coverage:* Utilities generally have large amounts of preferred stock in their capitalizations. Much of the analysis that we are using here also is suitable for analysis of preferred stocks, except that the coverage ratio must be adjusted. Take our example which we have recast for an easier calculation.

	Revenue	$1,000
minus	Operating expenses	500
equals	Pretax operating income	500
minus	Interest charges	300
equals	Pretax net income	200
minus	Income taxes (50% rate)	100
equals	Net income	100
	Preferred dividends	50

In a previous illustration, we have shown pretax interest coverage to be:

$$\frac{\$500}{\$300} \quad = 1.67 \times$$

Using our example, many analysts would calculate preferred dividend coverage as:

$$\frac{\$100}{\$\ 50} \quad = 2.00 \times$$

But, as Graham and Dodd pointed out long ago,[8] that would be an absurdity. How can the senior security have less coverage than the junior security? Is the preferred stock really safer than the debt? Thus, preferred coverage has to take into account the senior claims ahead of the stock. Unfortunately, that cannot be accomplished easily because the debt has a claim to earnings before taxes, while the preferred claim is junior to taxes. The solution is to put the preferred claim on a pretax basis too. We can then ask how much income before taxes has to be earned to pay the preferred dividend.

Under that formulation, preferred dividend coverage becomes:

$$\frac{\text{Income before interest charges } + \text{ Income taxes}}{\text{Interest charges } + \left(\dfrac{\text{Preferred dividend}}{1\text{-tax rate}} \right)}$$

The income tax rate is stated on a decimal basis, i.e. $34\% = 0.34$.

For those ratios that use Income Before Interest charges in the numerator, income taxes includes the taxes shown as operating expenses less income tax credits included in Other Income. The tax credits have been explained in the paragraphs above concerning income taxes.

Earnings per share (EPS) analysis is based on the average number of shares outstanding during the year. Because utility companies often sell common stock, using year-end shares could be misleading. For example, only a portion of the money received from the sale of shares may have been put to work to produce income during the entire year.

That point is illustrated in the following example, which shows two identical companies, each of which started the year with 800 shares outstanding and ended the year with 1,000 shares. Company A sold new stock at the beginning of the year and had 1,000 shares outstanding for almost the entire period and, therefore, had use of the money from the new shares for almost the full year. Company B sold new shares at the end of the year and had use of the funds for just a few days.

	Company A	Company B
Net income for year	$1,000	$1,000
Year-end shares outstanding	1,000	1,000
EPS based on year-end shares outstanding	$ 1.00	$ 1.00
Average shares outstanding	999	801
EPS based on average shares outstanding	$ 1.00	$ 1.25

If we were to calculate EPS on the basis of shares outstanding at the end of the year, the investor could conclude incorrectly that the shares of both companies have equal earning power. Is it not likely that Company B, once it puts into use the cash derived from the sale of stock near the end of the year, would show greatly improved earnings per share in the following year?

What happens to earnings? A portion of earnings is retained and the rest is distributed as dividends to stockholders. The *dividend payout ratio* is the standard measure of how much of the earnings available to common stockholders is paid out in the form of dividends. One comparison we can make is that between the payout ratio and the *percentage of earnings derived from AFUDC*. Here are two examples:

	Company A	Company B
Reported EPS	$2.00	$2.00
less AFUDC	1.00	0.50
equals EPS − AFUDC	1.00	1.50
Dividends	1.20	1.20
Payout ratio (Div.)/(EPS)	60%	60%
Payout ratio excluding AFUDC from EPS $\left(\dfrac{(DIV)}{EPS-AFUDC}\right)$	120%	80%

Other things being equal, we should be more comfortable with an investment in Company B, because that utility is neither borrowing money nor selling stock to raise the cash for its dividend. All calculations can be based on total dollars, not earnings per share or dividends per share.

$$\text{Dividend payout ratio} = \frac{\text{Common stock dividends}}{\text{Earnings available to common stock}}$$

The payout ratio is one indication of how well the dividend is covered by earnings. Unfortunately the tendency exists to look at the ratio for a single year and to forget that utility earnings have become less stable in recent years because of the timing of rate relief and the sensitivity of earnings to weather conditions. Investors in utilities expect stable or growing dividends. Companies do not raise or lower dividends to maintain a stable payout ratio. A company maintains a stable dividend and lets the payout ratio fluctuate. Most companies have a target payout ratio, which represents an average goal. Remember too that the higher the payout ratio, the less able the company will be to raise the dividend, and the smaller the funds the company will retain to finance future growth.

The Sources and Uses of Funds Statement

In this era of high cost money, the need to borrow money or to sell stock at inconvenient times in the market cycle could have a serious effect on profitability. On the other hand, if a business can generate cash from operations, that money could be invested in profitable ways. Even in the best of times, electric utilities may require new cash because operations for the year do not generate sufficient funds to finance the purchase of expensive equipment that can serve customers for 30 years. Customers cannot be expected to pay so much for electricity in a single year that the utility can meet its needs for the next three decades.

The sources and uses of funds can be analyzed conveniently by using a standardized format:

USES OF FUNDS

Capital expenditures	$1,000
Purchase of nuclear fuel	100
Allowance for funds used during construction (AFUDC)	100
Total expenditures for plant account	1,200
Refunding	50
Working capital and misc.	50
Total uses of funds	$1,300

SOURCES OF FUNDS

Retained earnings	100
Depreciation and amortization	200
Deferred taxes	150
Total internal sources of funds	450
Debt	400
Common stock	300
Preferred stock	150
Total sources of funds	$1,300

Internal sources of funds (less AFUDC) as a % of expenditures for plant account (less AFUDC) =

$$\frac{(450 - 100)}{(1,200 - 100)} = \frac{350}{1,100} = 31.8\%$$

Internal sources of funds as a % of expenditures for plant account =

$$\frac{450}{1,200} = 37.5\%$$

We want to know how much of the money spent for construction came from internal sources. In the above example, the answer seems to be 37.5%. Part of the earnings, however, came from a non-cash source, the AFUDC. Again, part of the expenditures for plant may not represent cash outlay, but are for AFUDC. Therefore, we could develop a second ratio that excludes AFUDC and that shows that 31.8% of cash expenditures for construction (i.e., what was actually paid to the suppliers and builders) came from internal sources.

The above ratios show how much cash is generated from the sale of electricity. Sometimes utilities finance plant expenditures from sources other than their internal savings or from the sale of securities in the current year. For example, funds raised from the sale of securities last year could be used for financing plant construction in the current year. The utility also can sell assets to raise cash. Occasionally those sources are treated as if they were internal. Nevertheless, growing concerns cannot stay in business by living off assets. That leads us to an interesting conclusion. So long as the utility is growing rapidly (needs new plant), the company is not likely to raise sufficient money from internal sources to pay for its new equipment. The company will only be able to generate cash in excess of current needs (cash that can be used to pay debts contracted in the past) when the company's growth slows or stops. At that time, however, the company may need cash for other items. For example, when growth stops, deferred taxes will have to be paid. For that matter, the plant will cease to expand when demand weakens—a time when revenues could decline badly enough to make it difficult for the company to pay debts incurred in the past. Technological changes make obsolete many products and services. Therefore, a prudent management should try to meet its cash needs to the extent possible when that can be done easily and should not put off until tomorrow that which can be paid for today.

That brings up the question of how money should be raised. If an industrial firm builds a factory that will last for 10 years, the company might borrow money for the construction and pay the loan over a ten year period. Because the firm is unlikely to build a plant each year, the loan will probably be paid from the proceeds of the operation. The loan, in short, will be self-liquidating. Electric utilities, on the other hand, may borrow annually, plow all cash back into plant, and funds to repay the loan can only come from sale of additional securities.

Inflation adds to the problem. A utility's cash flow from internal sources is derived from a return on and depreciation of the original cost of assets. Original cost is not adjusted for increases in price levels. Accordingly, the utility can only recover by means of depreciation the actual cost of the asset, not the cost of replacement at current price levels. The utility has to sell additional securities to raise cash with which to replace the asset.

How is that problem different from that of other businesses? Most other businesses do not have so much of their money invested in long-lived fixed assets. Other businesses can raise prices on inventory so that the firms can replace the inventory with a like quantity of more expensive goods. They can also raise prices, if the competition allows, to make sure that they have enough cash to replace fixed assets that now cost more. The utility, of course, cannot raise prices at will. So long as regulation and depreciation are based on original cost of property, the utility has a hard time meeting its needs from internal sources in an inflationary economy.

Other Ratios

In our previous examples, we have examined ratios derived entirely from a single financial statement. Yet, several key ratios use items from several financial statements.

Investors and regulators want to know *rates of return*—how much profit is made for every dollar invested. When creditors lend the business $100 in return for $10 a year of interest plus repayment of the $100 principal at the end of a given period, they accept a 10% return ($10 a year for every $100 borrowed). When a stockholder puts money into a new business expecting the business to earn $20 for each $100 invested by stockholders, the investors expect a 20% return ($20 a year for every $100 invested). Shareholders also expect to sell their shares for at least $100, so that the $20 a year does not have to be offset against a capital loss. If the business is set up with $100 from creditors, who expect a return of $10 a year, and with $100 from stockholders, who expect a return of $20 a year, the *return on the total investment* of $200 is:

Debt	$100	×	10%	=	$10
Equity	100	×	20%	=	20
	$200				$30

$$\frac{\$30}{\$200} = 15\% \text{ return on investment}$$

We will discuss several ratios that can be calculated either to present a picture of the utility's profitability or to approximate the return as calculated by the regulatory agency.

Net Operating Income as a Percentage of Net Plant is one of the easiest returns to calculate. Utilities are generally allowed to earn a given return on the rate base. Commissions differ in their calculations of both income and rate base. The ratio that we are discussing is rarely used by a regulatory agency but it is helpful to investors. It is a calculation of ability to earn a return on net plant from operations alone (and excludes AFUDC and other nonoperational income). Consider the following example:

SAMPLE UTILITY
INCOME STATEMENT*
($ Millions)

Revenues	$100
Operating expenses	
Fuel	20
Operations and maintenance	20
Depreciation	10
Income taxes	20
Total operating expenses	70
Operating income	30
Other income	
Allowance for funds used during construction	3
Other income and deductions (net)	1
Income before interest charges	34
Interest charges	10
Net income	24
Preferred dividends	3
Earnings on common stock	21

*Restated to include both allowances for funds used during construction in one section as part of Other Income.

SAMPLE UTILITY
BALANCE SHEET
Assets

Plant ($400 in service and $100 construction work in progress)	$500
Depreciation	100
Net plant	$400
Current assets (all materials and supplies)	$ 50
Deferred charges	5
Total assets	$455

Liabilities

Capitalization	
Common stock and retained earnings	$125
Preferred stock	50
Long term debt	210
	$385
Current liabilities	$ 60
Deferred credits	10
Total liabilities	$455

Rate of return on net plant:

$$\frac{\text{Operating income}}{\text{Net plant}} = \frac{\$ 30}{\$400} = 7.5\%$$

We can also calculate *Income Before Interest Charges us a Percentage of Net Plant.* Many utilities argue that the AFUDC is good income and should be included in calculating returns. Some regulators include CWIP in the rate base and derive the rate of return by using income before interest charges, rather than by using operating income. For the investor who is interested in determining a rough rate of return on the basis of a rough approximation of the rate base, the ratio under discussion serves the purpose.

$$\frac{\text{Income before interest charges}}{\text{Net plant}} = \frac{\$ 34}{\$400} = 8.5\%$$

Return on Rate Base, as used in regulatory proceedings, is often calculated differently from the two previous ratios. Here is one method that can be used, with working capital approximated as materials and supplies plus one-eighth of operating and maintenance expenses.

Rate base calculation (no CWIP in rate base):

Net plant in service =
   Plant in service − Depreciation = $300.00
Materials and supplies   50.00
One-eighth of operations and
   maintenance expense   2.50
     ———
Rate base = $352.50

Rate of return on rate base:

$$\frac{\text{Operating income}}{\text{Rate Base}} = \frac{\$ 30}{\$352.50} = 8.51\%$$

Return on Common Equity measures the return on the common stockholders' investment. Return on common equity is a vital component of overall rate of return. A low return on equity usually means that the utility needs (and has a good chance of obtaining) rate relief. On the other hand, a high return on equity might mean difficulty when the company seeks to justify relief.

An extraordinarily high return could indicate that the return has no place to go but down and that relief is unlikely before the return has reached a sub-par level.

Return on common equity:

$$\frac{\text{Income available to common stock}}{\text{Common stockholders' equity}} = \frac{\$\ 21}{\$125} = 16.8\%$$

We have based our calculations on the balance sheet at the end of a period. Actually, all the assets may not have been in service for the full year, and therefore may not have contributed to profits. Accordingly, a more meaningful return might be calculated on average plant or on average equity. Rate base may not fit the mold either. Some regulators subtract deferred taxes or plant that was not prudently constructed from the rate base. Regulators use different methods for calculating the working capital component of rate base. Some include part or all of the CWIP in the rate base. When regulators calculate earnings, they make adjustments for unusual items. Some will add all or part of AFUDC to the earnings component. As a result, we should know the formula used or we can simply make approximations for purposes of comparison.

Chapter 27

Market Ratios and Ratings

. . . a stock is worth the present value of its future dividends, with future dividends dependent on future earnings. . . .[9]

John Burr Williams

The financial statements tell us how much the company earns, where the money comes from and where it goes, and how much has been invested in the business. Statements do not tell us the present worth of nor do they indicate how much investors are willing to pay for the flow of cash coming to them from the business. Statements cannot tell us what the company would have to pay for additional funds, nor do they show the amount that could be realized from sale of the business. Managements need that information to make investment decisions, and regulators need the information to determine the utility's cost of capital.

The common stockholder is concerned with stock price, dividend, earnings per share and book value per share.

Price of stock in market	$20.00
Earnings per share (EPS)	4.00
Dividends per share	2.40
Book value per share	30.00

The *price/earnings ratio,* P/E, or multiple for the stock is the price divided by earnings per share. In the above case:

$$\frac{\text{Price}}{\text{Earnings per share}} = \frac{\$20}{\$4} = 5 \times$$

Generally speaking, the market is willing to pay a higher multiple for each dollar of earnings when the company is extremely solid (risk is lower) or when earnings are growing rapidly. In the case of a rapid-growth company, investors may be willing to pay 8 times earnings on the theory that earnings are increasing so fast that by next year earnings will have doubled. Accordingly, the multiple is actually just 4 times earnings for next year. In some instances the investor will pay a higher multiple because net for the current year is unduly depressed and will spring back quickly. Conversely, the investor may pay a low multiple for this year's earnings, which are unduly high and are expected to fall.

The reciprocal of the P/E ratio is the *E/P* ratio or earnings yield:

$$\frac{\text{Earnings per share}}{\text{Price}} = \frac{\$\,4}{\$20} = 0.20\% = 20\%$$

If investors paid $20 for the stock and all earnings were distributed to shareholders, the return on the investment would be 20%. Some regulators have confused the earnings yield with the return that the investor expects. The investor buys not only current but also future earnings. Most investors expect earnings to rise in time. Accordingly, current earnings may not provide a return on current price that fully reflects the return expected by investors.

Because utility stocks are generally purchased for current income, the *Dividend Yield* is an important element in the investment decision. Although the price-earnings ratio is generally meaningful, there can be temporary distortions in earnings per share (caused by weather, delays in rate relief, plant breakdowns, and so forth). Investors could view the dividend as an indication of normalized earning power. If so, then it might be better to examine the dividend yield in relation to that of other stocks. The dividend yield is:

$$\frac{\text{Dividends per share}}{\text{Price}} = \frac{\$\,2.40}{\$20.00} = 0.12 = 12\%$$

Other things being equal, the investor will accept a lower current dividend yield from an investment in a strong company with good prospects for growth than from an investment in a weaker company with poorer prospects. A lower risk produces a lower return. The prospect of more income in the future will induce investors to accept less income in the present. The

Total Return of a stock is the current dividend yield plus growth in value of the shares. Thus, assuming that earnings, dividends and stock price move together over time, a stock with a 12% dividend yield and a 5% anticipated growth rate would have an expected total return of 17% per year.

Investors often look at the *Book Value* of a stock. (Book value is the total amount of stockholders' equity, as shown on the books of the corporation, divided by the number of outstanding shares of common stock.) In many businesses, book value is only of academic interest, because changes in the value and earning power of assets make it likely that a purchaser of the corporation would pay far more or far less than book value for outstanding shares. In the utility business, rates of return are allowed on book value, and, therefore, book value is a key to the potential earning power of the company. The market/book ratio is:

$$\frac{\text{Price of stock}}{\text{Book value of stock}} = \frac{\$20}{\$30} = 67\%$$

The *Market/Book Ratio* indicates to existing shareholders whether new common stock financing will increase or will dilute book value and earning power of their shares. The ratio also indicates to regulators whether return being earned is satisfactory (i.e., high enough to bring the stock to book value). In the following example, new stock offerings are made at 50%, 100%, and 150% of book value. The regulator allows the company to earn a 15% return on equity.

	Before Stock Offering	*Situation After* $1,000 is Raised by Sale of Stock at		
		50% of Book Value	100% of Book Value	150% of Book Value
Common equity	$1,000	$2,000	$2,000	$2000
Number of shares	100	300	200	166.7
Book value per share	$10	6.67	10	12
Net income	$150	300	300	300
Earnings per share	$1.50	$1.00	$1.50	$1.80

A low market price/book value ratio means that new financing will be dilutionary. On the other hand, if the ratio is low, the company is probably under earning and potential for improvement exists. The investor must judge whether financing plans will lead to considerable dilution and whether potential for improvement can be realized within a reasonable time.

The various market ratios are affected by the prospects of individual companies and by alternative investments that are available. A change in prospects for a company or for an entire industry will cause investors to pay higher or lower P/E ratios or to accept lower or higher dividend yields. A change in the returns offered by alternative investments would have the same effect.

The following table illustrates the effect on stock price and ratios of a shift in bond yields from 10% to 13% to 8%, in cases where the alternative is to invest in bonds and investors demand a dividend yield on stocks one percentage point below the interest rate on bonds.

	10% bond yield	13% bond yield	8% bond yield
Dividend per share	$2.40	$2.40	$2.40
Earnings per share	4.00	4.00	4.00
Book value	30.00	30.00	30.00
Stock price	26.67	20.00	34.29
Dividend yield	9.0 %	12.0 %	7.0 %
P/E ratio	6.67×	5.0×	8.57×
E/P ratio	15.0%	20.0 %	11.7 %
Market/book ratio	88.9 %	66.7 %	114.3 %

The same logic would apply if a utility has steady earnings, and the returns from other investments rise sharply. Assume that investors had been used to buying stock in manufacturing firms that could only earn 10% on stockholders' equity and that investors pay a 10% earnings yield (10 × P/E) for that level of earnings. Because utility shares supposedly involve lower risk, investors are satisfied when the utility earns 9% on equity, and the stock sells at a 9% earnings yield (11.1 × P/E). If the earnings of the manufacturing firm surge upward to 15% on equity, and higher yields are available from alternatives such as bonds, the investor would now expect a 15% earnings yield (6.67 × P/E) on the manufacturer's shares. Because of regulation, however, the utility cannot raise its return above 9%. Yet, the investor demands a higher return (14%) on the market value of the utility investment. Consequently, new investors lower the price they are willing to pay for the utility stock, and thus obtain a competitive earnings yield from the shares. In fact, that is what happened to utility stocks in the period after 1965.

	Manufacturers earn 10% and shares sell at 10% E/P	*Manufacturers earn 15% and shares sell at 15% E/P*
Utility Stock		
Earnings per share	$ 0.90	$ 0.90
Book value	$10.00	$10.00
Stock price	10.00	6.43
Market/book ratio	100.0%	64.3%
E/P ratio	9%	14%

Bonds provide a fixed return (interest) if held to maturity. The *Coupon Yield* is based on the face value of the bond. For example, the 12% series first mortgage bond, due January 1, 2000, pays 12% a year on every $100 of face value. On January 1, 2000, the investor will get back $100 for every $100 face value of bonds issued. Some investors do not choose to hold the bond to maturity and, therefore, sell it at whatever market price is offered. The price offered rises and falls with interest rates. Suppose the market for a bond is as follows:

Years to maturity =	20
Coupon =	12%
Price of bond per $100 of face value =	90%

If we ignore the payment of a bond at maturity, we calculate *Current Interest Yield* as:

$$\frac{\text{Coupon rate}}{\text{Price of bond}} = \frac{12}{90} = 0.133 = 13.3\%$$

If the acceptable interest rate on the above quality of bond rises to 15%, the price for the bond would have to decline to $80 to give new investors a 15% return.

$$\frac{\text{Coupon}}{\text{Price}} = \frac{12}{80} = 0.15 = 15\%$$

The current yield, however, does not really indicate the total return picture. If investors hold the bond to maturity, they receive not only the coupon every year, but also an extra $10 (in the first case) or $20 (in the second) because they paid less than $100 for the bond. That capital gain is really part of the return expected by investors. The return that includes both coupon and capital gain (or loss) is *Yield to Maturity*. Tables provide accurate yields to maturity. The investor, however, can calculate an approximate yield to maturity.

Where:

$100   = Face value of bond
C   = Coupon rate (for each $100 of face value)
P   = Price of bond
Y   = Years to maturity

The approximate yield to maturity (A) equals

$$\frac{C + \left(\dfrac{100 - P}{Y}\right)}{\left(\dfrac{100 + P}{2}\right)}$$

In the above examples

$$A = \frac{12 + \left(\dfrac{100 - 80}{20}\right)}{\left(\dfrac{100 + 80}{2}\right)} = \frac{13}{90} = 0.144 = 14.4\%$$

and

$$A = \frac{12 + \left(\dfrac{100 - 90}{20}\right)}{\left(\dfrac{100 + 90}{2}\right)} = \frac{12.5}{95} = 0.132 = 13.2\%$$

Yields calculated by the above formula should be regarded as approximations, and not as substitutes for numbers found in bond tables.

Bonds have quality *Ratings* determined by rating agencies. The largest agencies—Moody's and Standard & Poor's—use letter guides, in declining order of quality:

Moody's	S&P	Comment
Aaa	AAA	Best quality, extremely strong.
Aa	AA	High quality, very strong ability to pay.
A	A	Upper medium grade, strong capacity to pay.
Baa	BBB	Medium grade, adequate strength.
Ba	BB	Speculative, future not assured.
B	B	Speculative, undesirable as an investment.

A plus or minus or a number (the lower the better) after the letter rating is often added to indicate further gradations in quality. Generally, ratings below Baa and BBB are not considered to be of investment quality. Bonds with ratings that begin with the letter C (not shown here) are of companies in or near bankruptcy or are extremely speculative in nature. Many investors are prohibited by law from buying bonds with ratings below certain limits.

A utility may have several kinds of debt with varying degrees of seniority. First mortgage bonds have the greatest seniority and, in theory, must be paid before securities junior to them. Other kinds of debt have lower credit standings and lower credit ratings. Thus, the investor should not be surprised to see the senior debt with a Aa rating and the junior debt of the same utility rated A.

For that matter, the ratings for particular issues may differ from rating agency to rating agency. As a rule, ratings do not differ sharply, but it is not unusual for a bond to be rated Aa by one agency and A by another. That is called a split rating.

The market demands a higher yield from riskier bonds. Therefore, bonds with lower ratings generally provide higher yields to maturity than bonds with higher ratings. A drop in rating (the ratings are re-examined and revised periodically) can lead to a drop in bond price (to produce the higher interest rate). Accordingly, investors watch the trend in financial ratios for the companies in which they invest.

Utilities also seek to keep financial ratios at levels that will retain or improve ratings. A lower bond rating might make the bond difficult to sell to certain investors and might force those investors to sell the bonds if the rating fell below desired levels. When investors expect a bond rating to change, they adjust the price that they will pay for the bond (thus requiring a different yield). Accordingly, some bonds provide yields that seem out of line with their present ratings.

As a final point, the difference in yield between rating groups varies over time. When the market is worried about the state of the economy and the ability of weaker companies to weather the storm, a greater yield differential often exists between low and high quality bonds. At such a time, investors see greater risk in low quality securities and demand to be compensated accordingly.

Chapter 28

Financial Results on
The Books and in The Marketplace

A public utility company is not permitted to enjoy the full fruits of its business successes inasmuch as regulation prohibits a return higher than that which is required to attract capital and provide service at reasonable rates. As a result, it does not have the resources available to absorb the major adversities which it encounters.[10]

Corporation Commission of Oklahoma

In the postwar era, investors in electric utilities rarely did extraordinarily well in the market, although profitability was respectable over time. In less than half the years did utilities provide a total return (dividends plus capital gains) greater than that of industrial stocks[11] just as utilities only occasionally earned a return on equity close to that for industrial corporations. Of course, return should be commensurate with risk, and the investor will accept a lower return for lower risk. At the same time, acceptable return is a relative concept and depends on the returns available elsewhere. When investors can get get only 3% interest annually from a bond, they are satisfied to put their money in a utility that can earn 10% on stockholders' equity or in an industrial company that can earn 13% on stockholders' equity. If, on the other hand, investors can collect a 13% interest rate on bonds, they will not be satisfied with a utility investment that earns just 10% on shareholders' money while an industrial firm returns 17% on equity.

Current investors cannot affect the return being earned by the company in which they invest. If competitive returns rise, but the return earned by their company does not, current investors have lost the opportunity to do better elsewhere. New investors, however, can make a choice. New investors will not buy a security unless the expected flow of future income provides an adequate return on the price that they pay. Because future flow of income cannot be changed by the investor to provide an adequate rate of return, the investor instead regulates the price for the security.

Table 28-1 provides information on market activity in the postwar period (1946-1986). Table 28-2 summarizes that same information for five year periods.

250

Table 28-1

Stock and Bond Yields and Performance 1946-1986

Year	S&P 400 Industrials					Moody's Electric Utilities					Bonds	
	Total Return (%)	Year-end Market Book Ratio (%)	Return on Year-end Common Equity (%)	Year-end P/E Ratio (x)	Year-end Dividend Yield (%)	Total Return (%)	Year-end Market Book Ratio (%)	Return on Year-end Common Equity (%)	Year-End P/E Ratio (x)	Year-end Dividend Yield (%)	Total Return Long-Term Corporate Bonds (%)	Year-end Yield on Moody's Average Utility Bond (%)
1946	-8.3	132	11.2	11.8	4.45	9.6	119	8.0	14.9	4.52	1.7	2.77
1947	8.3	122	15.4	7.9	5.48	-17.0	92	7.7	11.9	6.17	-2.3	3.02
1948	5.9	104	16.9	6.1	6.19	8.6	93	7.9	11.8	6.22	4.1	3.06
1949	16.0	109	14.0	7.7	6.87	23.0	107	8.3	13.0	5.50	3.3	2.79
1950	32.9	123	16.5	7.5	7.27	6.5	104	8.8	11.8	6.00	2.1	2.87
1951	18.5	130	13.5	9.6	6.02	16.0	110	7.9	13.9	5.61	-2.7	3.27
1952	16.5	133	12.2	11.0	5.42	17.5	122	8.4	14.4	5.07	3.5	3.19
1953	-2.5	120	12.4	9.7	5.91	10.0	126	8.8	14.2	5.28	3.4	3.37
1954	55.6	169	12.2	13.8	4.24	25.5	148	9.1	16.2	4.50	5.4	3.10
1955	34.8	193	14.3	13.5	4.02	8.4	148	9.7	15.4	4.60	0.5	3.34
1956	7.2	190	13.3	14.3	4.04	3.9	142	9.7	14.6	4.84	-6.8	3.93
1957	-10.5	146	12.0	12.1	4.52	7.7	138	9.4	14.8	4.89	8.7	4.29
1958	41.9	192	9.6	20.0	3.14	36.9	178	9.8	18.3	3.87	-2.2	4.39
1959	12.7	200	10.8	18.6	3.02	3.0	170	9.8	17.2	4.01	-1.0	4.86
1960	-1.6	182	10.1	18.1	3.26	20.9	191	10.8	18.6	3.57	9.1	4.58
1961	26.5	217	9.7	22.5	2.79	33.0	235	10.3	22.9	2.88	4.8	4.62
1962	-9.9	181	10.5	17.2	3.34	0.1	217	10.7	20.4	3.18	8.0	4.41
1963	23.7	208	11.1	18.7	3.05	9.4	221	10.8	20.5	3.25	2.2	4.49
1964	16.3	223	12.1	18.5	2.97	16.3	236	11.1	21.4	3.18	4.8	4.54
1965	13.0	226	12.6	17.9	3.34	2.8	227	11.7	19.4	3.50	-0.5	4.82
1966	-10.4	187	12.9	14.5	3.05	-4.1	203	12.1	16.8	3.94	0.2	5.65
1967	26.8	220	11.8	18.7	2.97	-3.3	179	12.2	14.7	4.52	-5.0	6.57

Table 28-1 — Continued

Stock and Bond Yields and Performance 1946-1986

Year	S&P 400 Industrials					Moody's Electric Utilities					Bonds	
	Total Return (%)	Year-end Market Book Ratio (%)	Return on Year-end Common Equity (%)	Year-end P/E Ratio (x)	Year-end Dividend Yield (%)	Total Return (%)	Year-end Market Book Ratio (%)	Return on Year-end Common Equity (%)	Year-End P/E Ratio (x)	Year-end Dividend Yield (%)	Total Return Long-Term Corporate Bonds (%)	Year-end Yield on Moody's Average Utility Bond (%)
1968	10.5	225	12.3	18.3	2.84	10.5	180	11.5	15.6	4.40	2.6	6.85
1969	-7.3	196	11.9	16.6	3.28	-14.2	140	11.4	12.2	5.47	-8.1	8.39
1970	2.6	192	10.3	18.7	3.17	10.3	138	10.8	12.9	5.33	18.4	8.45
1971	15.0	204	10.8	18.9	2.77	2.0	129	10.8	12.0	5.62	11.0	7.92
1972	19.9	226	11.7	19.3	2.48	3.4	119	11.0	10.8	5.87	7.3	7.48
1973	-14.7	174	14.2	12.3	3.35	-21.2	85	10.5	8.1	8.28	1.1	8.17
1974	-26.5	113	14.2	8.0	4.97	-24.4	56	10.4	5.4	11.73	-3.1	10.02
1975	36.8	142	12.1	11.8	3.73	47.3	73	10.3	7.2	8.97	14.6	9.87
1976	22.6	157	14.0	11.2	3.65	28.4	86	10.6	8.1	7.92	18.7	8.61
1977	-8.2	127	14.0	9.1	4.90	11.2	87	11.0	7.9	8.33	3.8	8.65
1978	7.5	120	14.6	8.2	5.16	-3.9	75	10.8	7.0	10.01	0.3	9.67
1979	18.5	123	16.5	7.5	5.27	4.8	69	11.0	6.3	11.24	-2.2	11.68
1980	33.0	143	14.9	9.6	4.24	8.1	65	10.7	6.1	12.26	0-5	14.48
1981	-6.7	118	14.4	8.2	5.11	19.7	70	12.43	5.6	12.52	2.3	16.18
1982	20.2	133	11.1	11.9	4.56	34.9	85	13.1	6.4	10.87	35.5	13.50
1983	22.9	153	12.1	12.6	3.96	14.5	87	14.3	6.1	11.11	9.3	13.46
1984	3.6	150	14.6	10.4	3.99	22.7	94	14.9	6.3	10.44	16.2	12.96
1985	30.1	186	12.1	15.4	3.30	28.1	108	14.3	7.6	9.17	25.4	10.56
1986	18.6	217	11.7	18.7	3.02	29.9	126	14.5	8.7	7.89	16.3	9.00

Sources: Moody's, Standard & Poors, Merrill Lynch estimates. Total return on long term corporate bonds 1946-1976 from: Roger g. Ibbotson and Rex A. Sinquefield, *Stocks, Bonds, Bills and Inflation: The Past (1926-1976) and the Future (1977-2000)* (Charlottesville: Financial Analysts Research Foundation, 1977), and Merrill Lynch Corporate Index—All Corporate Bonds for 1977-1986.

Table 28-2

Stock and Bond Yields and Performance by Periods 1946–1983

	1946-1950	1951-1955	1956-1960	1961-1965	1966-1970	1971-1975	1976-1980	1981-1983
Total return/yr. (%)								
Industrials	10.2	23.1	8.6	13.3	3.6	3.4	13.4	11.3
Utilities	5.3	15.7	13.8	11.7	-0.7	-1.4	9.2	22.7
Bonds	1.8	2.0	1.4	3.8	1.2	6.1	4.0	8.7
Market/book ratio (%)								
Industrials	118	149	182	211	204	172	134	135
Utilities	103	131	164	227	168	92	76	81
Return on equity (%)								
Industrials	14.8	12.9	11.2	11.2	11.8	12.6	14.8	12.5
Utilities	8.1	8.8	9.9	10.9	11.6	10.6	10.8	13.3
P/E Ratio (X)								
Industrials	8.2	11.5	16.6	19.0	17.4	14.1	9.1	10.9
Utilities	12.7	14.8	16.7	20.9	14.4	8.7	7.1	6.0
Yields (%)								
Industrial dividend	6.1	5.9	3.6	3.1	3.1	3.5	4.6	4.6
Utility dividend	5.7	5.0	4.2	3.2	4.7	8.7	10.0	11.5
Utility bond yield	2.9	3.2	4.4	4.6	7.2	8.7	10.6	14.4
ROE – Bond yield (%)								
Industrials	11.9	9.7	6.8	6.6	4.6	3.9	4.2	-1.9
Utilities	5.2	5.6	5.5	6.3	4.4	1.9	0.2	-1.1
Div. yield – Bond yield (%)								
Industrials	3.2	2.7	-0.8	-1.5	-4.1	5.2	-6.0	-9.8
Utilities	2.8	1.8	-0.2	-1.4	-2.5	0.0	-0.6	-2.9

In the earliest period (1946-1950), the economy recovered from World War II and fears of renewed depression. Utility holding companies were being broken up, and shares of operating companies were being distributed to security holders. The deliberate policy of the Federal Reserve kept down interest rates. Price controls were being dismantled. The earnings and dividends of industrial firms rose rapidly as did profitability. Gains in the utility industry were more moderate, and return earned on equity was far less than in the industrial sector. At the same time, the return offered by bonds was low and steady. In that period, industrial shares sold at roughly one-fifth above book value and utilities sold at close to book value, an indication that industrial companies were probably earning more than cost of capital, while utility earnings were about equal to cost of capital. Utilities sold at consistently higher P/E ratios and provided a slightly lower dividend yield than that of industrials. The total return on an investment in industrial stocks was far greater than that produced by utility stocks or by bonds.

The next period (1951-1955) may have been more representative. The Treasury and the Federal Reserve reached an accord freeing the Federal Reserve System from the responsibility for keeping down interest rates. The rise in long term interest rates, however, was still modest. The profitability of industrial corporations (measured by return on equity) dropped but remained well above that for utilities. Profitability of electric utilities rose. Electric utility stocks maintained higher P/E ratios and provided lower dividend yields than did industrial shares. Both utility and industrial stocks sold above book value. Again the industrials provided a higher total return for investors.

At the beginning of the second half of the Eisenhower Administration, industrial profitability declined further while utility profitability continued to rise. In 1956-1960, utility and industrial shares sold at similar multiples, although utility shares provided slightly higher dividend yields. For the first time since 1936, the dividend yield on electric utility stocks in 1957 was lower on average than the yield for utility bonds.

Interest rates also rose, but not enough to discourage investors who bid the prices for industrial and utility shares up above book value. Electric utility shares also provided a better total return than either industrial stocks or bonds. In fact, the supposedly golden age for utility shares was 1957-1962, during which total return averaged 16.1% a year vs. 8.2% a year for industrials and 4.5% for bonds.

The golden age ended in the 1961-1965 period. Interest rates rose slightly. Return in the utility sector picked up, but not substantially. On the other hand, industrial companies made a dramatic recovery in profitability, despite a poor beginning. Investors obviously had euphoric expectations, because market/book ratios and multiples reached their highest levels, levels which have yet to be equalled since the Great Depression. In the period, electric utility shares sold at higher market/book ratios than industrial stocks. On a total return basis, industrial stocks once again did better than utility stocks and bonds.

By 1966-1970, interest rates began a sharp upturn that was not accompanied by a commensurate rise in return on equity for either the industrial or the utility sector. Oddly enough, despite dull corporate results, the period marked the beginning of the era of performance investing—the go-go years on Wall Street. Utility shares were shoved aside because investors knew that the group could not provide the necessary growth for superior performance. Instead, investors put their money into shares with greater risk. The market/book ratio began to fall for all shares, but even more precipitously for utilities. The P/E ratio for utility stocks declined while that for industrials issues. held. As for total return on investment, industrial issues and bonds outperformed utility stocks.

As the 1970s began, the illness of the utility sector became more evident. In 1971-1975, prices for utility stocks fell below book value, as return on utility equity declined while yields on bonds rose further. Industrial companies, on the other hand, were able to raise profitability. With bonds providing a high yield alternative, the market revalued equities. Multiples and market/book ratios fell. Yields rose. Bonds gave investors a higher total return than did industrial stocks, and utilities provided an even lower total return than that for industrial shares.

In 1976-1980, interest rates continued to rise, profitability for utility companies was flat and profitability for industrial companies improved. Because neither group was able to earn a return that rose in line with bond yields, market/book ratios and multiples slid, and dividend yields rose. Nevertheless, industrials closed above book value in every postwar year. On the other hand, electric utility stocks closed at a price below book value in each year 1973-1980. In terms of total return, industrial stocks again outpaced utility shares and bonds. In 1981-1986, roles reversed, as utility shares responded to improving profitability and lower interest rates. By 1987, in fact, the average electric utility share had moved above book value.

Investors in bonds expect to assume an interest rate risk. They want the credit-worthiness of their investment to remain stable or to improve. A higher bond rating indicates more strength. Accordingly, investors will pay more for the better quality issue. Even if interest rates remain stable, bond investors can show a profit or loss if the bond rating rises or falls.

Table 28-3 shows the rating distribution of a sample of operating electric utilities that are not associated with holding companies. The same companies represent more than 70% of the industry's operating income and long term debt in 1975.[12] Between 1946 and 1950, the percentage of ratings in the two highest quality groups (Aaa and Aa) remained static. In the decade from 1950 to 1960, the sample changed drastically in quality and quantity because of the addition of several companies, and because the quality of the industry improved dramatically in the eyes of the credit experts. Further improvement took place through 1965. Thus, from the end of World War II to the end of 1965, investors were able to depend on a rising trend of credit-worthiness to add value to utility bonds. A modest

Table 28-3

Debt Ratings and Ratios
Percentage Distribution of Long Term Debt Outstanding by Rating Category
(Year-end, 73 Independent Electric Companies, Unweighted, in %)

	1946	1950	1955	1960	1965	1970	1975	1980	1983
Moody's Ratings (%)									
Aaa	17.2	13.8	12.1	16.2	19.3	15.5	5.1	1.4	0.0
Aa	34.5	37.9	47.0	57.4	69.3	62.6	44.0	35.6	32.9
A	39.7	43.0	33.3	20.6	7.2	18.9	32.5	46.6	34.2
Baa	6.9	10.3	7.6	7.4	4.2	3.0	18.4	16.4	28.8
Ba	1.7	0.0	0.0	0.0	0.0	0.0	0.0	0.0	4.1
	100.0	100.0	100.0	100.0	100.0	100.0	100.0	100.0	100.0
Standard & Poors Ratings (%)									
AAA					19.2	14.0	0.0	0.0	0.0
AA					68.0	65.6	39.1	32.9	31.5
A					8.0	17.4	44.2	43.8	30.1
BBB					4.8	3.0	16.7	21.9	28.8
BB					0.0	0.0	0.0	1.4	9.6
					100.0	100.0	100.0	100.0	100.0
Percentage of Ratings (%)									
Aaa and Aa (Moody's)	51.7	51.7	59.1	73.6	88.6	78.1	49.5	37.0	32.9
AAA and AA (S&P)	—	—	—	—	87.2	79.6	39.1	32.9	31.5
Ratios for Industry (all departments)									
Debt ratio:									
Long term debt as % of permanent capitalization (excludes short term debt)	46.0	48.9	51.0	52.6	51.7	55.3	52.6	50.2	48.4
Total debt as % of total capitalization (includes short term debt)	46.2	49.3	52.2	53.4	52.4	56.4	53.7	51.8	49.2
Pretax interest coverage ratio									
Operating income (x)	4.57E	4.79	5.44	5.03	5.15	2.80	2.25	1.94	2.34
Income before interest charges (x)	4.85E	5.14	5.68	5.17	5.27	3.11	2.66	2.53	3.06

Notes: When ratings are not available, sample size is reduced, to 58 in 1946 and 1950, 66 in 1955, 68 in 1960. Income before interest charges includes all allowance for funds used during construction.

Sources: Moody's, Standard & Poors, EIA, FPC, Edison Electric Institute, Merrill Lynch estimates (E).

decline in ratings began in 1965-1970, and a disastrous falloff occurred through 1975. Many seem to believe that the 1973-1975 drop in credit-worthiness (induced by the Yom Kippur War, the oil embargo, a drop in demand for electricity, higher interest rates, and Con Edison's omission of a dividend) produced the low point for the industry. In reality bond ratings continued to decline afterwards. Weak utilities with double or triple B ratings find it expensive to sell debt because many institutions will not buy such low quality securities.

What caused the decline in credit-worthiness? A basic reason is that utilities continued to rely on debt ratios that were inappropriate to the changing circumstances. The companies concentrated on maintaining debt as a given percentage of capital without taking into account that coverages could not be maintained when higher interest rates increased unless the debt ratio was reduced. Thus, when the industry ran into hard times, bond investors suffered along with equity investors. Fortunately, with interest rates down and a modest spending scheduled for the late 1980s, the industry should be able to improve its financial standing. Many companies are in the midst of programs to replace high cost debt and preferred stock with lower yielding securities, which should raise interest coverage ratios. Most utilities anticipate higher equity ratios, too, as they finance future spending more with retained earnings and less with debt.

Chapter 29

Summary

... the current regulatory climate is sending a very clear signal to utility stockholders, investors and management. That signal is that if you want to protect your economic interest you should liquidate the utility business you are in.[13]

Charles J. Cicchetti

The electric utility's financial structure is based on the heavy use of fixed income securities. In fact, almost two-thirds of capital is derived from sale of debt and preferred stock. The industry is also capital intensive and requires large amounts of fixed assets to produce revenues. As a result, the industry bears a heavy load of fixed costs: interest, preferred dividends, depreciation, and taxes on real property.

Because profitability is controlled and expenditures on long-lived new plant are often huge in relation to funds generated by operations, utilities have not been able to finance the bulk of their capital needs from internal sources. The companies must raise large sums of money in the markets on a regular basis. The need to raise large sums of money at a time of rising capital costs combined with unexpectedly poor demand for power puts a crimp on profitability and reduces the coverage of interest charges.

As Table 29-1 shows, in the period from 1965 to 1970, the financial ratios of the electric utilities dropped precipitously. Companies pushed up the debt ratios. More money was tied up in incomplete plant (construction work in progress). The industry became less capable of funding its needs from internal sources. Interest coverage ratios collapsed because interest rates rose by far more than the return earned by the utilities on the money invested. Furthermore, even the reported earnings of the companies fell in quality, as non-cash credits became a larger percentage of earnings. From 1970 on, utilities reduced their use of debt, but most other ratios continued to deteriorate. The return earned on assets rose, but not by an amount sufficient to offset the sharp increase in fixed charges. As a result, profitability for the common shareholders dropped. To make matters worse, the decline in return on stockholders' equity occurred despite the inflation of earnings by non-cash credits. The market's reaction to the deterioration in financial strength and profitability, in the face of the availability of rising returns elsewhere, was predictable. Prices for utility stocks fell as investors, who demanded higher returns, marked down the stocks until the returns were adequate to attract new investors.

Table 29-1

Financial Data
Electric Utility Industry
(All Departments)
1965-1986

	1965	1970	1975	1980	1985	Est. 1986
Capitalization %						
Long term debt	50.6%	53.0%	50.8%	48.6%	48.1%	48.3%
Short term debt	1.8	3.4	2.9	3.2	1.0	1.2
Preferred and preference stock	9.3	9.5	12.1	11.7	9.5	8.7
Common equity	38.3	34.1	34.3	36.5	41.4	41.8
	100.0	100.0	100.0	100.0	100.0	100.0
Construction work in progress as % of net electric plant	5%	14%	20%	29%	26%	22%
Internal sources of funds as % of construction expenditure						
Including AFUDC	55%	30%	42%	39%	70%	75%
Excluding AFUDC	54	26	36	29	61	70
Pretax interest coverage — all debt						
Operating Income	5.15×	2.80×	2.25×	1.94×	2.42×	2.57×
Income before interest charges	5.27	3.11	2.66	2.53	3.02	3.09
Rates of return on						
Average net plant	7.0 %	7.4 %	8.4 %	9.5 %	11.2 %	10.8 %
Average common equity	12.5	11.8	11. 1	11.4	12.5	13.2
Net income for common stock						
Dividend payout ratio	65%	68%	67%	76%	76%	70%
% of net/common from AFUDC	4	20	35	55	50	37
Average cost of money (Moody's)						
New debt	4.7%	8.9%	9.8%	13.1%	11.8%	9.5%
New preferred	—	9.0	10.6	12.3	10.1	8.3
E/P ratio (common)	5.1	8.7	15.2	16.4	14.4	11.8

Sources: Moody's, Edison Electric Institute, FERC, EIA, Merrill Lynch estimates.

During the dramatic declines of the 1960s and 1970s, analysts, academics, and industry executives applied the ruler method of projection. They extrapolated from the trend line and predicted disaster. Yet, it should have been obvious that the electric industry could not afford to continue to invest in projects that produced a return below the cost of capital. Investors would refuse to buy the securities needed to finance the projects. As shown in Table 29-1, conditions did improve in the 1980s.

The industry is paying off short term debt, refinancing high cost securities through the sale of lower cost issues, and cutting down construction projects to reduce the need for outside financing. A handful of companies are in extreme difficulty, facing the writeoff of major portions of their assets, unable to pay or continue dividends, but most companies are showing improvement.

As a result of two decades of financial difficulties, though, utilities have modified their strategies for growth. Most are reluctant to commit funds to large, regulated projects for fear that the capital invested will not receive proper compensation. That attitude could control managerial decisions that previously have been made on an engineering basis. As a result of declining interest rates, winding down of big construction programs, and a cautious attitude toward new spending, the financial picture for electric utilities is improving.

Notes

[1]Haskins & Sells, *Public Utilities Manual* (New York: Deloitte Haskins & Sells, 1977), p. 33.

[2]The Averch-Johnson effect was first hypothesized in a 1962 article: Harvey Averch and Leland L. Johnson, "Behavior of the Firm under Regulatory Constraint", *American Economic Review* (December 1962).

[3]"From the financial point of view . . . earnings are limited but . . . more stable than most industrial companies, bonds . . . are widely used in capital structures, and the risk is usually less than for industrial companies because of the essential nature of the service . . . and protection against competition." Ralph E. Badger, Harold W. Torgerson, and Harry G. Guthmann, *Investment Principles and Practices* (Englewood Cliffs, N.J.: Prentice Hall, 1961) p. 296.

[4]Badger, Torgerson and Guthmann, *op. cit.,* p. 273.

[5]Ambrose Bierce, *The Devil's Dictionary* (New York: Dover, 1958), p 26.

[6]Haskins & Sells, *op. cit.,* p. 7.

[7]Benjamin Graham, David L. Dodd, and Sidney Cottle, *Security Analysis* (New York: McGraw-Hill, 1962) p. 1.

[8]Graham, Dodd and Cottle, *op. cit.,* p. 386.

[9]John Burr Williams, *The Theory of Investment Value* (Cambridge: Harvard U. Press, 1938) p. 397.

[10]Corporation Commission of the State of Oklahoma, *Application of Public Service Company of Oklahoma* (Cause No. 27068, Order No. 206560, Jan. 15, 1982), p. 63.

[11]The total returns for utilities are understated to the extent that in the period

1946-1965, many utilities sold new stock to shareholders at a below-market price. Shareholders who did not choose to exercise their rights to purchase the shares could sell those rights, thereby adding to income. In the late 1960s, rights offerings lost popularity. The addition of the value from sale of rights to total return would not change the conclusions of the discussion.

[12]For details, see Leonard S. Hyman and Carmine J. Grigoli, "The Credit Standing of Electric Utilities," *Public Utilities Fortnightly*, Mar. 3, 1977, pp. 24-30.

[13]Charles J. Cicchetti, "Conservation Financing—Its Rate Impact," in Edison Electric Institute, *Proceedings, Sixteenth Financial Conference, October 4-7, 1981* (Washington, D.C.: EEI, 1982), p. 7.

Part Six

The Future of The Electric Utility Industry

Chapter 30

Introduction

The data indicate that actually generated electricity at current prices, as a way to deliver energy services is already uncompetitive in several energy service markets. Raising the price may just exacerbate the problem. As one of us has suggested. "To say you can solve utilities' problems by raising rates is much like saying we could solve the problems of Chrysler by raising the price of their automobiles."[1]

Roger W. Sant

A few years ago, this section would have been titled "The Electric Utility Industry: Does it Have a Future?" Too many managements were fighting tooth-and-nail to continue strategies that seemed to make little business sense. Too many regulators either pursued short range political goals or showed little appreciation of the economics of the sector that they regulated. The coerciveness of central station power, the virtues of nuclear energy, and the date of the millennium when the lights would go out were favored subjects for theological-like debates. Meanwhile, customers reduced their consumption of power and the industry sank into a slough of financial despond.

Economic and political conditions have not been kind to the industry. As a large borrower of funds, the industry was hurt by high interest rates. As an industry that can only raise prices after a delay, it was hurt by inflation.

As a major user of oil and gas, it has had to spend scarce resources on projects that switch fuels rather than increase productive capability. Because its generating plants dam running water, spew out pollutants and use radioactive matter, and because its transmission lines cut a swath through the landscape, the industry became a target for environmental activists.

During the Reagan administration, the drop in interest rates, de-emphasis of environmental protection activity, and the free market approach to energy policy all reduced the pressure on the hard-pressed electric utilities. But the improvement really came about because the industry was finishing the massive construction projects that had been such a drain on resources.

No longer faced with cash outflows and outraged customers, the average electric company can plan for the future rather than fight battles for survival.

The future, though, may not be an idyllic period in which the sale of electricity grows steadily while utilities harvest a bumper crop of cash that will be used for diversification, higher dividends and stock repurchases. Demand could grow faster than expected, thereby bringing up the question of who will build the next power plant. Customers want competitively priced electricity, not electricity priced to provide the correct rate of return to the local utility. New suppliers of power can help the utility meet its needs, or they can compete with the utility by selling directly to the utility's own customers. Utilities will have to become flexible organizations. And regulatory agencies will have to reformulate policies that were relevant when electric utilities really were natural monopolies.

Chapter **31**

Building For The Future

Investment based on genuine long-term expectation is so difficult today as to be scarcely practicable . . . There is no clear evidence from experience that the investment policy which is socially advantageous coincides with that which is most profitable.[2]

John Maynard Keynes

Spending (in real terms) in the electric utility industry is a function of the need to:

1) Increase plant to meet the requirements of new customers and the additional requirements of existing customers.

2) Replace old equipment.

3) Assure an adequate margin of safety in the level of service.

4) Modify equipment in order to burn a more available fuel instead of a scarce fuel, or to reduce the emission of pollutants.

In 1987, electric utilities had a high reserve margin and heavily depended on coal as a fuel. By 1996, taking into account current construction plans and the industry's 2.0% forecasted growth in peak load, reserve will fall sharply, as can be seen in Table 31-1. Coal will remain the most important fuel, Non-utility generators will account for a small but increasing proportion of capacity. The industry has reduced its demand forecast downward again and again since the days of the energy crisis of the 1970s. The sharp increases in the price of electricity and the resulting conservation effort certainly pushed demand down. So did the United States' retreat from heavy industry to a service-oriented economy. But we now face a different situation. The price of electricity may not rise much in real terms, while the downfall of the dollar could reinvigorate American manufactur-

268   America's Electric Utilities: Past, Present and Future

Table 31-1

Total Electric Utility (Contiguous USA):
Sales, Capacity, Demand and Fuel Mix
Projected 1987 and 1996

| | *Projected* | | *Annual Rate* |
	1987	*1996*	*of Growth (%)*
Annual energy production (billions of kwh)	2,550	2,994	1.8
Summer capability (thousands of MW)	645	708	1.0
Summer peak (thousands of MW)	484	577	2.0
High voltage (over 230 kv) transmission (thousands of circuit miles)	144	157	0.9
Summer reserve margin (%)	33	23	—
Generating capacity by fuel (%)			
Nuclear	13.9	15.2	
Coal	44.4	43.4	
Hydro	10.4	10.0	
Oil and Gas	28.0	26.2	
Other	3.3	5.2	
Total	100.0	100.0	
Production by fuel (%)			
Nuclear	19.2	21.4	
Coal	54.8	52.9	
Hydro	9.8	8.4	
Oil and gas	14.4	12.8	
Other	1.8	4.5	
Total	100.0	100.0	
Generating capacity by ownership (%)			
Utility	98.5	96.5	
Non-utility	1.5	3.5	
Total	100.0	100.0	

Source: North American Electric Reliability Council, *1987 Reliability Assessment* (Princeton, N.J.:NERC, 1987).

ing. No doubt that conservationists will argue, rightly, that Americans can do far more to control consumption of electricity and growth in peak load. In the glutted market for electricity that presently exists, though, utilities want to encourage—not discourage—demand. Moreover, if they attempt to influence demand through the price mechanism, in the competitive market of today they will drive customers to competing suppliers of energy during a period when the electric industry needs the revenue, but may get the customers back when the energy surplus has shrunk and the customers want to return to a low, controlled price. A free market may not be conducive to rational decision making that involves facilities that last 30-40 years.

If we accept the industry's estimates, we must conclude that capacity should be adequate for the nation's needs in 1996. A large fraction of the projected capacity additions, though, consists of facilities on which no work has begun, and of non-utility stations, In addition, greater transmission capability would make it easier to move electricity in volume, and would assure greater reliability of service, but little expansion of transmission is planned. Undoubtedly, if demand for electricity rises faster than expected, the utilities will respond by building peaking units and other small power stations that can be put up quickly, and non-utility suppliers will come forth with additional projects. Nuclear power will not play its hoped-for role in the energy market, but it should produce about one-fifth of our electricity. Of the 26 nuclear stations scheduled for service after January 1, 1987, perhaps 17 will go into operation. The nuclear option appears to have been killed off, a victim of cost overruns, technical difficulties, loss of public confidence, lack of political backing, the fall in fuel prices, and slower than expected growth in demand for electricity. Loss of that option could become a problem if fuel prices rise, or foreign nations embargo their energy exports, or if fossil fuel combustion must be reduced in order to prevent damage to the climate. Otherwise, it appears as if most utilities in the United States could find replacements for cancelled nuclear projects.[3]

Capacity additions reached a five year peak in 1986, declined in 1987, and should fall rapidly into the 1990s. Capital spending, however, hit an all time high in 1983, showed a gradual decrease through 1986, and then began a faster drop. As can be seen in Table 31-2, the need to raise money from external sources should decline.

The industry's projections for demand may not fully take into account the potential of load management devices that can reduce demand during peak periods. Most companies are still experimenting in this area and may not emphasize load management until new generating facilities are in service and excess capacity is reduced. Demand can also be controlled by means of time-of-use pricing accompanied by computer controls on the premises of the consumer. For instance, the computer could turn on or off certain appliances, based on the price of electricity, and the price would depend on the time of day or the cost of generation at a particular time.[4] That type of system has even greater applicability to industrial processes in

Table 31-2

Estimated Spending and Financing—Investor Owned Utilities
($ billions)

| | Actual | | | Estimated | | |
	1984	1985	1986	1987	1988	1989
Spending						
Capital spending	26.0	24.9	25.3	23.0	21.8	19.7
Nuclear fuel	1.8	2.2	1.7	1.7	2.0	2.0
Allowance for funds used during construction	8.2	7.9	6.5	4.9	3.6	3.5
Total	36.0	35.0	33.5	29.6	27.4	25.2
Internal funds						
Retained earnings	5.8	3.8	5.2	5.8	5.2	6.0
Depreciation and amortization	10.1	12.8	12.4	13.2	15.5	15.8
Deferred taxes	6.9	6.7	6.8	5.0	3.8	3.8
Total	22.8	23.3	24.4	24.0	24.5	25.6
External funds, working capital and sale of assets	13.2	11.7	9.1	5.6	2.9	(0.4)

Note: Capital spending includes non-electric utility capital expenditures.
Sources: Electrical World, EEI, Merrill Lynch estimates.

which power plays an important role. Ideally, sales promotion and demand side management (such as load management or special pricing) should be integrated into a comprehensive marketing strategy that will encourage profitable and discourage unprofitable demand.[5]

In addition, the industry can improve the operating performance of existing power stations. Doing so should be more cost effective than building new generating units. Proper regulatory incentives to encourage more efficient operations would benefit customers and utility owners.[6]

Fortunately, the industry can tackle expansion in ways that do not require huge, risky projects that have long lead times. New technological options (such as fluidized bed combustion, gasified combined cycle or fuel cell) might be built economically in relatively small sizes, are less polluting, and can be constructed in a few years. Furthermore, non-utility generating firms might supply the industry by erecting units that range from hydro projects, to windmills, to cogeneration. It is too early to judge the importance of superconductivity in the industry's plans. Certainly, developments in that field will have an impact.

In other words, now that the bulk of the industry's major construction projects are completed, capital expenditures can be brought under control by utilization of new technologies, demand side management, improved pricing of the product, and shifting some construction from the utility to independent power producers. But it remains necessary for the utilities to maintain a flexible stance, because they could be moving into a period in which demand grows faster than expected.

Chapter 32

Market, Structure and Regulation

Competition is an indispensable mainstay of a system in which the character of products and their development, the amount and evolving efficiency of production, and the prices and profit margins charged are left to the operation of private enterprise. In our conception . . . it is . . . crucial . . . that the customer should be in a position . . . to exert effective discipline over the producer. . . . Otherwise, government would . . . undertake discipline . . . — as it does in the field of public-service industries.[7]

John Maurice Clark

Electric utilities long regarded themselves as the monopoly suppliers of central station power, a narrow view of the market encouraged by the regulatory process. Some competition existed for the end use of that power: oil or gas could be used for heating, as an example. And private generating units could reduce or eliminate the need to purchase electricity from the central station. But that competition seemed trivial. The government regulated electric utilities because they were supposed to be natural monopolies.

Now, the natural monopoly rationale for regulation is under attack. Economies of scale may no longer exist for the generation of electricity, in which case generation could be deregulated, provided that a transmission system exists that could connect competitive generators to customers.[8] Competition exists now in the sense that large customers choose between producing their own electricity or buying it from the local utility. In some instances, customers have even chosen which of neighboring utilities should serve them, basing the choice on price and quality of service.

Perhaps competition has not come faster because of the regulatory process. When regulation depresses the price of central station power below its true economic value, there is no incentive for consumers to self generate or for competitors to bring on new sources that must be priced at current costs in order to show a profit. Thus, where regulators price electricity artificially low, they protect the monopoly status of the electric utility by preventing the development of competitive power resources, until a revolutionary new technology appears that can produce electricity below the regulated price. However, where regulators (or the utility) attempt to price central station power above its economic worth to the consumer, or above what it costs for a customer that self generates, they encourage competitive sources of electricity, thereby endangering the, utility's monopoly. Protection from competition has fostered a method of doing business that may have been—in the end—riskier than allowing competitive entry into the market. The protection of regulation, the appearance of monopoly, encouraged utilities to build large, long-lived generating stations that took a decade or more to construct. From an engineering standpoint, such plants seemed to represent the least cost way to service customers. The engineers assumed that the monopoly existed, that risk was low, that the regulators could and would provide the revenue needed to support and pay for the new facility. Yet, if a major change in technology were to occur, enabling non-utilities to offer electricity to some customers from a cheap, unregulated source, raising utility rates to make up for the loss of business that goes to the new source will only drive more consumers to the new source. The low depreciation rates and return earned by the utility are premised on monopoly power through the life of the plant. Technological innovation by a competitor might lead to a situation in which the utility's revenue is insufficient to provide a profit on and recover the cost of its facility. If the utility built smaller, faster-to-construct plants, it could adjust its plans to shorter range considerations and could adjust to what the competition could offer.

A number of utilities are trying to avoid the regulatory and technological risks inherent in large, central stations by offering to purchase power generated by others. Shifting the burden of supply to an outside party does not—in itself—shift risk, unless the outside supplier is better able to do the job than the utility. A commitment to purchase power represents a risk, too. The electricity might not be needed, but it will have to be paid for, anyway. Or it might prove to be more expensive than subsequently discovered alternatives. In either case, regulators could disallow the contract expense from what the utility can charge its customers.

The questions of who should build and who should purchase have become intertwined with the question of whether the industry needs competition as a spur to better performance. Some have concluded that competition should be introduced into the electric industry by separating the distribution, transmission and generating functions. Local distribution would remain regulated, because the function continues to be a natural monopoly, although there could be opportunities for competition for customers along the borders between distribution companies. The transmission system is the key to making competition more than a local phenomenon, bringing power from competing generating stations to the purchasers, and permitting distribution systems and large users to tap into power from the cheapest sources. In a competitive market, transmission might have to remain regulated, perhaps as a common carrier, in order to prevent the transmission firms from exercising their monopoly power in a way that strangles the development of competing generating sources. In the competitive scenario, the generating sector (including industrial producers) would be unregulated, because generation has lost economies of scale, no longer has the characteristics of the natural monopoly. Low cost producers should get the business. Distribution companies should not be associated with generating entities that they would favor as opposed to picking the low cost source. Therefore, the separation of functions.

Arguments for competition encompass two issues: capital attraction and efficiency. Some proponents of competition really want to encourage the flow of new capital into the generating business. They fear that the electric utilities have been so discouraged by past regulatory actions that they will not invest in new, needed generating capacity. They advocate that new generation should be built in response to requests by utilities. The utility would select the lowest bidder who agrees to build the plant and sell the electricity to the utility. Presumably, the bidders would select prices for output that included their minimum cost of capital requirements, given the level of risk. No firm would build unless the price reflected this *ex ante* assessment of required profit. That would be unlike the present procedure in which the utility builds not knowing what profit level will be set by the regulator on an *ex post* basis, once the facility is completed. Regulators would approve the bidding procedure, and accept the price without questioning the return built into it, because the return is what the market (as indicated in the bidding procedure) requires. The competition is between bidders. To the extent the bidders are more efficient than the local utility, customers might benefit. If the winning bidder suffers cost overruns or runs into operating problems, he suffers the consequences, not the customer of the electric company, because the latter is getting the electricity at the set price, whether the winning bidder makes his expected profit or not. At least, that is the situation in theory. The bidders have to raise funds, too, and suppliers of capital may not accept those ideal terms, or might exact a high price for money that diminishes the attractiveness of a process that makes the builder fully responsible for his actions.

If competition is limited to the auction at which the winner of a generating contract is chosen, does that produce an efficient, competitive market for electricity? Some consumers might do better if they could find their own electric supplier, cutting out the local distributor (except as a conduit) or generator. Competition (and freedom from rate of return regulation) only for new supply discourages investment in conservation or cost cutting for existing regulated generation. Limiting new suppliers by means of rigid contracts might prevent the development of a fluid market in which many generators move in and out (and customers choose to take or not take electricity) depending on short term price fluctuations. Certainly, if the utility signs a long term contract with a supplier, the utility's flexibility has been lessened in dealing with new, more competitive power sources.

For the customer or the distributor to get the cheapest power available, perhaps there could be a market for electricity analogous to the stock market. Prices in the marketplace—registered on customers' computers—would depend on supply and demand, affected by plant availability, outages, weather, and fuel costs. Customers would pay for some combination of capacity or access to the system, perhaps, on a steady basis, and then make decisions on current usage depending on short term market prices. When prices rose or fell, the consumer would adjust demand when, for instance, the price exceeded the electricity's value to the customer. Price would clear the market through the interplay of supply and demand This system would reduce the need for a high reserve margin, because during shortages price would rise until customers cut down on usage, which they presumably would do if they had to pay for what they were getting. Furthermore, firms would have an incentive to build power plants when the market looked profitable, because they could collect a price that reflected the current value of what they were selling. Customers would have reason to reduce usage when price went too high. To continue the stock market analogy, it might be possible to create a futures market for electricity, with those who expect to require the electricity to buy future delivery, and those who plan to supply it taking the money to help finance the construction of the means of supply.

Several variants of a competitive system have been proposed. Skeptics cite numerous problems. The transmission network was not designed to handle the anticipated power flows. Access to the transmission network must be assured. The bid and contract procedure could lead to lawsuits from losing bidders and disputes reminiscent of some of the Defense Department contract fiascos. And, what is the nature of the utility's obligation to serve customers in its territory if the utility does not control the source of power, and if the customers need take the utility's service only when it is advantageous to them, but the utility is obligated to serve the customer under adverse circumstances? The prospect of the utility acting as supplier of last resort, with only the most unprofitable accounts wedded to it is an unpleasant but probable one that would be forced on it by authorities that want both competition and service for those who cannot afford to pay the going rate. (The economist's answer, that the utility should charge the right price, and the government should give the poor customer the funds to buy the electricity, has never been acceptable to politicians in this country, because it would mean exacting a visible tax from voters instead of exacting a hidden tax through cross subsidy of one customer by another.) Unfortunately, the utility could play the role of redistributor of wealth when it had a monopoly, when one service could cross subsidize another. It will not be able to play the role once competition forces down the prices on the highly profitable sales, leaving no means of cross subsidy.

The desire for reform is based on the belief that the regulatory system has not worked: it has produced an industry not mindful of costs, because all costs could be passed on to captive customers. Now that regulators have refused to pass on all costs, the industry has retreated from the needed future investment for fear of another round of hindsighted refusals to pay. Anything, even an imperfect new system, would be better. Industry executives reply that America's electric industry is exceptionally reliable and economical despite its travails, that the regulatory system should be modified not junked, that incentives to make regulated companies more efficient would work, and that risk of construction could be reduced through continuous regulatory oversight and approval.

The Public Utility Regulatory Policies Act of 1978 (PURPA) reintroduced independent power generation, but produced bizarre results, too. Independent power producers that met PURPA requirements could sell to the local utility at the utility's avoided cost, as defined by local regulators. Some contracts were written in a way to force the utility to reduce its own low cost production in order to buy the PURPA power. The added costs were passed on to its customers, of couse. Utilities could participate in but not control PURPA projects. Because of the nature of the contracts, many PURPA producers were able to earn profits far higher than what would have been allowed the local utility on a regulated basis. PURPA was a success in that it created a new group of electricity suppliers, rejuvenated interest in cogeneration, and convinced many that independent producers could be integrated into the existing network. But it may not lower costs to customers unless PURPA generators are forced to compete to supply the utility. The utility should not be forced to compete to supply the utility. The utility should not be forced to buy from all comers just because they have power to sell. PURPA's limit on utility ownership has laudable motives: to bring new entrants to the market and to prevent self dealing between a utility and its PURPA subsidiary. It also limited the participation of the most experienced power producers in the alternative power production business, and may have inadvertently created a combination of a hothouse and a cottage industry: one consisting of small firms that require a rigid and high price to survive. Electricity is electricity no matter the ownership of of the generator. Why is PURPA electricity worth more than utility electricity? If higher prices are needed to bring forth new sources of electricity, why are they payable only to non-utilities?

Much of the debate about competition and deregulation has a Rube Goldberg-like quality to it. Academics, government officials and regulators want to determine in advance the optimal format of the new system, and in the process they seem determined to erect a complicated structure that will deal with all questions in advance of implementation. In reality, the market will evolve and provide *ad hoc* solutions while the debate drones on. Radical measures that involve wholesale disintegration of utilities or complete repricing of the tariffs will be avoided because of the financial, political and social dislocations that would follow.[9] Mortgage bond indentures make it difficult to split utilities into generation, transmission and distribution segments without careful and time-consuming preparation. Piecemeal implementation might be necessary. Consumers buying electricity at a low, regulated price would not want to give up that benefit. High cost producers of electricity would not want to risk losing no longer captive customers to more competitive utilities. Competition and deregulation are more likely to come on a gradual, incremental basis. The easiest route would be to follow the British Telecom model: retain the integrated utility, but declare certain sectors of the business to be competitive and unregulated, and make certain that customers of the unregulated sector really have choices. If the utility wanted to keep the unregulated customers, it would have to run an efficient operation, and it could not overcharge the other customers because they would be protected by the regulator.(At present, many industrial customers are acting as if they were unregulated customers and the utilities are acting as if they could lose those customers if they do not provide economic service. Perhaps that is the beginning of competition and deregulation.) Severe regulatory problems might induce some utilities to take their chances in a competitive market, on the theory that they could be no worse off than under regulation. Wholesale power contracts, electricity from small producers, and sales to large industrial customers might be deregulated to some extent. Certainly those buying unregulated power should have the opportunity to shop around for the best contracts. It appears that the industry is evolving into a group of integrated utilities surrounded and served by many non-utility producers that are partially owned by the integrated utilities. Depending on the regulatory process and developments in the marketplace, some integrated utilities may move some of their assets into the unregulated arena. Piecemeal evolution of the industry may disturb economic purists who object to the inefficiencies produced by mixing regulated and unregulated elements, but it has an advantage: small mistakes are easier to correct than massive ones.

Regulators have tried to modify the system in order to encourage efficiency by granting higher returns to more efficient companies, or by letting the utility keep part of the profit over the allowed return as long as that extra profit comes about through better operating procedures rather than through rate relief. On the whole, though, regulators prefer the stick to the carrot. It must be easier to penalize a company than to reward it.

Meanwhile, regulators and utilities struggle with interrelated problems of rate shock, prudency, phase-in, and accounting for assets. When a large, expensive power station is placed in rate base, the price of electricity may have to be raised sharply to cover the operating and capital costs of the new unit. That sudden price increase is rate shock. (It could have been avoided by gradually raising prices before the plant was finished, but that would have meant including construction work in progress in rate base, which is illegal in many jurisdictions.) Customers may react to the price increase by cutting consumption, so the utility does not collect the desired revenue. Regulators may react by seeking to reduce the shock, either by gradually phasing in the rate increase over a period of several years, or by disallowing some or all of the plant from rate base, thereby making it unnecessary for customers to pay for it. To make the disallowance, the regulators might determine that the expenditures for the plant had not been prudent, and therefore should not be a burden to ratepayers. All of that brings the accountants into the picture. They had assumed that all assets were good because regulators would authorize rates that would provide for timely recovery of and return on investment, and customers would have no choice but to pay those rates. Clearly this is no longer the case. Refusal of regulators to let the utility earn a return on an asset, or to raise rates in a fashion that provides an adequate return for the entire life of the asset reduces the value of the investment, which might have to be written down or written off altogether. The combination of inability to collect rates (either because of regulation or due to consumer resistance), risk of disallowance of investment, and the fact that accountants will require immediate writeoffs if there is any question about recovery of or return on investment all pushes the utility managements in the direction of risk aversion. That means avoiding expenditures on large plants and, possibly, shunning innovation in the regulated part of the business.

If the utility avoids investment in large, regulated projects, perhaps management attention and company funds can be directed toward diversified activities, best defined as any venture outside the regulated, central station power business. Electric companies have diversified in three ways: portfolio investment, energy related, and unrelated. A number of companies have invested in portfolios of leases and tax-advantaged securities, often planning to liquidate the portfolio when the funds are needed in the utility business. Energy related activities have included fuel production and transportation, conservation activities, engineering, and unregulated electricity production. Unrelated activities, so far, have encompassed everything from banking and insurance through subliminal anti-shoplifting operations to orange groves. If one regards the total market for energy, or the end uses to which energy is put, as the market served by the utility, perhaps the utility could better serve the customer by providing a service other than central station power. If that is the case, the utility should have an opportunity to do so. Regulators often assert that diversification could add to the risk of the business and therefore raise cost of capital to the utility. Yet, inability to be flexible in meeting the needs of the customer could increase the risk of investing in the utility. Being locked into a one service, one technology business in an ever-changing world is perilous. At the same time, moving into unfamiliar, unrelated businesses just to expand could be just as perilous.

If the market for electricity becomes more competitive, if utilities find a way to reap the benefits of better management, if regulation becomes looser, then well run utilities would see an advantage in taking over and running the laggards. Firms might acquire companies with strategic but unexploited assets. Regulators could step in to force shotgun marriages, too, in order to rescue troubled firms. Utilities might buy and sell assets that are of more value to another company. The complications of regulation, though, could hinder rational asset distribution as well as mergers and acquisitions in the real world. Furthermore, mergers are not always economically rational. They may produce no benefits to customers or shareholders of the acquiring firm, although they may build empires for managements.

America seems to be moving gradually toward electric deregulation, incrementally rather than in a dramatic, all-or-nothing fashion. The move toward diversification comes just as many other firms are divesting themselves of unrelated activities, after poor experiences. Diversification may be the wave of the past. Why do utility managers know better than those who have tried it? As for mergers, benefits might be hard to prove, except in the case of troubled companies. But there might be real benefits to some asset sales and swaps. One conclusion is certain, though. Utilities cannot be run in the old fashioned way. That is too dangerous.

Chapter 33

Conclusion

However, it is clear that a critical American industry is being enervated by slow regulatory ... reactions and reform is critical ... Even those talking about how important reform is have been overly timid.[10]

Richard L. Gordon

When analyzing the problems of the electric utility industry, there has been a tendency to cite a string of difficulties and to act as if they were unrelated. If that were the case, the industry's recovery might have had to await another string, this time of unrelated miracles. One could, however, regard the industry's difficulties as the result of one problem: inability to properly price the product. If the price for electricity approximated its incremental cost, power demand would have been lower (making much of the construction program unnecessary) and the industry would have had less trouble financing what it had to build. Less resistance to environmental improvement might have existed ifthe costs could have been easily passed on to customers. Fuel costs, and the use of oil as a fuel, might have been kept down if the utility could have priced in a way to cover the cost of fuel conversion. At the same time, incremental pricing would have encouraged the development of competition for the utility, possibly in ways that would have reduced oil consumption even more.

Although regulators have become increasingly responsive to the need for prices to reflect the cost of doing business, they are not ready to set prices in a way that would simulate the results of a free market. Some makeshift pricing procedures that try to set rates for high use or for peak load periods closer to marginal costs should have some positive results. If regulators are unwilling to use price to dampen demand, they might instead endorse or force load management or energy conservation, because those measures are usually more cost effective than building power plants to meet unfettered demand. That compromise may produce more rational results —economically speaking—than if prices were simply kept down. Without control of demand, the result might be more demand for power placed on an industry that would be hard pressed to finance additional construction.

The industry is completing facilities the construction of which was induced by improper pricing and the costs of which were raised by the inability to finance easily, caused, in turn by the same improper pricing. Once the plants go into service, there could be a hiatus in building as utilities grow into excess capacity, make increasingly efficient use of existing plants, and engage in vigorous conservation efforts.

Diversification is regarded by some as a means of adding zip to an industry that has for too long been zapped. Others dismiss it as inconsequential. How can a huge utility develop sufficient outside business to meaningfully affect financial statements? Diversification should be the means by which the utility can best capitalize on its assets and expertise, and a way in which to meet the needs of a changing marketplace for energy. That the utility has both the ability and the structure to be flexible is important to the survival of the corporate entity. The utility might not need to develop nonutility services, but it should be able to do so if necessary.

The industry, though, will undergo more change than through diversification. The market for electricity is becoming more competitive. Utilities cannot run in the old, regulated manner because the consumers will not tolerate that. Inefficient companies will suffer, losing business and even their independence. But, at the same time, the transition to more competition and less regulation could come gradually. The efficient, flexible, market-driven company will come out ahead. So will the customers and power suppliers that understand how to take advantage of the more open environment. Competition, though, does not mean more profits for all. It does mean less certainty for an industry that used to project its future with a ruler.

Notes

[1]Roger W. Sant, *Eight Great Energy Myths: The Least Cost Energy Strategy, 1978-2000* (Pittsburgh: Carnegie-Mellon University Press, 1981), p. 36.

[2]John Maynard Keynes, *The General Theory of Employment Interest and Money* (New York: Harcourt, Brace & World, no date), p. 157.

[3]U.S. Congress Office of Technology Assessment, *Nuclear Power in an Age of Uncertainty* (Washington, D.C.: U.S. Government Printing Office, 1984).

[4]Fred C. Schweppe, Richard D. Tabors, and James Kirtley, *Homeostatic Control: The Utility/Customer Marketplace for Electric Power*, MIT Energy Laboratory Report, MIT-EL 81-033, September 1981.

[5]Ahmad Faruqui, "Marketing Electricity—A Military Approach," *Long Range Planning*, Vol. 20, No. 4, pp. 67-77, 1987.

[6]Wallace A. Stringfield, James V. Barker, Jr., and Harinder Singh, "Power Plant Productivity," presented at the Association of Rural Electric Generation Cooperatives, 31st Annual Conference, June 9-11, 1980, Des Moines, Iowa.

———, "Power Plant Productivity and State Regulation," presented at NARUC Biennial Regulatory Information Conference, September 3-5, 1980, Columbus, Ohio.

[7]John Maurice Clark, *Competition as a Dynamic Process* (Washington, D.C.: The Brookings Institution, 1961), p. 9.

[8]Some recent comments on deregulation include:

William W. Berry, "Let's End the Monopoly," presented at the Edison Electric Institute Fall Financial Conference, October 6, 1981, Palm Beach, Florida.

Edison Electric Institute, *Deregulation of Electric Utilities; A Survey of Major Concepts and Issues* (Washington, D.C.: EEI, July 1981).

——, *A Survey of Deregulation Experience in Selected Industries* (Washington, D.C.: EEI, February 1982).

——, *Alternative Models of Electric Power Deregulation* (Washington, D.C.: EEI, May 1982).

Bennett W. Golub, Richard D. Tabors, Roger E. Bohn and Fred C. Schweppe, "Deregulating the Electric Utility Industry: Discussion and a Proposed Approach," MIT Energy Laboratory Working Paper, MIT-EL 81-043 WP, July 1981, revised August 1981.

Ernst Habicht, Jr., "Restructuring the Role of Electric Utilities: Cogeneration, Conservation, Construction and Competition," presented at Merrill Lynch Economics Seminar on Electric Utility Industry, April 28, 1981, New York City.

Leonard S. Hyman, "Should Electric Utilities be Regulated?", *Public Utilities Fortnightly,* August 14, 1980.

Leonard S. Hyman and Ernst R. Habicht, Jr., "State Electric Utility Regulation: Financial Issues, Influences and Trends", *Annual Energy Review,* Vol. II, 1986, pp. 163-183.

Roger W. Sant, "Cutting Energy Cost," *Environment,* May 1980.

Richard E. Schuler and Benjamin F. Hobbs, "Spatial Competition—Applications in the Generation of Electricity," presented at 1981 Annual Meeting of the Southern Regional Science Association, April 15, 1981, Washington, D.C.

[9]Bennett W. Golub and Leonard S. Hyman, "The Financial Difficulties and Consequences of Deregulation Through Divestiture," *Public Utilities Fortnightly,* February 17, 1983.

Pennsylvania Governor's Energy Council, *Report to Lieutenant Governor William W. Scranton, III from the Pennsylvania Electric Utility Efficiency Task Force,* (Harrisburg: Pennsylvania Governor's Energy Council, March 29, 1983).

[10]Richard L. Gordon, "Reforming the Regulation of Electric Utilities—Priorities for the 1980s", MIT Energy Laboratory Working Paper MIT-EL 81-033 WP, June 1981.

Appendix: Canada

Canada has the most electricity-intensive economy and the third largest electric utility industry in the industrial world, Canada will be a significant source of electricity to the United States through an export of power that accounts for one-tenth of the industry's sales. All of this from a country with a population of 26 million. To put the figures in perspective, with a gross national product and a population roughly half of West Germany, Canada's generating capacity and electricity production exceed that of Germany, the industrial powerhouse of Europe. Perhaps those astounding statistics are due, in part, to the low price of Canadian electricity, half that of the United States or West Germany and one-third that of Japan, And the reason for the low price is the abundance of hydroelectric power in Canada.

International Comparisons

Country	Capacity 12/31/84 (Thousands of MWs)	Generation 1985 (Billions of Kwh)	Consumption per capita (Kwh)	Consumption per unit of 1985 GDP (Kwh/ 1980 US$)
U.S.A.	672	2,499	9,651	0.85
Japan	163	677	4,963	0.52
Canada	96	446	17,590	1.53
W. Germany	90	409	6,736	0.48
France	85	344	5,817	0.50
U.K.	67	297	5,252	0.51

Source: Energy, Mines and Resources Canada

The production and sales statistics demonstrate the importance of hydro and exports.

Production and Sales
(Thousands of Mwh and %)

	1985	1986
Utility generation		
Hydro	271,076	278,409
Fossil steam	79,203	71,583
Nuclear	57,095	67,233
Other	1,269	1,200
Utility total	408,643	418,425

Production and Sales — Continued
(Thousands of Mwh and %)

Industry generation	1985	1986
Hydro	29,612	29,235
Fossil steam	6,118	5,985
Other	1,988	2,189
Industry total	37,718	37,409

All generation		
Hydro	300,687	307,645
Fossil steam	85,321	77,567
Nuclear	57,095	67,233
Other	3,258	3,389
Total	446,361	455,834
Sales		
Canada	363,022	382,922
USA-		
Firm	12,305	9,756
Non-firm	30,711	29,178
Total	406,038	421,856

%		
Utility generation		
% of total	91.5	91.8
Hydro generation		
% of total	67.4	67.5
Exports to USA		
% of sales	10.6	9.2

Source: Energy, Mines and Resources Canada

The National Energy Board of Canada authorizes exports. In doing so, the Board must determine that the export power is not needed in Canada, that the revenue from the export recovers the proper share of costs in Canada, that the price may not be lower than what Canadians would pay for the same power, and that the price must not be less than the lowest cost alternative to the purchaser.

Canada's industry is largely owned by government agencies. The production in 1985 was 85% by government utilities, 7% by investor-owned utilities and 8% by industrial firms. The status by province is:

Newfoundland—Newfoundland and Labrador Hydro is a provincially owned crown corporation that has enormous hydro generation resources, distributes electricity directly to customers in rural areas, and sells to investor-owned Newfoundland Light & Power most of the electricity that firm distributes to its customers in the more populated areas.

Prince Edward Island—Investor-owned Maritime Electric serves the island province, with most power coming by submarine cable from New Brunswick.

Nova Scotia—Nova Scotia Power, owned by the province, serves the entire population.

New Brunswick—Provincially owned New Brunswick Electric Power Commission generates electricity, serves the bulk of the customers directly, and the balance through municipal systems.

Quebec—Hydro-Quebec, owned by the province, controls vast hydroelectric resources, and generates and distributes throughout the province.

Ontario—Ontario Hydro, provincially owned, generates electricity, sells it mainly through municipally owned distribution systems, and also sells directly to large industrial firms and to customers in rural areas.

Manitoba—Manitoba Hydro-Electric Board, another provincial crown corporation, produces and sells throughout Manitoba except for the territory of municipally owned Winnipeg Hydro.

Saskatchewan—The Saskatchewan Power Corporation, property of the province, generates and sells electricity and distributes natural gas.

Alberta—An investor-owned company, TransAlta Utilities, generates 80% of the province's electricity. Another investor-owned firm, Canadian Utilities, provides 17%. The balance is furnished by city owned Edmonton Power. The companies operate an integrated network.

British Columbia—Provincial crown corporation British Columbia Hydro & Power Authority generates and sells most of the province's electricity, as well as natural gas in some areas. Cominco Ltd. and West Kootenay Power are small investor-owned utilities in the province.

In terms of size, Ontario Hydro is the largest Canadian utility, Hydro-Quebec is a close second, and B.C. Hydro is a distant third.

Regulation for investor-owned utilities in Canada is similar to that of the U.S.A. Pricing approval policies for the provincially owned agencies vary, but some government approval is required for their tariffs.

In 1985, Canada had 95,000 MW of capacity, and a 31% reserve margin. Potential additions in the coming 15 years could more than double capacity, with 80% of the additions being hydro.[1] Some of that increase in capacity, if made, could go to the export market. Clearly, Canada and the United States will be doing more business in the electricity market.

---

[1]William A. Vaughan, *Canadian Hydropower* (Washington, D.C.: Electricity Consumers Resource Council, June 1987.)

Selected Bibliography

This bibliography is designed to give the reader the standard sources of information, with emphasis on those sources that are easily found and easily understood. In addition, there is a huge body of speeches and technical papers that circulates within the industry in a *samizdat* manner. And, of course, there are many articles in learned journals and an abundance of extremely technical books. The bibliographic references are grouped by general topic. The readings are grouped by one category, although some ought to be in several categories.

Statistics and Reference

The standard sources are publications of the Energy Information Agency, Edison Electric Institute and the various financial services, as well as *Electrical World, Public Utilities Fortnightly* and *Electric Light & Power.*

Deloitte Haskins & Sells, *Public Utilities Manual* (No place of publication: Deloitte Haskins & Sells, 1980).

Edison Electric Institute, *Statistical Year Book of the Electric Utility Industry* (Washington, D.C.: Edison Electric Institute, various years).

———— , *Year-End Electric Porter Survey* (Washington, D.C.: Edison Electric Institute, various years).

———— , *EEI Pocketbook of Electric Utility Industry Statistics* (Washington, D.C.: Edison Electric Institute, various years).

Electric Light & Power (various issues).

Electrical World (various issues).

Electrical Energy Branch, *Electric Power in Canada 1985* (Ottawa: Ministry of Supply and Services, 1986).

Haskins & Sells, *Public Utilities Manual* (New York: Deloitte Haskins & Sells, 1977).

Moody's Public Utilities Manual (New York: Moody's Investors Service, various dates).

Pacific Gas and Electric, *Resource: An Encyclopedia of Utility Industry Terms* (San Francisco: Pacific G&E, 1984).

Public Utilities Fortnightly (various issues).

Statistics Canada, *Electric Power Statistics,* December 1986 (Ottawa: Ministry of Supply and Services, 1987).

U.S. Department of Commerce, National Oceanic and Atmospheric Administration, *State, Regional, and National Monthly and Seasonal Cooling Degree Days, Weighted by Population (1980 Census)* (Asheville, N.C.: U.S. Department of Commerce, various dates).

———— , *State Regional, and National Monthly and Seasonal Cooling Degree Days (Heating Degree Days), Weighted by Population (1980 Census)* (Asheville, N.C.: U.S. Department of Commerce, various dates).

U.S. Department of Energy, Energy Information Administration, *Statistics of Privately Owned Electric Utilities in the United States* (Washington, D.C.: U.S. Government Printing Office, various years).

———— , *Electric Power Monthly* (various issues).

———— , *Monthly Energy Review* (various issues).

U.S. Department of Labor, Bureau of Labor Statistics, *Monthly Labor Review* (various issues).

U.S. Federal Power Commission, *Statistics of Privately Owned Electric Utilities in the United States* (Washington, D.C.: U.S. Government Printing Office, various years).

Regulation and Economics

Numerous texts on regulation have been written. Probably almost everything that has been or will be said was covered by Bonbright. Kahn's work deals with all aspects of regulation, not exclusively with utilities. *Public Utilities Fortnightly* is an excellent source for keeping up with current issues. Welch's book provides a clear exposition of regulatory law and texts of cases as well. The EEI studies cover the issues well. The Pennsylvania study represents one of the few recent governmental efforts to examine regulation.

Adelaar, Richard H., and Leonard S. Hyman, "The Comparable Earnings Approach as a Useful Tool in Utility Regulation, *Public Utilities Fortnightly.* Vol. 87, No. 5, March 4, 1971.

American Association for the Advancement of Science, *Proceedings of the Conference on National Energy Policy, May 17, 1977* (Washington, D.C.: AAAS, 1977).

Anderson, Douglas D., *Regulatory Politics and Electric Utilities* (Boston: Auburn House, 1981).

Arthur Andersen & Co., *Return Allowed in Public Utility Rate Cases* (Vol. I 1915-1954 and Vol. II 1955-1961). No date or place of publication.

Bain, Joe S., *Industrial Organization* (New York: John Wiley & Sons, 1959).

Balk, Walter L., and Jay M. Shafritz, eds., *Public Utility Productivity: Management and Measurement* (Albany: The New York State Department of Public Service, 1975).

Bechtel, Stephen D., Jr.,"America's Industrial Future is Clouded," *Bechtel Briefs,* July/August 1982.

Bonbright, James C., *Principles of Public Utility Rates* (New York: Columbia University Press, 1961).

Cicchetti, Charles J.,"Conservation Financing—Its Rate Impact," in Edison Electric Institute Proceedings, *Sixteenth Financial Conference October 4-7, 1981* (Washington, D.C.: EEI, 1982).

Clark, J. Maurice, *Studies in the Economics of Overhead Costs* (Chicago: The University of Chicago Press, 1962 impression).

———— , *Competition as a Dynamic Process* (Washington, D.C.: The Brookings Institution, 1961).

Clemens, Eli Winston, *Economics and Public Utilities* (New York: Appleton-Century-Crofts, 1950).

Crew Michael A., ed., *Issues in Public-Utility Pricing and Regulation* (Lexington: D. C. Heath, 1980).

Edison Electric Institute, *Economic Growth in the Future* (New York: McGraw-Hill, 1976).

———— , *Deregulation of Electric Utilities; A Survey of Major Concepts and Issues* (Washington, D.C.: EEI, July 1981).

———— , *A Survey of Deregulation Experience in Selected Industries* (Washington, D.C.: EEI, February 1982).

———— , *Alternative Models of Electric Power Deregulation* (Washington, D.C.: EEI, May 1982).

Glassman, Gerald J., "Discounted Cash Flow Versus the Capital Asset Pricing Model (Is g Better Than b?)," *Public Utilities Fortnightly,* September 14, 1978.

Gordon, Richard L., *Reforming the Regulation of Electric Utilities* (Lexington: D. C. Heath, 1982).

Hyman, Leonard S., and Ernst R. Habicht, Jr., "State Electric Utility Regulation: Financial Issues, Influences and Trends," *Annual Energy Review,* Vol. II, 1986, pp. 163-183.

Kahn, Alfred E., *The Economics of Regulation* (New York: John Wiley & Sons, 1970-1971).

Metcalf, Lee, and Vic Reinemer, *Overcharge* (New York: David McKay, 1967).

Morin, Roger A., *Utilities' Cost of Capital* (Arlington, Va.: Public Utilities Reports, 1984).

Pennsylvania Governor's Energy Council, *Report to Lieutenant Governor William W. Scranton, III from the Pennsylvania Utility Efficiency Task Force,* (Harrisburg: Pennsylvania Governor's Energy Council, March 29, 1983).

Phillips, Charles F., Jr., *The Regulation of Public Utilities: Theory and Practice* (Arlington, Va.: Public Utilities Reports, 1984).

Primeaux, Walter J., Jr., "A Reexamination of the Monopoly Market Structure for Electric Utilities," in A. Phillips, ed., *Promoting Competition in Regulated Markets* (Washington, D.C.: Brookings Institution, 1975).

Resources for the Future, *Price Elasticities of Demand for Energy—Evaluating the Estimates* (Palo Alto: Electric Power Research Institute, September 1982).

Rodgers, Paul, J. Edward Smith, Jr., and Russell J. Profozich, *Current Issues in Electric Utility Rate Setting* (Washington, D.C.: National Association of Regulatory Utility Commissioners, 1976).

Roberts, Keith, ed., *Towards an Energy Policy* (San Francisco: Sierra Club, 1973).

Saltzman, Sidney, and Richard E. Schuler, eds., *The Future of Electrical*

Energy: A Regional Perspective of an Industry in Transition (New York: Praeger, 1986).

Sant, Roger W., *Eight Great Energy Myths: The Least Cost Energy Strategy, 1978-2000* (Pittsburgh: Carnegie-Mellon University Press, 1981).

Schurr, Sam H., and Bruce C. Netschert, *Energy in the American Economy, 1850-1975* (Baltimore: Johns Hopkins Press, 1960).

Stalon, Charles D., "Deregulation of the Electric Generating Industry: Some Unsystematic Observations," *Proceedings: Edison Electric Institute Sixteenth Financial Conference October 4-7, 1981* (Washington, D.C.: Edison Electric Institute, 1982).

Vandell, Robert F., and James K. Malernee, "The Capital Asset Pricing Model and Utility Equity Returns," *Public Utilities Fortnightly*, July 6, 1978.

Welch, Francis X., *Cases and Text on Public Utilities Regulation* (Washington, D.C.: Public Utilities Reports, 1968).

Westly, Steven, ed., *Energy Efficiency and the Utilities: New Directions* (San Francisco: California Public Utilities Commission, 1980).

Wilcox, Clair, *Public Policies Toward Business* (Homewood, Ill.: Richard D. Irwin, 1960).

Finance

Although it was not written for the purpose, Dewing's text provides extraordinary insight into the regulation, finance and development of the electric utility industry. Most recent writings seem to concentrate on the financial straits and imminent demise of the industry. The classic text on security analysis is still Graham and Dodd.

Badger, Ralph E., Harold W. Jorgenson, and Harry G. Guthmann, *Investment Principles and Practices* (Englewood Cliffs, N.J.: Prentice Hall, 1961).

Dewing, Arthur Stone, *The Financial Policy of Corporations* (New York: The Ronald Press, 1953).

Graham, Benjamin, David J. Dodd, Sidney Cottle, with Charles Tatham, *Security Analysis* (New York: McGraw-Hill, 1962).

Hyman, Leonard S., "Utility Stocks in 1967-72: A Tale of Woe," *Public Utilities Fortnightly*, Vol. 93, No. 5, Feb. 28, 1974.

———, "Market to Book Ratio: Statistical Confirmation or Aberration?", *Public Utilities Fortnightly*, Dec. 19, 1979.

———, and Carmine J. Grigoli, "The Credit Standing of Electric Utilities," *Public Utilities Fortnightly*, Vol. 99, No. 5, March 3, 1977, pp. 24-30.

Ibbotson, Roger G., and Rex A. Sinquefield, *Stocks, Bonds, Bills and Inflation: The Past (1926-1976) and the Future (1977-2000)* (Charlottesville: Financial Analysts Research Foundation, 1977).

O'Brien, Betsy, and Andrew Reynolds, *Impacts of Financial Constraints on the Electric Utility Industry* (Washington, D.C.: U.S. Government Printing Office, 1982).

Young, Harold H., *Forty Years of Public Utility Finance* (Charlottesville: The University of Virginia, 1965).

History and Structure

For an industry that just got over its centennial, one would have expected more solid new material on how it got the way it is. Even some of the oft-cited classics seem to have some amazing blind spots. The *EPRI Journal's* special issue probably puts together the story as well as any source.

Commager, Henry Steele, ed., *Documents of American History* (New York: Appleton-Century-Crofts, 1949).

Conot, Robert, *A Streak of Luck* (New York: Seaview Books, 1979).

Dillon, Mary Earhart, *Wendell Willkie* (Philadelphia and New York: J. B. Lippincott, 1952).

Electrical World, June 1, 1974. Special Issue: The Electric Century.

EPRI Journal, March 1979. Special Issue: Creating the Electric Age.

Friedel, Robert, and Paul Israel with Bernard Finn, *Edison's Electric Light: Biography of an Invention* (New Brunswick: Rutgers University Press, 1986).

Hughes, Thomas P., *Networks of Power: Electrification in Western Society, 1880-1930* (Baltimore: The Johns Hopkins Press, 1983).

Joskow, Paul L., and Richard Schmalensee, *Markets for Power: An Analysis of Electric Utility Deregulation* (Cambridge: The MIT Press, 1983).

Josephson, Matthew, *Edison* (New York: McGraw Hill, 1959).

McDonald, Forest, *Insull* (Chicago: The University of Chicago Press, 1962).

Plummer, James, Terry Ferrar and William Hughes, eds., *Electric Power Strategic Issues* (Arlington, Va. and Palo Alto, Cal.: Public Utilities Reports and QED Research, 1983).

Ripley, William Z., "From Main Street to Wall Street," in Louise Desaulniers, ed., *Looking Back at Tomorrow* (Boston: The Atlantic Monthly, 1978), p. 125.

Rodgers, William, *Brown-Out* (New York: Stein and Day, 1972).

Schlesinger, Arthur M., Jr., *The Age of Roosevelt: The Crisis of the Old Order* (Boston: Houghton Mifflin, 1957).

Sporn, Philip, *Energy—Its Production, Conversion, and Use in the Service of Man* (New York: Columbia Graduate School of Business, 1963).

————— , *The Social Organization of Electric Power Supply in Modern Societies* (Cambridge: MIT Press, 1971).

Wyatt, Alan, *Electric Power: Challenges and Choices* (Toronto: The Book Press, 1986).

Operations and Environment

Environmental literature tends to get argumentative and operational literature technical. The *EPRI Journal* provides easily read studies, and *Science* and *Environment* are good sources of information on energy and environmental issues. The Commoner and Schumacher books, although ostensibly about economics, are more ecological-philosophical-political in tone.

Abelson, Philip H., ed., *Energy: Use, Conservation and Supply* (Washington, D.C.: American Association for the Advancement of Science, 1974).

———— , ed., *Energy II: Use, Conservation and Supply* (Washington, D.C.: AAAS, 1978).

Broecker, W. B., T. Takahashi, H. J. Simpson, T. H. Peng "Fate of Fossil Fuel Carbon Dioxide and the Global Carbon Budget," *Science,* Vol. 206, 26 October 1979, p. 409.

Brown, Harold J., editor, *Decentralizing Electricity Production* (New Haven: Yale University Press, 1983).

Commoner, Barry, *The Poverty of Power: Energy and the Economic Crisis* (New York: Alfred A. Knopf. 1976).

Electric Utility Task Force on the Environment, *The Electric Utility Industry and the Environment, A Report to the Citizens Advisory Committee on Recreation and Natural Beauty by the Electric Utility Task Force on Environment* (no place or date of publication Library of Congress Card No. 68-57661).

Environment (various issues).

EPRI Journal (various issues).

Holdren, John, and Philip Herrera, *Energy: A Crisis in Power* (San Francisco: Sierra Club, 1973).

Komanoff, Charles, *Power Plant Cost Escalation* (New York: Komanoff Energy Associates, 1981).

Madden, Ronald A., and V. Ramanathan, "Detecting Climate Change Due to Increasing Carbon Dioxide," *Science,* Vol. 209, 15 August 1980, p. 763.

Moss, Thomas H., and David L. Sills, eds., *The Three Mile Island Nuclear Accident: Lessons and Implications* (New York: N.Y. Academy of Sciences, 1981).

North American Electric Reliability Council, *1987 Reliability Assessment* (Princeton: North American Reliability Council, 1987).

Sant, Roger W., "Cutting Energy Cost," *Environment,* May 1980.

Schindler, D. W., "Effects of Acid Rain on Freshwater Ecosystems," *Science,* 8 January 1988, Vol. 239. pp. 149-157.

Schumacher, E. F., *Small is Beautiful: Economics As If People Mattered* (New York: Harper & Row Perennial Library, 1975).

Science (various issues).

Swanson, Christina, and Patrick Reddy, "A Risky Business," *Environment,* July/August 1979, p. 28.

U.S. Congress Office of Technology Assessment, *Nuclear Power in an Age of Uncertainty* (Washington, D.C.: U.S. Government Printing Office, 1984).

Vaughan, William A., *Canadian Hydropower: Potential Resources and Implications for U.S. Industrial Competitiveness* (Washington, D.C.: Electricity Consumers Resource Council, 1987).

SUBJECT INDEX

INDEX OF NAMES